The Horse's Pain-Free Back and Saddle-Fit Book

Also by Dr. Joyce Harman

The Western Horse's Pain-Free Back and Saddle-Fit Book
English Saddles: How to Fit Pain-Free (DVD)
Western Saddles: How to Fit Pain-Free (DVD)

The Horse's Pain-Free Back and Saddle-Fit Book

*Ensure Soundness and Comfort
with Back Analysis and Correct Use of Saddles and Pads*

Joyce Harman, DVM, MRCVS

Illustrations by Susan E. Harris

TRAFALGAR SQUARE BOOKS
NORTH POMFRET, VERMONT

First published in 2004 by
Trafalgar Square Books
North Pomfret, Vermont 05053

Printed in China

Photo credits: All photographs courtesy of Joyce Harman, except 1.2 B by Audrey Petschek; 4.3 A, 4.4 A, 9.8 D & E, 14.1, 14.2, 14.6 B by Mandy Lorraine of *Practical Horseman*; 6.3 B by Equine Photography; 7.4 A by Carlotta Schaller. Illustration 14.5 by Vanessa Preast, DVM.

Library of Congress Cataloging-in-Publication Data

Harman, Joyce.
The horse's pain-free back and saddle-fit book : ensure soundness and comfort with back analysis and correct use of saddles and pads / Joyce Harman.
        p. cm.
ISBN-13: 978-1-57076-292-5 (pbk.)
ISBN-10: 1-57076-292-9 (pbk.)
1. Saddlery. 2. Horsemanship. 3. Horses—Health. I. Title.
SF309.9H368 2004
636.1'0837—dc22   2004009968

Book design by Carrie Fradkin
Cover design by Heather Mansfield
Typeface: Stone Serif, Stone Sans, Rockwell

Color separations by Tenon & Polert Colour Scanning Ltd., Hong Kong

10 9 8 7 6

Dedication

This book is dedicated to my mother, Ann Harman. Also to my horse Rummy (now sadly departed) who put up with hours of computer saddle testing in a ring while much preferring to go hunting and trail riding.

Table of Contents

Acknowledgments

Many people and horses have contributed to this book, but it could not have been written without three key people to whom I am most indebted to for their teaching and sharing of experience. Wendy Murdoch encouraged me from the very beginning and taught me how to really see riders and horses move correctly. She would not let me give up until I had it right. Andy Foster opened my mind to questions I had not begun to ask and put into words questions I was almost ready to ask. Blake Kral broadened my knowledge and taught me about Western saddle fit, which added to my knowledge of English saddle fit, since the concepts are the same.

In my opinion, the illustrations done by Sue Harris make the book. No one but Sue could have taken the concepts and turned them into such wonderfully clear drawings. I will be forever indebted to Debbie Kral, without whom many of the photographs would not have happened.

Bruce Gerrish, Pat Paris, Phyllis Poore, and Wendy Murdoch all took time out of their busy schedules, cleaned up their horses, and posed in all sorts of uncomfortable saddles to make the photographs.

Susie Coffey showed me how creative flocking and adjustments could fix many saddles that I thought could not be helped. Larry Large showed me that foam panels could be adjusted. Kerry Ridgway, DVM, has been a wonderful friend and staunch supporter of my work from the beginning, always there when I needed him. Other friends and colleagues who have given me encouragement include, but are not limited to Hilary Clayton, MRCVS, and Jim, Gwen, and Kendra Helfter. George and Heather Humphries, Kate Riordan, and my mother proofed many of the early versions. Dale Myler taught me a new way of looking at bits and their relationship to the back. Dan Marks, DVM, supported my work and contributed some valuable ideas. Jon

Zahourek's courses taught me three-dimensional muscle anatomy, which helped me see horses in a completely different way. Mandy Lorraine kindly allowed the use of some of her wonderful photographs.

A most important thank you has to go to my clients for providing horse backs, saddles, and feedback. Without them, I would have no experience to draw upon. The horses have been the greatest teachers, as they are so patient and tolerant even when their saddles are not perfect. My thanks also to the veterinarians, chiropractors, and horse owners who have taken my teaching to heart and have spread the knowledge to othcrs.

Caroline Robbins and Rebecca Schmidt at Trafalgar Square have done a masterful job of taking the text from a very rough manuscript to an incredible finished book. They put in countless hours organizing the text and illustrations and overseeing the design. I cannot thank them enough for their dedication to making this book happen.

Preface

When I opened my equine veterinary acupuncture practice in 1990, I realized I had little training about the function of the horse's back, back pain, or saddle fitting. As I started to recognize back pain and treat it with acupuncture and later with chiropractic, the horses made promising advances in their soundness and ability to perform. When I added correct saddle fit to my treatments, the horses did even better. I was blessed with many teachers, both human and horse, who helped me see and understand the relationship between the saddle, the horse's back, and the rider. And now over 75 percent of my work involves treating back pain.

In recent years, discussions of back pain and saddle fitting have become more frequent in the equine media, but many of the articles that have appeared discuss saddle fitting from the saddle maker's point of view, often without an explanation of how the horse's back functions and how the rider's comfort (and resulting effectiveness)

fits into the picture. Since I regularly saw horses suffering from pain caused by their saddle, I felt it was time the horse had a "voice"—a person not connected to selling any particular product, and one that would pay attention to the whole picture.

In 1994, when I was introduced to a computerized device designed to analyze pressures under a saddle, I knew I had to have one to advance my knowledge. Using this computer, I was able to document exactly what was happening under the saddle when a horse was ridden. I could also truly study the effects of various saddle pads. I then realized that I could teach saddle fit to people who do not have access to this sort of advanced equipment so the average horse owner can perform a credible job of fitting a saddle to horse and rider.

In this book, I address the entire horse—connecting his back through the saddle—and the rider and her ability to perform, no matter what the sport. It is a book, not only for pleasure riders who want a happy horse, but also amateurs and professionals who need maximum performance. I've tried to provide solutions and treatments to solve as many saddle-fitting and back problems as I can.

You should look at your quest for a pain-free back for your horse as a challenge—or a puzzle, if you prefer. The satisfaction that comes from getting all the pieces working together is enormous. For some, that journey will be brief while for others, many pieces of the puzzle will need to be put into place. However long it takes, you will have a more comfortable, happy, willing horse to ride, in the end.

Why Saddle Fit Matters

If you've ever used golf clubs that were the wrong length or gone out shopping all day in a pair of shoes that were too small, you know how painful and miserable poor fit can make a usually good experience. Yet, we routinely ask our horses to perform various tasks while wearing saddles that don't fit properly, primarily because we lack the knowledge necessary to recognize correct saddle fit or to rectify any problems that we might find.

Horses are being purchased at higher prices than ever before, and in many places, land for keeping horses is very costly, making their upkeep more expensive than ever. Whether we are in the horse business to make a living, or just to enjoy a weekend trail ride, owning and caring for horses costs money every day of the year. It is understandable, then, when owners are disappointed that a horse fails to live up to expectations. Often, such poor performance is simply due to pain and discomfort frequently caused by poorly fitted saddles. Sometimes, unproductive months—and often years—are invested in trying to train horses that are limited by back pain. Riders who are able to correct saddle-fitting problems are often amazed at the dramatic changes in their horses and regret the time wasted before they were able to understand, and ultimately solve, the problem.

"Equine welfare" is not just about saving starving horses; it is also about preventing pain and discomfort. Many horses are treated unfairly and roughly for behavior problems that are simply reactions to their pain. We need to understand that a large percentage of horse "disobedience" stems from such preventable causes.

When Saddle Fit is Correct

How do you know when you find the right saddle? You just "feel" it, because your horse is relaxed and willing under you, and your hours in the saddle are less hard work and far more pleasurable. Your saddle feels like a comfortable pair of shoes—the kind that when you slip your feet into them at the end of a long day, your whole body breathes a sigh of relief. You sit on your horse with ease, instead of struggling to find a spot that allows you to relax and stay in balance. Your riding instructor comments on how well you are riding, and you no longer hear, over and over, "Get your legs back underneath you," "Sit up straight," "Stop leaning over to one side."

When your horse wears a saddle that fits correctly, he can collect and turn fluidly, and when asked for a particular maneuver, he can happily comply. Your saddle does not interfere with how your horse receives your aids; in fact, it *enhances* communication.

Because this well-fitting saddle allows the horse to move freely with an easy stride, many lameness problems are prevented. He connects lightly with the ground, putting minimal stress on the joints in his lower legs. Other stresses normally caused by a horse moving stiffly are minimized as well, even if he has conformation faults.

When Saddle Fit is Incorrect

When you ride in a saddle that does not fit you, you "fight" it to stay in balance, and no matter how hard you struggle, you can't seem to please your instructor with your position. You are often in pain, and though you blame your own poor riding skills, it is actually caused by the saddle, which places you in the wrong position.

When a saddle does not fit your horse properly, it hurts him. It is difficult for him to respond

FITS ME LIKE A GLOVE!

movements that only the highest level dressage horses perform with a rider, but this generally only occurs for a brief time when the horse is highly excited and unencumbered by a saddle. Most horses travel stiffly, ewe-necked and with their backs hollow. This poor movement is usually caused, or accentuated, by pain, and at least 75 percent of that pain has been caused by a badly fitting saddle. When the rider is added to the mix, the problems are then compounded.

Circle of Muscles

The horse's back is central to the function of his musculo-skeletal system and its ability to carry a rider. In her book, *Horse Gaits, Balance and Movement* (see *Resources,* p. 211), Susan Harris describes the connection between the head, neck, back, and hindquarters as a *circle of muscles* (fig. 1.1). The first way you can tell if a horse is using his circle of muscles correctly is by determining if movement looks easy for him—his abdominal and hind-leg muscles (the lower half of the circle) contract, allowing the back muscles (the upper half) to work freely. You can see his back rise, his head drop, his neck extend, and his back muscles soften. The movement goes around the circle of muscles in a forward-and-up direction, through

correctly to your aids because he is preoccupied with pain. Resisting is how he tries to tell you that he cannot do the task. This is often misinterpreted as a poor attitude or lack of willingness.

An uncomfortable horse hits the ground harder with his feet, increasing stress on his lower legs, which can result in lameness. The veterinary bills mount as treatments for his lower-leg problems yield no results because they originate in his back.

The Function of the Horse's Back

Sometimes, a horse can be observed running free and using his back correctly, maybe even doing

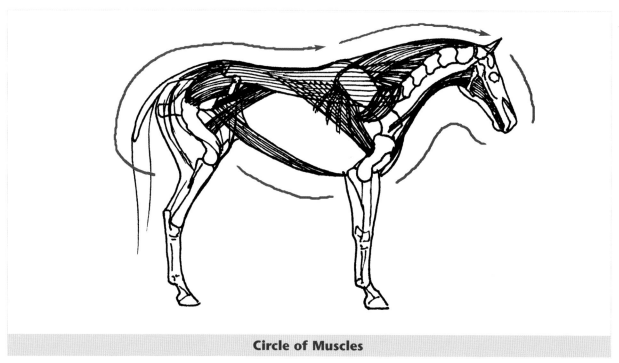

Circle of Muscles

1.1 The *circle of muscles* is formed by muscles in the hindquarters, back, neck, poll, jaw, lower neck, sternum, and abdomen. When these muscles work together correctly, the horse should move in a manner that feels and appears *forward* and *upward*.

the sternum. If you listen carefully to a horse being worked in an indoor arena, you can often tell if he is using himself correctly by the amount of noise his footfalls make. Less noise means he is lighter on his feet and is moving more correctly than a horse with loud, pounding footsteps (figs. 1.2 A & B).

When a horse is in pain, his back muscles contract, his abdominal muscles remain soft, and his back drops and becomes hollow. In this situation, his hind legs cannot effectively engage.

This hollow-backed position places unnatural strain on the stifles, hocks, tendons, suspensory ligaments, and feet—often causing lameness or soreness—because he cannot engage his hindquarters, or bring his hind legs up underneath his body properly. The circle of muscles won't be well developed if the horse has been ineffectively ridden, or ridden in a bad saddle for any length of time.

When observing a horse using his back and abdominal muscles incorrectly, resistance and tension are evident (figs. 1.2 C & D). The movement goes down through the sternum, toward the ground, instead of correctly forward and up. You actually see this quite often because the percentage of ridden horses using their backs correctly is, unfortunately, very small.

To feel how incorrect back muscle use can restrict movement, try this exercise. Hold on to a sturdy structure for support. *Hollow* your back, stand on one foot, and bend your other knee. Slowly lift it as high as you can. *Be careful! You could hurt yourself if your back is tight!* Now, *round* your back, tighten your abdominal muscles, and see how much further you can raise your bent leg. Compare the freedom your leg has when your back is round, to the stiffness in your hips and spine when your back is hollow (figs. 1.3 A & B).

Belly Lifts

The *belly lift* is a test that will help you ascertain whether your horse's back is hollow or rounded. Stand at your horse's side and run your fingertips (or, if he's not overly sensitive, the blunt end of a pen) along the midline of his abdomen, from the girth area back toward his hind end (figs. 1.4 A & B). Use caution, since a horse in pain may kick or bite.

Observe your horse's physical reaction. A normal horse's stomach muscles will contract, his back muscles will relax and soften, his back will rise, and his neck will drop and stretch forward. Look at the area right behind the withers for the most obvious change in his topline (figs. 1.5 A & B).

Evaluate the exercise results:

- If your horse looks like the horse in the photos 1.5 A and B before, and after, the belly lift, he is using his circle of muscles correctly. You can occasionally perform belly lifts to stretch his back, but you do not need to do regular exercises.

- If your horse raises his back one to three inches, this means his back has dropped but is still flexible. Perform this exercise regularly for a month or two and if you do not see positive change, you may need to have his back treated for pain (see chapter 14).

- If your horse's back looks hollow and he does not respond to the belly lift, his back is very stiff. In this case, you will probably need help in treating the stiffness (see *Resources,* p. 211).

- If your horse protests—kicks, bites, swishes his tail, stomps his foot—he's in pain and needs treatment. Try gently scratching his abdomen to see if you can get him to raise his back even slightly by making it an enjoyable experience instead of an uncomfortable one. Offer a treat when he attempts to lift his belly, though keep in mind that at this point, it's better to raise his back only a quarter of an inch and have him remain relaxed, than to raise his back high and have him tighten his muscles more to brace against the pain.

Evaluating Your Horse's Posture and Use of His Back

In order to evaluate your horse's use of his back, it is helpful to study photographs of other

A

B

C

D

Correct and Incorrect Use of the Circle of Muscles

1.2 A – D In A and B, the horse is using the circle of muscles correctly. Movement appears easy, fluid, forward, and upward. As you can see from photo B, the horse can support himself under a rider and perform a strenuous physical activity like the passage. In C and D, the circle of muscles is not engaged. Look at the horse in D with his hollow back and upside-down neck, and then compare him to the horse in B.

Back Muscle Test

1.3 A & B When you try to lift a leg with a hollow back, notice how stiff your back and hips feel. Now, round your back and try lifting the same leg again and see how much further you can bring your "hind leg" up under you!

horses, both standing still and in different phases of each gait, on the flat and over fences, and using themselves both correctly and incorrectly. You should also take photographs, or make a video of your horse standing and in motion. To get an accurate assessment, try to select photos in the same phase of the stride as those provided here, or if you're watching a video, use a VCR player that allows you to stop the motion so you can study each frame.

Standing

Have an assistant hold your horse on a level piece of ground. Do not try to make your horse

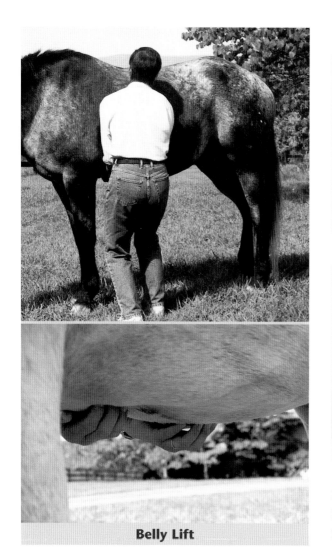

Belly Lift

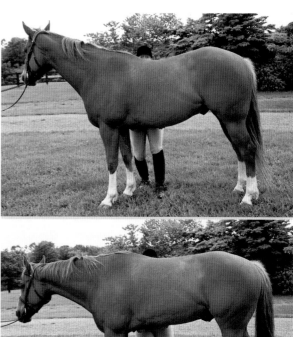

Effects of the Belly Lift

1.4 A & B Stand next to the horse's girth area, bend your knees if needed, and reach under the horse to the middle of his sternum (or belly) to where there is a groove in the muscles (A). Then, run your fingers down this center groove (B).

1.5 A & B As the rider prepares to perform the belly lift in A, this horse's head is up and his back is dropped. In B, see how the belly lift has caused the horse to raise his back, drop his head, and stretch forward. You can try different pressures and movements with your fingers to get a good reaction like this.

stand squarely, but just allow him to stop and place his legs wherever he is comfortable (figs. 1.6 A & B). Move him several times to see if he always puts his feet in the same place, and make a mental note of his preferred stance. Next, examine him from each side, front and back, from about 10 feet away. Notice his shape. Then, stand him squarely, stand at his tail, and look down his back facing his ears to evaluate his shoulders for evenness and his back for straightness (see figure 8.13 A, p. 126).

You can learn a lot about your horse's comfort level from this examination. Your horse compensates for pain by holding his body in an awkward way. What follows are some commonly seen postures.

Back

A *swayed back* is often considered a normal part of the aging process, but most horses under the age of eighteen with dropped, or slightly swayed, backs are showing signs of pain (see *Swayed Back*, p. 127).

Legs

Regardless of their conformation, horses that are comfortable generally stand with all four legs on the ground. When they rest a hind leg, they show no preference for one over the other. Any of the following stances are signs that your horse is attempting to relieve some sort of pain.

- "Stretched out" with front legs extended and hind legs stretched out behind the normal position.

- Front and rear legs close together tucked underneath body.
- Unable to stand in one position for very long.

Neck

A horse that stands with a ewe (inverted) neck—overly-developed muscles on the underside of the neck and a diminished natural curve along the top of the neck—is considered to have poor conformation (fig. 1.7). However, most have developed this neck due to pain and stiffness.

In Motion

Walk

At the walk, the horse in fig. 1.8 A is engaging his circle of muscles and back correctly. He looks "filled out" behind the saddle and through the loins, and his withers are raised because he is lifting his back. His neck rises in a smooth upward line from his shoulders, and his abdominal muscles are engaged and actively contracting. The lines of motion flow upward and forward, and the rider will be "lifted up" with them. In fig. 1.8 B, the same horse looks hollow through the loins, his equally hollow neck begins at his dropped withers and ends at his poll, and his abdominal muscles are relaxed and dropped. The lines of motion flow downward through the front legs, and the rider may find she hits the saddle harder or is less comfortable. In both photographs, the horse's hind legs are well under him, however, many hollow-backed horses show a much shorter stride, and will not reach up under themselves.

Evaluating Posture and Conformation

1.6 A & B When allowed to stop and place his legs wherever they are most comfortable, the horse in A halts fairly squarely and stands on all four feet with good posture. Though he has poor conformation, with a swayed back, high hind-quarters, and hind legs that are very straight through the stifle and hocks, this horse is an accomplished athlete and pain-free.

The horse in photo B halts with his front legs well behind the vertical and one back leg stretched out behind him. He is an example of a horse with good conformation and bad posture, which is a sign he is in pain.

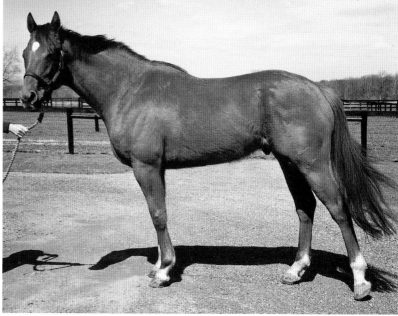

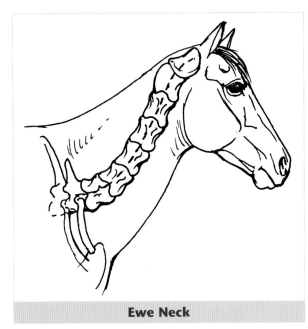

Ewe Neck

1.7 While a horse can be born with ewe-necked conformation, it is more often caused by him physically trying to compensate for pain. This can be due to an uncomfortable saddle, incorrect riding, or bad bridling and dental troubles. A horse with a neck like this cannot use his circle of muscles correctly.

Trot

Because the trot is a simple, two-beat gait, it is a bit easier to analyze than the walk or the canter. The horse in fig. 1.8 C is using his circle of muscles correctly. As could be seen at the walk, he looks filled out in the lumbar area, comes up through his withers, and his neck rises up out of his shoulders with his poll as the highest point.

His head is in the correct alignment, his abdominal muscles are engaged, and his stride is long. His hind leg is tracking up into the hoof print of the foreleg. The overall motion of this horse appears to be upward and forward. The horse in fig. 1.8 D is using his circle of muscles incorrectly and is hollow in the lumbar area. His withers have sunk, his neck extends in a straight line up from them, and his nose is in front of the vertical. His abdominal muscles are relaxed and dropped, and his stride is short with his hind foot landing behind the footprint of the front. This horse appears to move in a stilted, downhill manner.

Canter

The canter is more difficult to analyze because there are three distinct parts to the stride. In fig. 1.8 E, you can see the horse moving in the correct, forward and upward manner without a rider. With a rider, you will note that the characteristics seen at the trot are also apparent at the canter. The horse in fig. 1.8 F is moving upward and forward. He is slightly overbent in his poll, but he is "coming up" through his withers and his hind leg is reaching well under him. Fig. 1.8 G shows incorrect use of the circle of muscles. The horse's back is hollow, his neck juts awkwardly straight up in the air, and his overall motion is downhill.

Jumping

The same principles discussed in the walk, trot, and canter also apply in jumping. The horse that uses his circle of muscles correctly will display

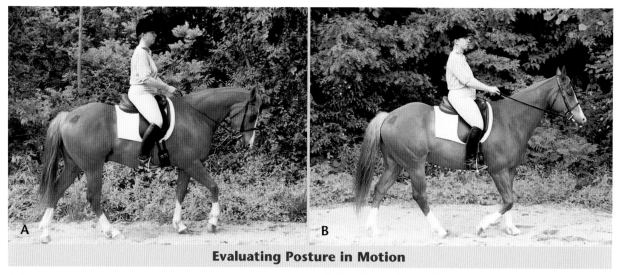

Evaluating Posture in Motion

1.8 A – G In A, the horse is engaging his circle of muscles at the walk. Note the forward and upward appearance of motion. In B, the same horse is walking with poor use of his circle of muscles. In photos C and D, you see a similar comparison at the trot. In E, the horse is cantering in the pasture and correctly engaging his circle of muscles at liberty. Compare this photo to F, where the horse is displaying the same correct, forward energy at the canter under saddle, and G, where his back is hollowed, his head is up, and his abdominal muscles are relaxed and dropped.

the same desirable characteristics over fences as he does on the flat and will incur less concussion on his lower legs as there is less downward energy flow and he is lighter on his feet. The horse in fig. 1.8 H is a good example as he makes jumping the fence look effortless. The incorrect horse in fig. 1.8 I displays hollow areas similar to the horses in figs. 1.8 B, D, and G. Horses that jump in this manner often look like they are "climbing" their fences or rushing at them, using speed rather than impulsion to clear the hurdle.

When a horse uses his back correctly and is free of pain, forward movement becomes effortless and supports the rider. When he uses his back incorrectly due to poor training or physical pain, he will have rough gaits, difficulty moving forward, and his hollow back will cause his neck position to be high and stiff. The physical pain associated with this incorrect movement is often caused by an ill-fitting saddle, so it is *imperative* that, before you ask a horse to use his back and move forward and round in a frame, you acquire a saddle that fits you and your horse properly.

C

D

E

F

G

Evaluating Posture in Motion (cont.)

1.8 H & I The forward and upward motion of the horse in H will carry him and his rider easily over the fence, but photo I shows a hollow horse that will not likely clear the jump with his hind legs.

CHECKLIST

Horse Evaluation

Consider the following list while observing your horse at the walk, trot, canter, and, if applicable, while jumping.

- Is his circle of muscles engaged?
- Is he "filled out" through the loins?
- Are his withers raised?
- Is his neck round?
- Is his poll the highest point?

- Are his abdominals engaged?
- Do the lines of motion move forward and upward?
- Is he "tracking up" with his hind legs?

The Horse's Pain-Free Back and Saddle-Fit Book

Recognizing
Saddle Problems

What are the signs of pain caused by the saddle? A horse's *physical* symptoms, *behavior* problems, and *performance* issues can all give clues.

Physical Symptoms

The following symptoms provide direct evidence that a saddle has caused or is causing problems for your horse.

A *sore* under the saddle clearly indicates a problem (fig. 2.1). Open sores are usually seen on endurance horses, fox hunters, and other horses that are ridden for extended periods of time. Sores should always be considered serious and should be investigated promptly.

If you have used a saddle for a long time and suddenly discover an open sore, carefully check the bottom of the saddle. Sores can be caused by

---

Physical Evidence of Poor Saddle Fit

- Obvious sores
- White hairs
- Temporary swellings after removing the saddle
- Scars or hard spots in the muscle or skin
- Muscle atrophy on the sides of the withers
- Friction rubs in the hair

---

a broken tree, or perhaps a nail or staple that has worked its way loose and is digging into your horse's back. An incorrectly reflocked saddle can cause sores if used on a long ride (see p. 29), and check your saddle pad for wrinkles or foreign objects, such as burrs.

White hairs appear as a result of inappropriate pressure from a saddle and sometimes, may be the only visual sign that a problem exists (fig. 2.2). The pressure alters the hair follicle, which then produces a white hair. White hairs can be subtle and often do not appear until a coat change occurs, either in spring or fall. If the damage is limited and you correct the saddle-fit problem, the white hairs may disappear at the next coat change. However, if the white hairs reappear, it means you have most likely failed in correcting the problem. Be aware that if you buy a horse with permanent white hairs in the saddle area, he may have residual back pain originating from a poorly-fitting saddle (see chapter 14, p. 189).

Temporary swellings that appear immediately after a saddle is removed, commonly referred to as "heat bumps," are often seen on endurance horses. They result from pressure created either by the saddle or the rider.

Scars or *hard spots* can occur on the skin surface or deep in the muscles on either side of the withers. Skin surface scars are most commonly seen on trail horses, but can occur on any horse in conjunction with any type of saddle. The scars deep within the muscle may not be apparent unless you feel into the muscle. The skin and sweat glands at these scars are often so damaged that even when the saddle-fit is corrected, they may be areas that cannot sweat.

Muscle atrophy can be recognized by deep pockets or depressions on either side of the withers or poor muscling over the entire back (fig. 2.3). The pockets bordering the withers are fre-

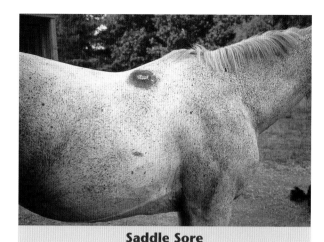

Saddle Sore

2.1 Open sores like this one clearly indicate a serious problem with the saddle or saddle pad.

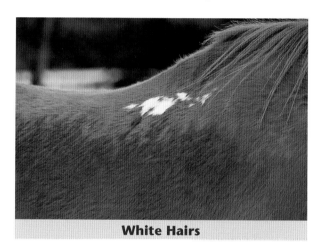

White Hairs

2.2 White hairs like these appear when pressure has damaged the hair follicles.

quently caused by saddles that are too narrow or by unnecessarily thick saddle pads that compress the withers (see p. 149). When a correctly fitted saddle is used, the atrophy process is reversed and

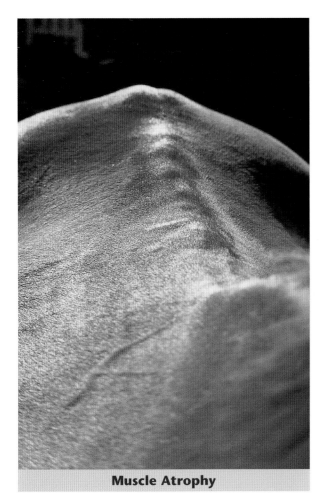

Muscle Atrophy

2.3 In this photo you can see "pockets" or depressions alongside the spine where the muscles have atrophied. This is because, due to poor saddle fit, there is excessive pressure on the muscle and the horse cannot use his back properly.

these hollow areas will generally fill out. Sometimes muscle regeneration occurs quickly; other times it requires several weeks or months. In some cases, treatment for back pain and changes in training techniques are necessary before muscle atrophy will improve (see chapter 14).

Friction rubs on the horse's hair are apparent when you remove your saddle after riding. Friction rubs can be, but are not always, sore. They occur when the saddle moves too much from side-to-side, usually from incorrect girth placement or uneven panels.

Behavior or Performance Problems

Behavior or performance issues related to saddle-caused back pain are often assumed to be training problems. Due to this misunderstanding, the horse is usually "disciplined," trained more intensely, or sold. When, and if, saddle fit is addressed and the source of pain is removed, these "training problems" are quickly resolved.

Behavioral Signs of Back Pain

If a horse *objects to being saddled or girthed*, he may be experiencing back pain. Most performance horses have sore backs to some degree, and many have pain originating from poor saddle fit. Often, when a properly fitting saddle is used, the protests desist.

Many horses are *unable to stand still* or are *fidgety when mounted*. They will paw the ground when tied and dance around on the cross-ties. If your horse fidgets at mounting time, or in other situations, it might be because every time you mount, the shifting saddle jams him at the base or sides of his withers. (High-withered horses suffer the most often from this.)

A horse with sore back muscles is often *hypersensitive to brushing*. When a person has the flu and her whole body aches, she does not want anything to touch her skin—even clothes. Similarly, this horse will not want to be brushed or touched.

A horse that is considered uncooperative, or to have a *bad attitude* about being handled or ridden, is often reacting to pain.

A horse with back pain has trouble standing with one leg up in the air and his back twisted, and is therefore often *difficult to shoe*. Misbehavior in this situation is often unfairly disciplined.

A horse may try to relieve pain by *bucking* or *rolling excessively* in his field or stall, while other horses are *too sore to move* at all in the pasture.

A horse may consistently *rearrange the bedding in his stall* in order to stand in a particular way that lessens or alleviates pain, usually with either his front legs higher than his hind, or vice versa. He may even "sit" on his water bucket or feed tub.

A horse with back pain may exhibit annoying *repetitive behaviors* like pinning his ears, swishing or wringing his tail, grinding his teeth, or tossing his head.

Performance Problems Indicating Back Pain

Performance problems can range from a mild protest when mounted, to an episode as an unmanageable bucking bronco. Many, if not most, of the difficulties encountered when training challenging horses can be traced to back pain, and training becomes much more productive when the problem is resolved. You can learn a great deal about saddle fit by observing how the horse reacts when you ask for different movements and exercises (figs. 2.4 A & B).

Some horses either sink down when being mounted or tighten and "hump" their backs during the first few minutes of riding. Others may actually buck early in the ride, then settle down after warming up. This is known as being *cold-backed*.

Some horses are very tense or stiff for the first part of the ride and appear to be *slow to warm up or relax.* Certainly, this may be due to arthritis or some other bone or joint pain, but often when back pain is discovered and the saddle fitted correctly, the problem disappears and the horse warms up easily.

Many riders and trainers believe that all horses *resist work* at different stages in training and that some horses are just resistant by nature. This is simply not true. There are times when the horse may not know how to respond correctly—when the messages or aids given by the rider are not clear—or when the horse is so sore that he refuses to move forward when asked, but it is not the nature of horses to resist constantly. To be able to do as their riders or trainers wish, they must be unimpeded by pain.

If the front third of the saddle restricts the horse's shoulders or withers, he will be *reluctant to stride out.*

Frequently, *obscure rear leg lameness or stiffness* originates in the back. Such lameness occurs because the hind legs cannot engage or come underneath the body with normal, strong movement. Instead, the hind legs tend to trail behind the horse. This causes excessive stress and concussion on the hind leg joints. *Reluctance to use the back and hindquarters properly* is caused by too much pressure from the back third of the saddle.

A horse that travels in a hollow-backed position from a back dysfunction hits the ground harder than a horse traveling with a free and loose back. Consequently, a hollow back can lead to heel pain, commonly assumed to be *navicular.* Conditions such as *front leg lameness,*

Performance Problems Indicating Back Pain

- "Cold-backed" during mounting
- Slow to warm up or relax
- Resists work
- Reluctant to stride out
- Hock, stifle, and obscure hind limb lameness
- Front leg lameness, stumbling, and tripping
- Excessive shying, lack of concentration on rider and aids
- Rushes to or from fences, or refuses jumps
- Rushes downhill, or pulls uphill with the front end (exhibits improper use of back or hindquarters)
- Demonstrates an inability to travel straight
- Is unwilling or unable to round the back or neck
- Displays difficulty maintaining impulsion or collection
- Twists over fences
- Falters or resists when making a transition
- Bucks or rears regularly
- Exhibits sudden, decreased speed on the racetrack or in any other timed sport
- Is slow out of the starting gate
- Ducks out of turns, turns wide
- Increases resistance as a riding session progresses

and *frequent stumbling or tripping* can be the result of shoulder movement inhibited by the weight of the saddle and rider on the shoulder blades.

A horse that *shies excessively* or *displays a general lack of concentration on the rider and the aids* is often in pain. This source of distraction manifests itself as a shortened attention span or as shying at every little thing.

Some horses *rush to* a fence to get it over with, while others come to the fence slowly, jump carefully, and *rush away* afterward. Some, of course, *refuse* to jump at all, or may become chronic stoppers. This "fight or flight" behavior is the horse's normal response to discomfort. Almost all of these horses are experiencing some degree of back pain and, more than likely, have pain in other areas of their body as well.

Many horses *rush downhill* in an unbalanced manner, usually on the forehand with a hollow back, a high head, and ewe neck, which stresses the front legs—particularly the suspensory ligaments. Horses that *pull*

Performance Problems

2.4 A & B Many performance problems can be related to back pain caused by saddle fit. Pinning the ears back, swishing the tail, or reacting like the horse in photo B are frequently seen responses to pain.

• The Horse's Pain-Free Back and Saddle-Fit Book •

B

• Recognizing Saddle Problems •

themselves uphill with their front legs are generally unable to properly use their backs or hind legs. Remember that the hollow position of the back leaves the hind legs trailing behind the horse, making a strong, upward push with his legs correctly underneath him impossible. When back pain is relieved, however, the horse will naturally balance himself on hills with his hind legs engaged, thereby decreasing the amount of stress on his front legs.

Some horses seem incapable of *traveling in a straight line*, even on flat ground, and are often much worse going downhill. A poorly fitting saddle, or a saddle with a twisted or broken tree, can cause this problem.

The horse that tends to *travel on his forehand* or is *unwilling to become round and engage his hindquarters* generally has back pain. If your horse is pinched or compressed somewhere in the front two-thirds of the saddle, he will be reluctant to lift his back and stretch his neck and head out and down.

When the horse's back is stiff or painful, he *has difficulty maintaining impulsion or collection* due to an inability to engage his hindquarters.

Faltering or *resisting during transitions* from trot to canter, and walk to trot, is a common symptom of back pain. Transition problems indicate pressure toward the back third of the saddle.

Horses that *twist over fences* are either unable to jump the height being asked or experiencing pain. Some upper-level, open jumpers are thought to have a "style" of jumping that involves twisting their backs; however, most of them are actually very sore and they twist to avoid hurting themselves further.

A horse that *bucks or rears regularly* is often directly reacting to a painful saddle. Rearing, in particular, commonly results from pain near the withers that is caused, or aggravated by poorly fitted tack.

Many promising horses start their careers showing a great deal of speed, only to slow down as time goes by. *Decreased speed on the racetrack or in other timed events* can sometimes be remedied by replacing a poorly fitting saddle and providing treatment for chronic back pain.

A horse will be *slow out of the starting gate or box* if he cannot crouch down and propel himself from his hindquarters. Back pain is a common cause of slow starts in many sports.

Turning issues can occur in all sports and are due to discomfort, poor balance, or poor riding. Crooked saddles or riders cause horses to *duck out of* or *become unbalanced in turns*.

Most horses will improve as they warm up, so a horse that *increases resistance as the ride progresses* usually has a saddle-fitting problem.

3

Saddle Construction

It is important to understand the saddle's construction and why one saddle may work for you and your horse, while another may not. Each piece of the saddle and how it is attached to another can influence the comfort of horse and rider.

Parts of the Saddle: An Overview

Interior

The *tree* is the foundation of the saddle upon which the leather is attached. There are two basic types of trees: *spring* and *non-spring*.

A *spring tree* is the most common type of tree used in modern saddles (figs. 3.1 A & B). It is made from wood or a synthetic material and is reinforced with metal head and gullet plates and the spring. The spring is made of two flat pieces of flexible metal that run along the bottom sides of the tree from the front to the back and around the cantle. A broken spring can be repaired, but a broken tree cannot, though it may be replaced.

A *non-spring tree* is constructed in a similar fashion as a spring tree but, as befits the name, without the spring (figs. 3.2 A & B).

The *head* is the wooden arch that makes up the shape of the pommel (fig. 3.3 A). It is also called the "iron arch" because it is lined with metal reinforcement on both sides (see *head plate* and *gullet plate*). The head can have a *regular-shaped* arch or a *cut-back* or "scooped-out" shape (figs. 3.3 B & C). The cut-back head allows the withers more clearance. The saddle may be cut back 1 to 4 inches, and the back of the head angles down so that it blends into the pommel of the saddle. A cut-back head cannot be

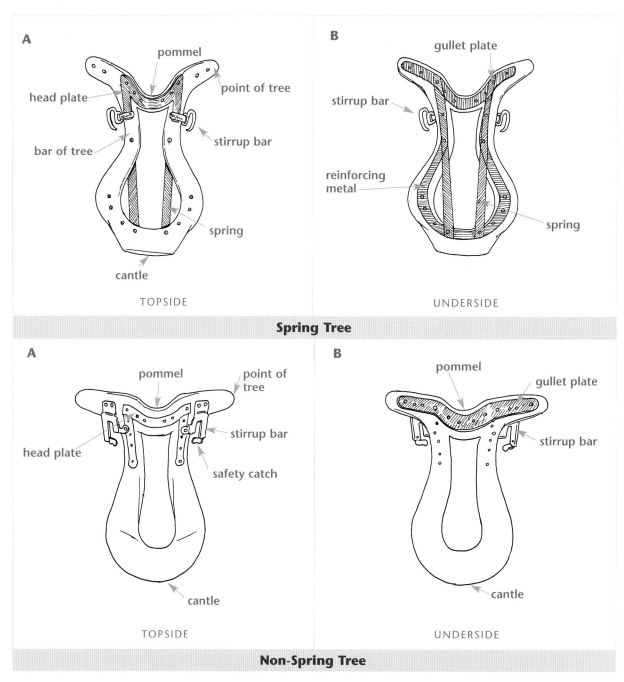

A

pommel

head plate

point of tree

bar of tree

stirrup bar

spring

cantle

TOPSIDE

B

gullet plate

stirrup bar

reinforcing metal

spring

UNDERSIDE

Spring Tree

A

pommel

point of tree

head plate

stirrup bar

safety catch

cantle

TOPSIDE

B

pommel

gullet plate

stirrup bar

cantle

UNDERSIDE

Non-Spring Tree

3.1 A & B and 3.2 A & B Parts of the spring tree and the non-spring tree.

The Horse's Pain-Free Back and Saddle-Fit Book

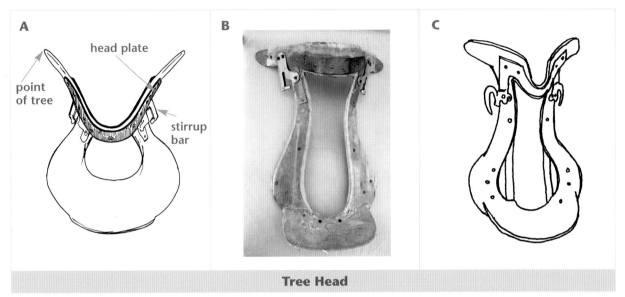

A

point
of tree

head plate

stirrup
bar

B

C

Tree Head

3.3 A – C In A, you can see the different parts that make up the head of the tree and the shape of the pommel. Photo B shows a regular-shaped pommel and C shows a cut-back head, or pommel.

adjusted, and if the head breaks, cut-back or not, it cannot be repaired.

The *head plate* is the piece of metal across the *topside* of the head that reinforces the arch so it does not break (see figs. 3.1 A and 3.2 A). The head plate's shape can be altered to adjust tree width, but if the head plate is broken, the tree is also broken and cannot be repaired.

The *gullet plate* is the piece of metal that adds strength across the *underside* of the head (see figs. 3.1 B and 3.2 B). Its shape can be altered to adjust tree width, but when the gullet plate is broken, the tree is broken and cannot be repaired.

The *points of the tree* are the ends of the head

and form the shape of the tree across the horse's withers (see figs. 3.1 through 3.3). This shape determines the width of horse the tree will fit. The points are normally the only parts of the tree you can see without tearing the saddle apart. To see them, lift the saddle flap and look for the U-shaped, *point pockets* at the front of the saddle. The points may be totally encased in leather. The angles of the points on some high-quality trees can be adjusted to fit different horses.

Surface
All of the *surface topside* and *surface underside* parts of the saddle that follow can be seen in figs. 3.4 A – D.

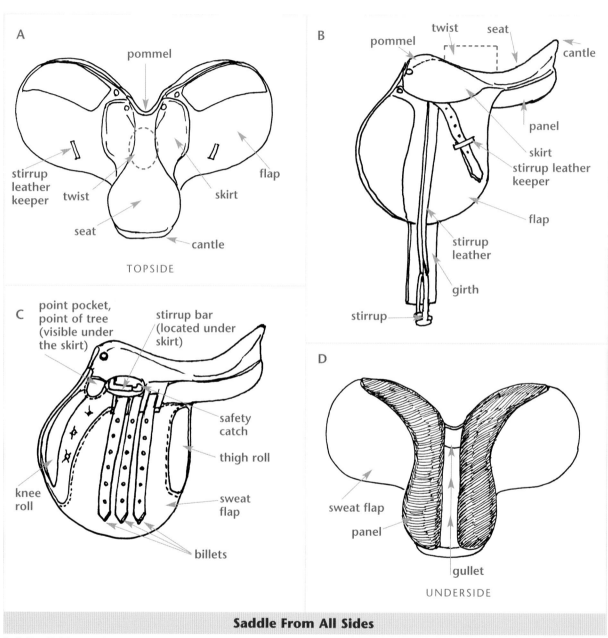

A TOPSIDE

pommel

stirrup leather keeper

twist

seat

cantle

flap

skirt

B pommel

twist

seat

cantle

panel

skirt

stirrup leather keeper

flap

stirrup leather

girth

stirrup

C point pocket, point of tree (visible under the skirt)

stirrup bar (located under skirt)

safety catch

thigh roll

sweat flap

knee roll

billets

D UNDERSIDE

sweat flap

panel

gullet

Saddle From All Sides

3.4 A – D Figure A shows the saddle as viewed from above, B is from the side, C has the saddle flap removed, and D is the underside—the part that actually comes in direct contact with the horse.

The *pommel* is the top of the front of the saddle. The leather of the pommel covers the head of the tree and cannot be adjusted.

The *saddle flap* is the flat piece of leather that is under the rider's leg to protect it from the girth billets. It is also the place where *knee rolls*, *thigh blocks*, and similar additions can be attached. Small straps or slots cut in the flap provide keepers for holding the extra length of the stirrup leathers. The flaps can be adjusted on some saddles and can be repaired if they wear out.

The *knee roll* can be a piece of soft foam sewn into the front of the flap or a thick roll of foam placed just in front of the knee under the flap. If sewn into the flap, it can be thinned or thickened, but not removed completely.

The *thigh block* is a roll of foam placed *in front* of the thigh above the knee and usually on the *sweat flap* under the saddle flap. If sewn into the sweat flap, it can be thinned or thickened, but not removed.

A *thigh roll* or *jumping block* can be added *behind* the thigh to stabilize the leg for different sports, either sewn into the saddle flap or, more commonly, sewn onto the sweat flap. It can be easily adjusted.

The *skirt* is a small piece of leather that protects the rider's leg from the stirrup leather buckle, safety catch, and bar. Adjustments cannot be made, though it can be repaired if worn out.

The *seat* of the saddle refers to the *back* of the sitting area, which is the widest part of the saddle. The shape of the seat influences the rider's position. A seat cannot be adjusted unless the saddler is very skilled, but it can be repaired if it wears out.

The *twist* or *waist* encompasses the *front* and *center* of the rider's sitting area and the *sides* of the saddle where the rider's upper thigh lies. The width and shape of the twist determines the comfort of the rider's hips and pubic area. The shape of the twist cannot be changed, but there are ways to make it more comfortable (see p. 96).

The *cantle* is the back of the tree and surface of the saddle. If a corner of the cantle is broken, it will not affect the performance of the saddle, but if it breaks across the wood, the tree will be unstable.

The *stirrup bar* is attached to the tree and holds the stirrup leather in place. The *safety catch* is a joint at the back of the bar that allows the stirrup leather to come loose and free of the saddle, should the rider fall. Stirrup bars cannot usually be adjusted.

The *stirrup leather* holds the *stirrup* in place. The *keeper* holds the extra length of leather. These can easily be adjusted, and do not affect the fit of the saddle.

Underside

The *panels* line the bottom of the saddle and are in direct contact with the horse's back. Panels come in many different sizes and shapes, and can be adjusted to fit a variety of horses.

The *gullet* is the space between the panels on the bottom of the saddle, creating clearance for the spine. The gullet can be adjusted on many saddles.

The *sweat flaps* lie directly against the horse's skin. They protect the *billets* from sweat, and the horse from the billets. They cannot be adjusted, but they can be repaired.

The *billets* provide a specific location and surface for attaching the girth. They can be repaired, and their location can be altered to fit different horses (see p. 76).

Parts of the Saddle: Specific Areas

Tree Construction

When a saddle is built, the tree is the starting point. It is the foundation of the saddle and greatly contributes to its safety and longevity. As mentioned previously, spring trees are most commonly used today. In many cases, the spring acts primarily as a support to make the tree lighter and more flexible. Sometimes, the spring actually helps shape and curve the tree to fit the horse's back. A tree made without springs is generally heavier and stiffer and there is no "give" to it at all, though from the horse's standpoint, the type of tree is less important than the fit. If you happen to have a choice between a spring and non-spring tree, the spring tree will offer a bit more flexibility and comfort for you and your horse.

The standard, good-quality tree is made from laminated beech wood—a strong, flexible wood that is layered and glued like plywood, allowing flexibility and minimizing weight. Laminated wood does not change shape and securely holds the screws, nails, or staples commonly used in saddle construction. The tree width of many

Crooked Tree

3.5 A crooked tree sitting on a flat surface. Note how the rear right-hand corner does not make contact with the table. A saddle built with this tree as its base will never fit a horse.

laminated trees can be changed if the head plate and gullet plate for that specific tree are available in the size you need. In some cases, it can be rasped to a custom shape without compromising strength. (For example, a saddler might want to adapt the shape of the tree under a rider's leg to create more room for her thigh to fit comfortably.) However, if the laminated tree is too thin, it is more likely to break than a heavier tree, and they can be manufactured crookedly (fig. 3.5).

Trees made from poorer quality wood may be cheaper but may not be laminated and will not have the strength and flexibility of the beech wood. They are more likely to become bent, or even break, when they are used. Trees can also be made from various synthetic materials. Well-constructed synthetic trees are made in a mold, which eliminates the possibility of crookedness. However, over time, some synthetic trees spread and change shape from the heat, weight, and forces generated by the rider, especially during jumping. They can be too flexible, and the rider's weight can create painful pressure points under the stirrup bars. And, a synthetic tree does not hold screws, nails, or staples as well as wood does, so your saddle may fall apart easily.

Most inexpensive wooden trees and some synthetic trees should not be adjusted, even if the head and gullet plates are available in the size you need, as the change will weaken the tree and increase the likelihood of a break at a later date. New head and gullet plates are usually only available from the original manufacturer, and the saddle must be sent back to the company for alteration, but a few are commercially available for use by saddle refitters. Be aware that manufacturers offering to change a tree size are actually only changing the head and gullet plates, and while this can work very well, do not misconstrue this as a whole new tree.

Some manufacturers claim that their synthetic trees can be adjusted, either by heating or spreading them, but in my experience many tend to revert to their original shape, and you are left with a saddle that does not fit.

Saddles made with *adjustable trees* are an excellent idea, but unfortunately, they have not been perfected. The goal is to be able to use the same saddle on different horses, negating the need to own several saddles. However, the adjustable trees that are currently available have several worrisome tendencies.

The main concern is that the adjustment tends to change only one part of the tree, usually the angle of the front of the tree at the points, and if only *part* of the tree fits the horse, it has basically the same effect as when the *whole* tree doesn't fit. Also, most adjustments originate at the center of the pommel, and the points of the tree may no longer lay parallel to the horse's withers (see *Tree Fit*, p. 55). Imagine an "A" shape, instead of an upside-down "U" shape, fitting over the withers. The A-shape is not as "horse-shaped" as the U-shape.

An adjustable-tree saddle is also not easily changed accurately. A rider cannot expect to be able to use it on multiple horses in quick succession. Once you get it right for one horse, it will usually take quite a bit of fiddling to adjust it for another. Also, moving parts tend to wear out, especially under pressures such as those placed on saddles during riding.

Panel Construction

Panels are basically shaped sacks filled with one of a variety of materials. One sits on each side of the spine with a space between the two, which creates the gullet of the saddle. They form a soft interface between the hard tree and the soft muscle of the horse's back, distributing the rider's weight over as large an area as possible. Materials used in panel construction differ greatly and directly affect the comfort of the horse, perhaps more than any other part of the saddle.

Panels are generally covered with the same material used in the rest of the saddle. There is no real advantage to leather over synthetic material, though panels covered with poor quality leather may crack easily due to constant contact with sweat.

Some Australian stock saddles, and a few English saddles, have panels covered with *wool serge*, a strong, fairly loosely woven material. While slightly less durable than leather, these panels can be adjusted by using an awl or ice pick to push through the wool serge to the flocking material inside. You can customize these panels until the saddle fits well, but take great care when moving the flocking around. Lumps and unevenness in the panel can be created as well as corrected.

Panels are filled with wool flocking, foam, synthetic or acrylic fleece, horsehair, or a variety of other materials. There are advantages and disadvantages to all the materials used. In better quality saddles, wool and foam are most common, and truthfully, there is no one best material, as long as it is soft and smooth against the horse. The majority of panels will need to be refilled, reflocked, or replaced at regular intervals during the life of the saddle.

To determine the flocking material in your saddle, look through the *reflocking slot.* This slot is difficult to see, but it can be felt by pushing your hand between a panel and the tree and feeling for the break in the smooth leather. Pull a bit of the material out and look at it. Overly soft flocking may let the tree poke through, and very

hard panel material may have hard edges that create pressure points. If the material is synthetic, feel the bottom of the panel for lumps. If the flocking is of poor quality, a saddler can replace it with good quality flocking.

Wool is an excellent material to use to fill panels. Good wool flocking has natural softness and will conform slightly to the shape of the horse's back. It can also be carefully rearranged to create a more customized fit. Its disadvantages are that it does not stay in place permanently, it packs down over time and can become lumpy or hard. Wool flocking should be checked regularly and reflocked by a qualified individual every six to twelve months, depending on how many hours you ride.

Many types of *foam* also make excellent panel material. Depending on quality, some foam may last the lifetime of the saddle, while other foam may become compressed and hard long before the saddle has worn out. Foams come in different densities and degrees of softness. To make sure the foam in your panels is soft enough to be comfortable, you should be able to easily make a dent in it with your finger. However, if the foam is very thin or too soft, it may not serve as a protectant. Ask the manufacturer of your foam panels how long his foam lasts, or have a saddler examine the foam for signs of deterioration. A few times each year, feel the texture yourself and check for hardness or lumps forming. If you can feel the hard parts of the tree through the panel, the foam is breaking down.

The problem with foam panels is that there

are very few saddlers who are trained to work with them, and, unless professionally adjusted, foam panels that do not fit the shape of your horse will not change or adapt, so a hard square corner that creates a pressure point will always retain that shape and cause pain. Sometimes, foam panels can be removed and replaced with wool, though again, many saddlers are unfamiliar with changing panels from foam to wool, and if your saddler has never done the procedure, it might be too risky to proceed.

Synthetic fleece is used as panel material by some manufacturers and saddlers, but poor quality synthetic fleece quickly becomes lumpy and hard.

Air-filled panels have gained in popularity because they mold to the horse's back and the amount of air in them can be controlled by opening or closing a valve. This adjustment device is not always easily accessible, however. Air panels can feel unstable to some riders since the air moves around, and they become quite hard when under the pressure of a rider. They are also subject to sudden punctures, rendering the saddle temporarily unusable.

Horsehair was used in many older saddles and is still an appropriate material, but these days, few saddlers know how to work with horsehair, and it is not that easy to obtain. When horsehair is in good shape, it has some spring and resiliency. When it becomes packed down, it is very hard.

If panels are underflocked, or packed down and in need of reflocking, they will not evenly distribute the weight of the rider, and will appear lumpy and make poor contact with the horse's back. The entire panel should feel soft, inviting, and evenly stuffed. After all, your horse must wear this next to his skin. Normally, with a well-flocked saddle, you should be able to only gather a small pinch of leather from different parts of the panel. If you are able to take a large pinch of leather in your fingers, your saddle needs to be reflocked (fig. 3.6). In contrast, if the panels are overstuffed, the contact area will be narrow and hard, instead of flat and inviting (figs. 3.7 A & B).

The saddle should be reflocked with the same material it was originally filled with to provide the most consistent feel to the bottom of the saddle. If the texture of the flocking material is to be completely changed, however, the entire panel should be emptied and refilled. A poor quality saddler often takes shortcuts and may just add material without regard to what was done previously.

Selecting a skilled person to reflock your saddle can be a challenge. Many saddles have been permanently damaged, and even destroyed, by a poor reflocking job. Once a saddle has been badly reflocked—especially if the leather is stretched due to overstuffing—it will be impossible for even the best saddler to repair it. You have the right to ask any saddler about his credentials, and be sure to check out the person's work (see p. 185). Try to evaluate some saddles he has worked on, and talk to local people about the saddler's reputation and their experiences with him. The best referrals come from people you know and trust.

Understuffed Panels

3.6 A panel needs reflocking if you can take a significant pinch of the panel leather. This would be difficult to do with a properly stuffed panel.

Ideally, the saddler can evaluate the horse and saddle together before beginning to reflock. However, due to the scarcity of qualified saddlers in America, you may find you'll need to send your saddle away. If so, try to include pictures, videos, and measurements (see chapter 10).

Seat and Twist Construction

For the rider, the seat and twist are the most important parts of the saddle. "The seat," as I discuss it here, will also include the twist.

The seat determines where the rider will sit and how comfortable she will be. A correctly made seat supports the rider's seat bones and allows her to sit in the center of the saddle (the exceptions being saddles used for jumping, where

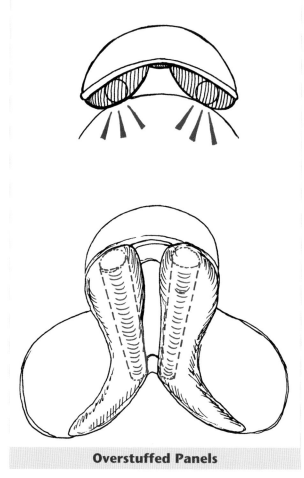

Overstuffed Panels

3.7 A & B Overstuffed panels are narrow and hard. They form two, small, cylindrical lines that distribute the rider's weight insufficiently and become severe pressure points.

riders need to sit slightly toward the front). Correct seat shape enhances the rider's ability, while an incorrectly made seat will cause her to struggle to stay balanced (see p. 89).

The saddle's seat is constructed from webbing material that is stretched over the top of the tree both lengthways and crossways. The location of the center of the seat is determined by the way the webbing is stretched. The ideal location for the lowest point of the saddle is the center of the saddle, as you measure from front to back (fig. 3.8 A). Many manufacturers of saddles are un-aware of the importance of the center and the balance point of the saddle (see *Balance Point*, p. 67). Instead, they locate the lowest part of the seat on each saddle randomly. This variation in centering the seat is the main reason you can ride in a specific saddle from a particular maker, and have it fit and feel great, while a different saddle of the same brand may not fit or feel good at all.

Many saddles are built with the lowest point of the seat near the rear. This concentrates the rider's weight at the back of the saddle and causes the rider's legs to drift forward in what is called the "chair seat" (fig. 3.8 B, see also *A Level Seat*, p. 66). A seat built like this will make it difficult to get out of the saddle in the rising trot.

The twist of a jumping saddle is generally longer and narrower than in a saddle designed for flatwork (fig. 3.8 C). This style is known as a *broken twist* and allows the rider to sit close to the front of the saddle and bring her knees and thighs closer together for increased stability.

Seat Sizing

The standard factory designation for seat size is a less-than-reliable gauge. As with our own shoes and clothes, manufacturers' sizing is not consis-

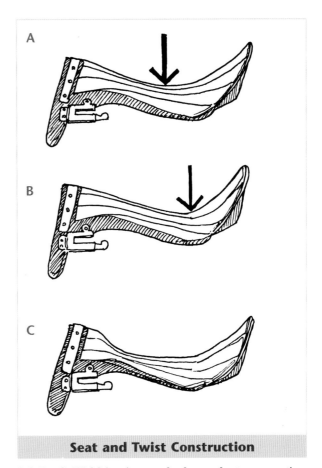

Seat and Twist Construction

3.8 A – C Webbing is stretched over the tree, creating the shape of the seat and the twist. In A, the center of the seat is ideally located in the center of the saddle. The center of the seat in B is near the rear of the sad-dle, which will cause you to sit too far back. The saddle in C is designed for jumping, and its twist—called a broken twist—is generally longer and narrower so the rider can bring her knees and thighs closer together.

Measuring Seat Size

3.9 To measure saddle seat size accurately, create a solid line across the front of the pommel, and using a tape measure, measure from the center of the back of the cantle to this line. To be precise, subtract a quarter of an inch to compensate for the leather roll sewn onto the front of the saddle.

tent throughout the industry. At one point or another, you have probably ridden in a saddle that, even though the seat was the "right" size, felt too big or too small. Saddles are commonly measured from the center of the cantle to the button on the pommel. However, a general lack of quality control permeates the industry and the saddle maker can locate the button anywhere, so seat measurements are not standard from one saddle to the next.

To consistently and correctly check seat size, measure the saddle yourself. Use a tape measure or ruler and measure from the center of the cantle to a solid line across the front of the pommel (fig. 3.9).

Subtract a quarter of an inch to adjust for the rolled leather seen in front of the tree at the pommel.

Billet Construction

Well-constructed billets are a very important safety feature. In the standard three-billet system, the two rear billets are attached to a strap that goes over the tree, and the forward billet is attached to a strap that is fastened to the tree on each side (fig. 3.10 A). This method of securing the billets distributes the pressure from the girth's action over the entire tree.

Occasionally, saddles are so poorly constructed that the billets are placed under the tree and above the panels (fig. 3.10 B). To check, pull on the billets and watch for panel movement, then slide your hand along the top of the billets, and if you can feel the edge of the tree, your billets are probably attached in this undesirable manner. Your horse may get white hairs or sore spots under the billets (fig. 3.10 C). This problem can usually be corrected by having a saddler move the billets from the bottom to the top of the tree.

On trees made of synthetic material or thin wood, it is possible for the screws, nails, or staples that attach the forward billets to the tree to become insecure. (Staples are less secure than nails, which are less safe than screws.) Evidence that a billet may not be safely attached include: very cheap workmanship overall; bits of nails or tacks sticking out underneath a flap of leather; visible staples; and loose or missing stitching on a newer saddle.

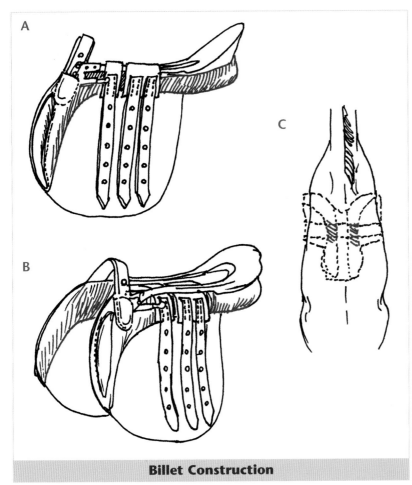

Billet Construction

3.10 A – C The inside view of the saddle in A shows how the billets should be placed over the tree. In B, they are incorrectly placed under the tree. Not only is this unsafe as the billets could easily separate from the saddle, but as you can see depicted by the red areas in C, can cause painful pressure points on your horse's back.

Stirrup Bar Construction

The stirrup bars are usually riveted onto the corner where the points and bars of the tree meet. Occa-sionally, on a dressage saddle, you will see them attached directly to the bar of the tree, which allows the rider's leg to hang down in the correct posi-tion (see figs. 6.1 A – C, p. 85). A correctly placed stirrup bar is parallel to the tree, neither pok-ing in toward the horse's back, nor out toward the rider's leg. Sometimes, a saddle maker in-tentionally recesses the stirrup bar, angling it in toward the horse's back, decreasing the bulk under the rider's leg. Unfortunately, the bar can then press into the horse's back (see *Stirrup Bars*, p. 75).

Stirrups

Stirrups are present to give the rider a base of support and a place to put her feet. They are usually made of metal, though some are made of plastic—espe-cially for endurance riding. It is important to check stirrups for weak areas or cracks, as a bro-ken stirrup can be a serious haz-ard (see p. 84).

Stirrups come in several designs (figs. 3.11 A – D). Some have a wider tread than others; some are jointed either in the middle of the side or near the tread; some are offset with the tread placed at an angle; and there are safety stirrups that are specially designed to free up the foot in an emergency. The treads can also be covered with various materials; usually rubber. These will act as a cushion to the feet as well as help keep them warmer in the winter.

Leather

Production factories, where most saddles are made, do not pay careful attention to details when selecting leather. Naturally, leather has a wide range of variation in thickness and flexibility, but it is often cut mechanically without regard to these characteristics. In order for each side of the saddle to wear evenly, leather parts should be carefully cut out in pairs from similar areas on the hide. When purchasing a saddle, compare each side for equality in cut, thickness, and grain.

Synthetic leather saddles, when well made and designed, look exactly like leather, can wear very well, and are very cost effective. Follow the manufac-

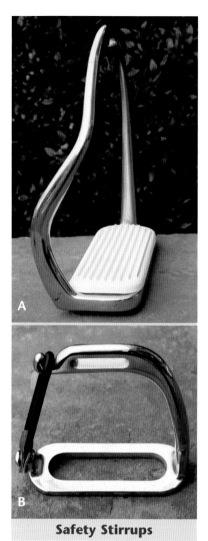

Safety Stirrups

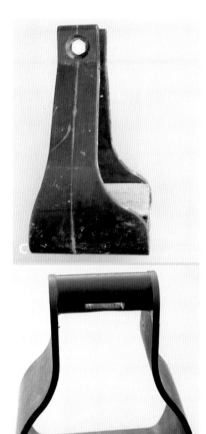

Endurance Stirrups

3.11 A – D Safety stirrups prevent the rider's foot from getting caught in an emergency. In A, you see a stirrup with a solid curved side, and in B, a stirrup with a rubber band forming one side. Endurance riders often favor stirrups made of plastic. Photo C is a plastic stirrup with sponge padding in the foot-rest area, and D is one that is slightly offset, which can create a more comfortable angle for the rider's leg.

turer's care instructions to properly care for a synthetic saddle, and it can last a very long time.

Good leather, well cared for, should last a lifetime, while cheap leather can wear out in a few years. Buy a saddle with the best leather you can afford, and care for it appropriately to get the longest life possible (see p. 186).

Saddle Innovations

Innovations in saddle type, adjustability, and material are regularly introduced to the market. As a consumer, you must be sure to critically examine claims of simplicity, versatility, or rider comfort. In my experience, such benefits often come at the sacrifice of your horse's health.

Treeless Saddles

The *treeless saddle* comes in different designs that have proven versatile enough for use in many sports (fig 3.12 A). Because there is not a tree, it fits many horses of different shapes and sizes—those with very high withers or big hollows on each side of the withers are the exceptions.

The treeless design does not have a gullet, so a horse with a spine visible *above* the back muscles will need a pad with a gullet to prevent the rider's weight from impacting his spine (fig. 3.12 B, and see sidebar, p. 141). A Quarter Horse or Morgan type, with a spine *below* the level of the muscles—the sort of horse that collects rain down the center of his back—does not need a special pad. The muscles themselves act like a gullet, which keep the saddle (and the rider) off the spine.

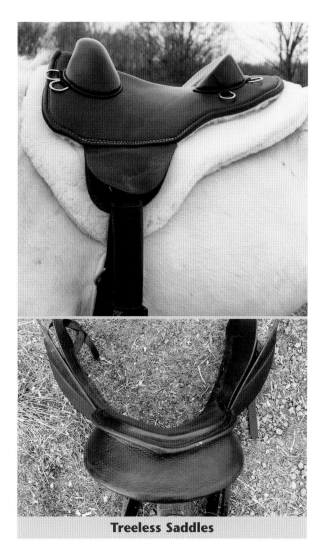

Treeless Saddles

3.12 A & B Photo A shows a treeless saddle. There is a small wooden piece at the pommel, and another at the cantle, which help stabilize the saddle, but essentially, the rider is sitting on the horse's back without a tree in between. In B, the underside view of a treeless saddle used for dressage clearly shows the lack of a gullet.

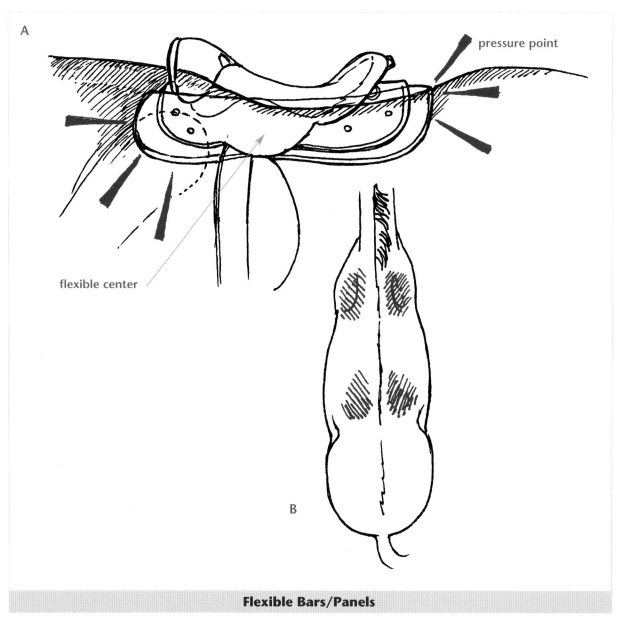

A

pressure point

flexible center

B

Flexible Bars/Panels

3.13 A & B Figure A shows a saddle with long, flexible bars (panels). Many of these saddles are made for endurance riding, but some are made in a more traditional English style. Unfortunately, the bars are often too long to conform to the shape of the horse's back so leave a gap in the center of the saddle, which puts extreme pressure on the tops of the shoulder blades and loins (B).

In some of the treeless saddles, the rider's weight causes both the pommel and cantle to lift, eliminating most of the pressure on the horse's back. The areas that contact the horse are under the rider's thighs and seat bones, and since there is no tree to provide sharp points, the pressure is typically quite soft.

Billet systems on these saddles are similar to traditional saddles. On many models, the stirrup attachments can be moved to the most comfortable place for the rider (see p. 84).

Partial-Tree Saddles

For years, the *partial-tree saddle* has been used for exercising racehorses, and in some countries, for endurance horses. This saddle is very comfortable for the rider, but the problem with the rider's weight concentrated over a short tree is that after a few months, the horse feels significant pressure points where the tree ends.

Flexible Bars

A *flexible bar* is another name for a flexible panel. It is similar in function to a traditional panel, except that it is one separate piece of flat material attached to bottom of the tree—often a piece of flat plastic covered with foam or fleece. It is attached with bolts, Velcro™, or other fasteners. It has long been used by endurance riders, but is now appearing on other types of English saddles.

Assuming modern plastics technology provides the correct materials, the flexible bar may eventually become an important part of saddle design, because the concept is excellent. It is soft, molds to the shape of the back, and moves with the horse. However, if a saddle with a flexible bar fits poorly, there are some significant problems. A bar that is too long, stiff, and flat to conform to the shape of the horse's back causes soreness on the shoulder blades, withers, and loins (fig. 3.13 A). The most critical problem is that the bar is generally attached to the four corners of the tree, creating four pressure points and not offering support to the center of the horse's back (fig. 3.13 B, see *Panel Fit*, p. 66).

Adjustable Panels

A few saddles are made with *adjustable panels* that the manufacturer states you can custom fit to the shape of your horse. Just remember, changing the panel shape will not necessarily make the tree fit the horse, and while adjustable panels are certainly a good idea, most still need to be perfected.

4 Saddle Evaluation

As it pertains to your horse's well-being, the importance of good saddle fit is indisputable, but finding the right saddle isn't easy. The variables of good fit are many. When evaluating a saddle, it is necessary to examine it both on and off the horse, with and without a rider. The first step in the process is to conduct a thorough examination of your current saddle, or one you are interested in purchasing, for safety, quality of construction, and symmetry.

Saddle price is generally based on the quality of the leather, since leather is its most expensive feature. In general, however, the leather is less important than the quality of the construction itself. "Stock," or off-the-rack, saddles are manufactured in factories. Workers are not highly paid, and many of them have never seen a horse—let alone ridden one—and most manu-

facturers do not have strict quality control. Custom saddlers, ideally, should be stricter about quality control, but be wary; some are not. While you can get a one-year warranty against manufacturing defects in a cheap coffee maker, in the world of saddles, you are lucky if you can get a warranty against the tree breaking. In many cases, you can't even test ride the saddle you are looking to buy!

In my experience, the initial cost of the saddle seems to have no bearing on the quantity or severity of structural defects. A $4000 saddle is just as likely to have major problems as a $400 saddle. A custom-made saddle is as likely to contain defects as an off-the-rack saddle. While a new saddle is not likely to have a broken tree, you should be aware that a saddle that has been used only a few times could have a cracked tree, without outward evidence of damage to the leather. And, some synthetic trees can warp if left in too much heat, such as in a car. This is why it is so important to be educated. It's your best defense against uninformed sales staff and a general lack of industry standards.

Saddle Pre-purchase Exam— Checking for Structural Soundness

Assessing Trees in New and Used Saddles

All saddles, including new ones, should be checked for broken or weakened trees. A broken saddle tree *is not repairable*. There are shops that claim to mend trees, but these repairs usually do not hold (fig 4.1). In some cases, and at a great expense, a new tree can be put in a used saddle. Replacing a tree is essentially building a saddle all over again, but if you love your saddle and it fits both you and your horse well, you may choose to go that route.

Look for worn areas or wrinkles in the leather of the saddle. Turn it over and look carefully at the bottom for any sharp protrusions that could also indicate a broken tree or spring. Slip your hand underneath the panels, next to the tree, and feel for anything sharp. A saddle with a healthy spring tree should have some give to it when you flex the seat area (figs. 4.2 A – D). If the seat flexes *a lot* when you push on it, and you do not see wrinkling of the leather, the tree may be thin and weak, or even possibly broken. If the flex feels different from one side to the other, the tree or the spring may be damaged. A saddle with a non-

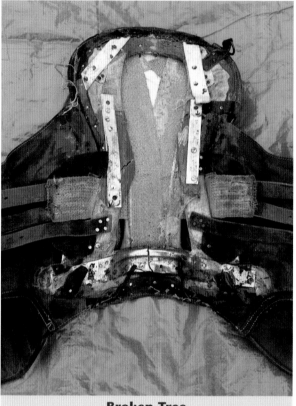

Broken Tree

4.1 This tree was broken, repaired, and then broken again. It is a good example of how tree repairs generally do not hold. It is important to recognize, for safety, that once a tree is broken, the saddle is no longer useable.

spring tree should not flex or give at all when you push on it. The lack of flex is not a problem if the tree and the saddle fit the horse.

Tree manufacturers are now using new materials, many of which may have as much, if not more, flexibility than a spring tree. Be open-minded, but cautious, about new tree materials. Remember that excessive flexibility may mean the tree will not be able to support your weight properly. Look for good independent research data before investing in a tree that feels very flexible.

Checking for Symmetry

Saddle Symmetry Basics

A well-made saddle is symmetrical when viewed from every angle. Many saddles are not symmetrical to begin with, and asymmetry can "creep up" on older saddles. While ideally, a saddle should be completely symmetrical on both halves, very small deviations can be tolerated. Here are some reasons why asymmetry occurs.

- Manufacturing issues: If the saddle leather was cut from two or more different hides, each hide will stretch in a different way as the saddle is broken in.
- Repair: If a repair is done using a different type of leather, or a piece of leather was cut in a different way than the original, then asymmetry can occur.
- Rider: A person who rides unevenly can, over time, make a straight saddle crooked. Regularly mounting from the ground on the same side can twist a tree.
- Horse: A crooked horse can alter the shape of a saddle over a period of time.

It is important to check all saddles, new and old, for symmetry in the *leather* and *stitching*. If pieces such as the knee rolls or flaps are stitched asymmetrically, it could cause the rider to feel unbalanced, and if the uneven part affects the way you sit in the saddle or the way the saddle sits on the horse, then the saddle becomes unacceptable.

Check the *topside* of the saddle, by holding the cantle against your thigh and grabbing the front of the pommel with your hand; then let the saddle swing or balance from your hands (fig. 4.3 A). Take your time and check and compare each side carefully. Examine the attachment of the panels (you can see the front and back corners of the panels from this top view), the location of the stirrup leathers, and the position of the flaps. Tip or roll the saddle slightly forward and backward to see each part clearly.

Any asymmetries observed from the top view will directly affect the rider. If the tree is distorted or the seat leather is sewn on unevenly, your pelvis may rotate and follow the imbalance. This can lead to back pain, or one leg may drift forward or backward. If the flaps are attached unevenly, one leg may appear to be further forward, and you will constantly hear your riding instructor telling you to move your leg, but you won't be able to comply (fig 4.3 B).

If the leather of the seat is worn unevenly in a used saddle—typically shown by worn spots or discoloration—it could have been caused by several factors. The previous owner may have ridden unevenly because of her own physical issues; because the tree, panels, or another part of the saddle is uneven; because the knee rolls, thigh blocks, and thigh rolls are attached unevenly; or because her horse was asymmetrical. Try to discover what the cause of the uneven wear was, and if it is in the construction, don't buy the saddle.

Once you have looked at the saddle from the top and are satisfied that there are not any major problems, turn the saddle over and study the *underside* (fig 4.4 A). Hold the saddle in good light, so you can see the panels and gullet clearly.

The panels are the most common areas for asymmetries. The panels need to be smooth, relatively soft, and symmetrical from side-to-side (fig 4.4 B). As you examine the bottom of the saddle, imagine whether you would feel comfortable with the panels in question on your own back. To demonstrate how important the bottom of the panel is, try this experiment. Next time you get in your car, carefully fold a shirt or sweatshirt, and place it between your back and the seat. Drive down the road, and notice how soon you notice all of the minor creases and wrinkles in the sweatshirt. As time goes by, focus on how your back muscles feel. Keep the "panel" there for as long as you can bear it. Add a marble or a bottle cap to simulate a lumpy panel if you're feeling daring.

The width of the gullet (the gap between the panels) determines how much room the horse has to move his spine. A consistently even space along its entire length, which can be as narrow as 2½ inches or as wide as 3¼ inches between the panels, is ideal. An uneven gullet width causes a lopsided saddle and an unbalanced rider (fig. 4.4 C). Gullets that are too narrow pinch and restrict the movement of the spine and create pressure points (fig. 4.4 D). Gullets that are too wide may allow the saddle to touch the spine, especially on a poorly muscled horse.

As you look down the gullet of an older saddle, you may notice two parallel ridges at the bottom (fig 4.4 C). These ridges are the springs of a spring tree showing through the thin leather lining. The panels should lie parallel to these ridges and almost cover them. If there is more space between a ridge and a panel on one side

Checking the Tree

4.2 A – D Hold the pommel against your thigh and pull the cantle toward you, as shown in A. You should feel only a slight "give" and you shouldn't see any wrinkles in the seat area. Now, place one side of the saddle against your knee, as in photo B, and pull the opposite side of the cantle toward you, flexing the saddle across the diagonal. Repeat across the other diagonal to check each side of the tree separately. Both sides should have an identical amount of "give." If one side is broken and the other is still intact, you will notice a distinct difference. Check for breaks in the pommel area by pushing the two sides of the saddle together as shown in C. Do not stand or kneel on the saddle to do this, or you could be the cause of a break!

Another Method...
If you have difficulty checking the sides of the tree as described in B, you can also do so by resting the pommel against your thigh and pushing down on one side of the seat at a time with the heel of your hand as shown in D. This is a particularly good alternative if you are not especially strong.

Checking Topside Symmetry

4.3 A & B With the cantle against your thigh and your hand at the pommel, allow the saddle to hang suspended for your inspection. The left and right sides should appear identical. (Do not assess symmetry based on the buttons near the pommel, as they are added by hand and are not part of the saddle's structure.) As you are looking down at your saddle, take note of the position of the saddle flaps. Figure B shows a saddle with a right flap that is farther forward, which will cause a rider's right leg to drift forward.

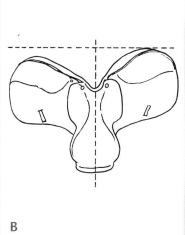

than on the other, the saddle is uneven. If you cannot see these characteristic ridges, you should reach under the panels to feel for the springs. Realize that when they are very prominent and the panels are thin, the springs could touch the horse's back and cause pressure points.

Put the saddle on a saddle stand or fence so you can examine it from the *front* and *rear* for overall symmetry (figs. 4.5 A & B). Examine the area where the panels attach and see if they are attached at the exact same spot on each side. To help your eye see this, you can mark the center of the pommel or cantle with chalk. The panels sometimes have a *gusset* added to increase the thickness of the cantle end of the panel, but gus-sets can be stitched unevenly, therefore creating an asymmetry (see p. 71).

Leave the saddle on the stand or place it on your knee and, using both arms, reach forward and touch each stirrup bar at the same point. Note if the position of your hands is identical (fig 4.5 C). If you are evaluating a used saddle, look down at the flaps and notice where the wear marks of the stirrup leathers are located. These marks should look the same on both sides. Check to see if the same holes were used in the leathers. If not, one stirrup bar could be placed higher than the other. If the stirrup bars are placed unevenly, you will have a very hard time keeping each leg in the same position.

Unevenly stretched stirrup leathers can also indicate asymmetrical stirrup bars. Uneven leathers can be the result of mounting from the ground regularly on one side, or riding with more weight in one stirrup. Take the stirrup leathers off the saddle and hold them together to see whether they are the same length. They should be checked on a regular basis for rotten or frayed stitching, or cracked leather.

Next, check the billets' placement. Billets are stitched onto a piece of canvas or nylon that crosses the tree under the seat (see *Billet Construction*, p. 34). They secure the girth and keep the saddle stable. Asymmetrical placement of the billets will twist the saddle when the girth is tightened. With the saddle on a stand or your knee, reach from behind the saddle, and put the same finger of both hands on the billets. Check to see if your hands are in the same place. This exploration technique is a bit difficult, since it can be challenging to notice a quarter of an inch difference between the sides. Sometimes it is helpful to have a friend stand in front of saddle to check your hand placement or to hold the flaps up so you can see where your hands are. Check the condition of the billets for cracks, rotten stitching, or weak places. Pull hard on them to be certain that they are anchored tightly, and if you feel any give, have them repaired immediately. Billet repair is easy and inexpensive, and it is dangerous to ride when they are weakened or torn.

If you discover serious, unrepairable defects in your current saddle, the only right thing to do is retire it. Reduce the likelihood of the saddle

When Custom Panels Have Gone Too Far

Horses frequently change shape. With a saddle that fits well and a conscientious training regimen, a horse usually acquires muscle or becomes more evenly muscled. After correcting a saddle-fitting problem, dramatic change in his musculature can occur very quickly.

When reflocking, some saddle fitters purposely create uneven panels in order to more closely fit a specific horse's back shape. However, unless the saddler is very skilled and you have the saddle rechecked every few months to adjust it to accommodate the newly developing back muscles, this process can be dangerous. It is often better to stuff panels symmetrically, as uneven panels can cause the horse's back to remain misshapen. Worse, if you use an uneven saddle on another horse, it will not fit, and may cause serious damage.

being used again by removing the billets, and donate it as a decoration to a non-profit organization (allowing you a tax break), or give it to a restaurant for decoration. Though it may be difficult to part with a saddle that you've had for many years, it is often the safe and responsible thing to do.

Checking Underside Symmetry

4.4 A – D Check the symmetry of the panels and gullet by holding the saddle upside down, as shown in A.

In B, you can see smooth, wide, even panels and a gullet width that can accommodate almost four fingers of a medium-size hand, allowing plenty of room for the horse's spine. This underside construction is very inviting to the horse's back.

The saddle in C has uneven panels: the panel on the right is visibly wider and flatter than the panel on the left, and lumps can be seen in the leather on both sides. Notice the two parallel lines in the gullet. These are wear marks from the tree's spring that are showing through onto the outside of the saddle. They indicate further asymmetry, as you can see that the space between the line indicating the spring and the left-hand panel is not identical on the right side. The gullet is also very narrow near the cantle, widening toward the pommel.

Photo D shows a saddle with a very narrow gullet. Only two fingers fit into the space, which means there will not be any room for the spine to move.

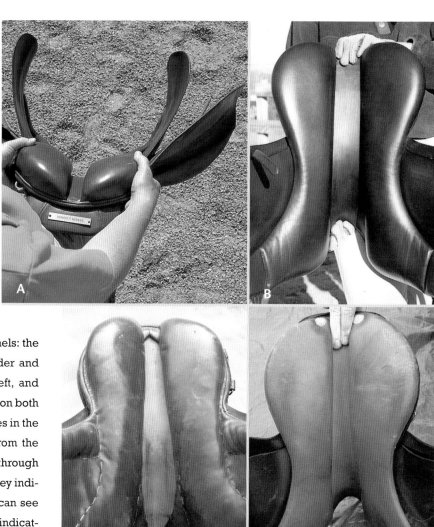

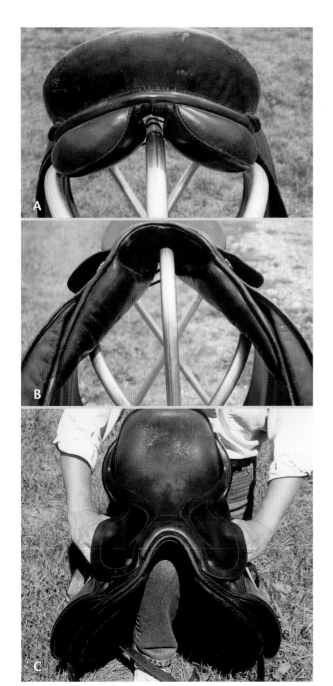

Checking Front and Rear Symmetry

4.5 A – C Sit the saddle on a rack, fence, or sawhorse, and stand directly behind it as in A. Look for the panels not only to be symmetrical, but to be attached to the saddle symmetrically. If you compare the left-hand panel to the right-hand panel on this saddle, you can see that the left is thicker than the right, and the stitching differs dramatically on each side.

Now, stand directly in front of your saddle as in B. The front view shows that the left side panel is attached to the saddle at a lower point than the other. It is also apparent that the gullet is not symmetrical. Imagine that the middle metal piece of the rack is your horse's spine, and you can see how the saddle would sit crookedly on his back.

Checking Stirrup Bar Symmetry

Leave the saddle on the rack and face it from the cantle side, or place the saddle on your knee with the cantle against your torso as shown in C. Reach forward with both hands on either side of the saddle and feel for the stirrup bars. Note if there is a significant difference in their placement on the saddle. You may need a friend to look from above and tell you whether or not your hands are in the exact same location on each side.

Saddle Evaluation

Saddle Feature	Factors to Consider		
Tree	■ Condition	*Leather*	■ Condition
	■ Width		■ Quality
	■ Symmetry	*Flaps*	■ Symmetry
Panels	■ Material		■ Length
	■ Thickness		■ Knee roll / thigh block Placement
	■ Hardness		
	■ Smoothness	*Seat*	■ Symmetry
	■ Symmetry		■ Wear
	■ Width		■ Seam condition
Gullet	■ Width		■ Location of deepest point
	■ Symmetry	*Stirrup leathers*	■ Stitching condition
Stirrup bars	■ Evenness		■ Leather condition
	■ Levelness		■ Evenness
	■ Safety catch condition	*Stirrups*	■ Condition
Billets	■ Location and style		■ Width
	■ Evenness		■ Style
	■ Condition		
	■ Leather quality		
	■ Placement		

5

Saddle
Fit on the Horse

" There is another consideration of great importance with regard to the place of the saddle—namely, that it should interfere the least possible with the action of the muscles of the horse's fore and back hands."

Francis Dwyer,
Seats and Saddles, Bits and Bitting, Draught and Harness, and the Prevention and Cure of Restiveness in Horses, 1869

Once your current saddle—or the one you are considering—has passed the soundness evaluation, you must assess how it fits your horse. This is a three-step process. First, you must examine your horse's back for structural or muscular maladies. Then, you must put the saddle on his back and determine if it accommodates your horse's shape and size. Finally, you should ride in the saddle and decide how your weight, your needs as an athlete, and the specific demands of your sport affect the way it fits your horse (see chapter 11).

Horse Examination

Before you place the saddle on your horse's back, a careful, physical examination of his back, neck, and hindquarters is in order. With patience and practice you can learn to evaluate the texture of the muscles for pain or tension. Healthy muscle has a soft feel and round look. Tight muscle looks and feels hard and has visible lines separating the different parts of the muscle. To help see and feel areas of tension, try examining a horse that is always relaxed and carries his head naturally low, then compare the look and feel with a horse that is generally uptight and carries his head high.

Always begin with a light touch and slowly increase the pressure. Observe your horse's reactions carefully. Small signs of discomfort can be very significant. A normal back has soft muscle—the consistency of a shelled, hardboiled egg—which you can probe quite deeply without signs of pain or contraction. Your first light and gentle touch may not reveal anything remarkable, or could simply trigger a normal reflex response (figs. 5.1 A – D). A reflex is a normal, nervous system reaction, like your knee jerking in a doctor's exam. Sometimes the normal reflex response can be mistaken for soreness, especially if you move your fingers quickly along the back and hindquarters rather than probe each area individually.

Gradually increase the pressure along the back muscle, and watch for contractions or twitches anywhere—not just under your fingers—in response to pain. Pain reactions can vary from a mild contraction of the muscle near your finger, to severe and sudden sinking of the back accompanied by a hardening of the back muscles. Some horses twitch or seem ticklish when you perform this examination, especially in response to a light touch. With others, this twitching, ticklish response may be caused by pain, and will go away when that pain is relieved. If you discover areas of muscle that are painful, tight, or hard, make note of them and then check your saddle for the corresponding pressure points.

Splinting, or bracing the back muscles so that they do not move, is a common response to this exam, because when a painful muscle is held rigid, it hurts less. This is sometimes misinterpreted as an absence of pain because the muscles don't move or sink away from the pressure.

Riderless Saddle Fit Examination

Under a saddle, the muscles surrounding the horse's withers are like your foot in a shoe (figs. 5.2 A & B). If the shoe is too tight, there is very little you can do to make your foot feel better. If the shoe is too loose, it may help to add a sock. If your shoe has uncomfortable pressure points, fit may be improved by adding an orthotic or some other device, but it is likely that there is nothing you can do to correct the basic fit. The truth is, if your shoe hurts your foot, you probably want to change the shoe. Saddle-fitting should be much the same.

It is important to realize that *perfect* fit is elusive. Once you have matched a saddle to both horse and rider as best you can, don't worry about "perfect." Sometimes "good" is good enough, especially if you ride recreationally. If, on the other hand, your horse exhibits performance or behavior problems that could be related to saddle fit, it is best to keep trying to improve the situation.

Position

Begin by placing the saddle in question on your horse in a kind manner. An English saddle is usually less than 20 pounds, sometimes even less than 10 pounds, so it should be easy to lift and set down gently. If you have trouble with this, try standing on a stool. At this point in the evaluation, use the saddle only—no pads or girth. If the saddle is brand new and you need to keep it clean, use a *very thin* piece of cloth or towel on the horse's back to protect it.

The most critical aspect of saddle fit is the position of the saddle on the back. A correctly positioned saddle that fits well allows the horse to move freely and the rider to stay balanced. Con-

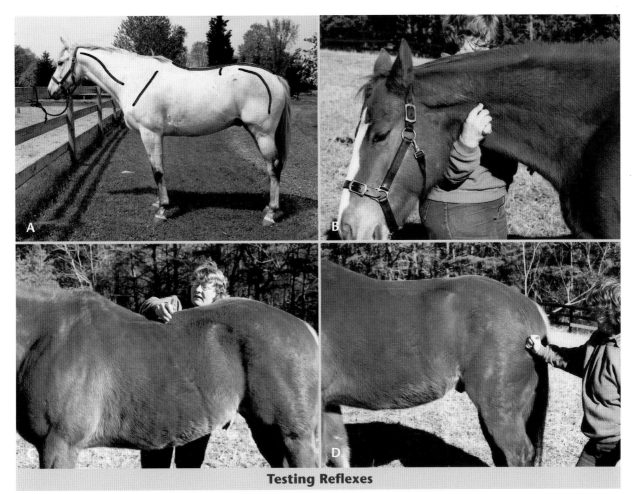

Testing Reflexes

5.1 A – D The lines drawn on the horse in A represent areas where a reflex movement away from pressure can occur. If your horse is not sore, he will simply move away from your touch, but if he is sore when you touch these areas, he may bite, kick, or pin his ears. To test your horse's reflex response, begin by running a pen along his neck as shown in B. Your horse should bend his neck away and tip his nose toward you. Next, run the pen along your horse's back as in C. He should respond by "dipping" his back down as you move from his withers toward his tail. Then, run the pen down around his hip as in D. Your horse should tuck his rear end and move away from you. (Note: I am standing on his other side only for photographic purposes in B and C).

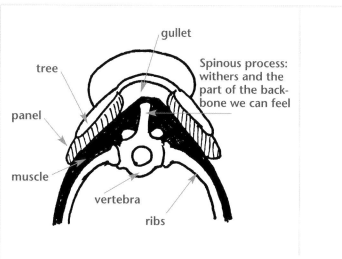

5.2 A & B Figure A shows a cross section of a saddle and a horse's rib cage (thorax) and how the soft muscle of the back lies over the hard bone of the ribs and vertebrae. Compare this fit to a shoe on a person's foot, as shown in

B. The tree is the shoe's upper layer, the horse's back muscle is the foot, and the rib cage is the inner sole of the shoe.

versely, an incorrectly placed saddle will restrict the horse's movement and unbalance the rider. To check the position of the saddle, have an assistant hold your horse, and stand him squarely on a level surface. If he rests a hind leg or shifts his legs constantly, it will be very difficult to assess saddle position. Be patient, since a horse that will not, or cannot, stand still usually has some type of back pain or other body pain (see p. 17).

A horse has only one place on his back where the saddle will sit naturally. This is behind the shoulder blades (figs. 5.3 A & B). When positioned there, the saddle, assuming it fits your horse's shape, will generally be stable. To correctly place the saddle, hold a hand over your horse's shoulder and have a friend lift that same front leg and gently pull it forward. Feel the hard shoulder blade move back. When it comes to freedom of movement, the shoulders of the horse are as important as the spine, so you must be sure they are free from pressure and can rotate efficiently. The saddle should be placed about 2 inches behind the shoulder blade when the horse is standing squarely (figs. 5.4 A & B). Initially place the saddle forward on the shoulder blades, then slide it backward until it settles into place.

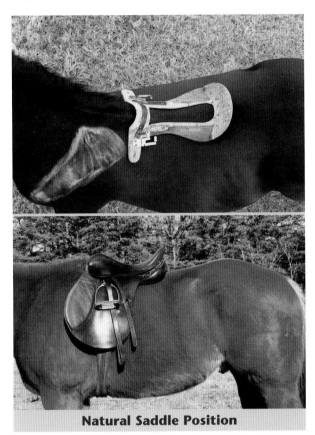

Natural Saddle Position

5.3 A & B Photo A shows a view of a saddle tree placed correctly behind the shoulder blades. (The left shoulder blade has been marked with chalk.) The position of this tree will not interfere with the motion of the shoulder. In B, you can see the correct placement of a saddle in its natural position.

The most common positioning mistake is placing the saddle too far forward (fig 5.4 C). In this position, the rigid points of the tree sit directly over the muscles above the shoulder blades, restricting movement in the horse's shoulders and front legs, and tipping the saddle down toward the cantle. Once the saddle is moved to the correct position, your horse's stride will generally lengthen immediately, and his head carriage will improve. If the saddle is placed too far back, the saddle will tip down at the pommel, the panels may rise at the back, and the rider will feel like she is tipped forward (fig. 5.4 D).

For jumping sports where a rider uses a short stirrup, the flaps need to extend over the shoulders to provide space for the rider's legs, especially with the more forward-cut flaps seen in cross-country and steeplechase saddles (fig. 5.5 A, and see also *Eventing*, p. 169). Because the leather is not stiff and weight is not placed on the flaps, they do not interfere with shoulder movement. A correctly placed dressage saddle should *not* have flaps that extend over the shoulder blades (fig. 5.5 B).

Tree Fit

The tree is the backbone of the saddle. Ideally, the "naked" tree, before leather or panels are added, will follow the contours of the horse's back and maintain even contact all along the muscles so the panels can easily fit (figs. 5.6 A – C). In order to attain the best fit possible, saddles come in all different tree widths and shapes. Some manufactured brands have a range of sizes, while others offer a rather limited selection. As is often found with human shoe fit,

"In the perfect world the tree would be fitted to the back before the saddle was built."

Elwyn Hartley Edwards

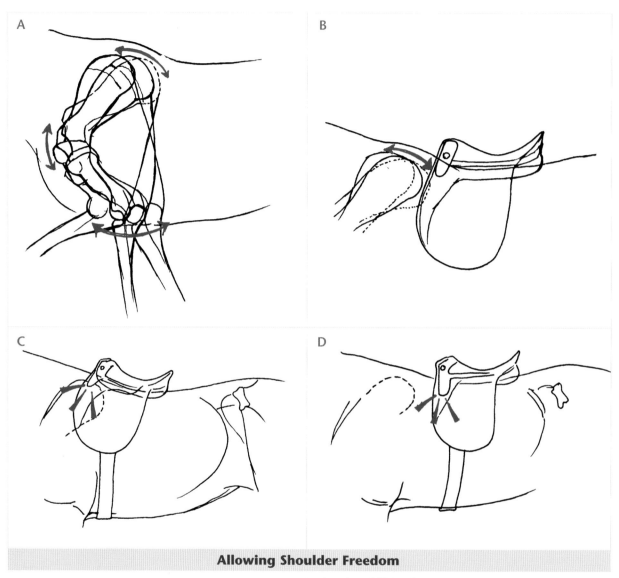

Allowing Shoulder Freedom

5.4 A – D Figure A shows how the top of the shoulder blade rotates backward and downward as the horse's leg moves forward. In order for that motion to occur, the saddle must be placed about 2 inches behind it, as in B. In C, the saddle is placed too far forward so the tree hits the shoulder blades. Note that the saddle also tips downhill backward to the cantle, which puts all of the rider's weight at the back of the saddle. A saddle placed too far back from the shoulder blades, as in D, will tip down in front and create painful pressure at the points of the tree.

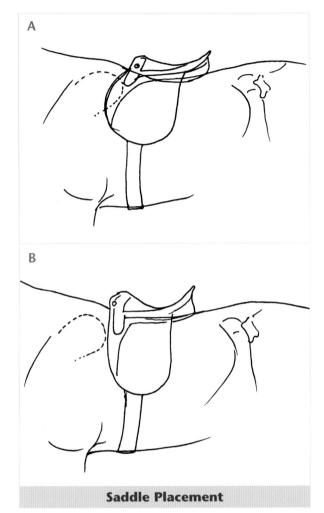

A

B

Saddle Placement

5.5 A & B Figure A shows a jumping saddle correctly placed. Though the flaps extend over the shoulder blades, they don't create a problem because the rider does not put weight on them. In B, a dressage saddle is shown correctly placed behind the shoulder blades.

Saddle Position and Different Sports

It is impossible for a horse that is being jabbed in the shoulders by his saddle to round and properly use his circle of muscles. Most competitive horse sports reward a rounded back and neck. For example, the fairly low head carriage and rounded back desired for the show hunter is much easier to achieve with a saddle that does not inhibit the shoulder blades. A jumper rider who puts his saddle too far forward can't expect his horse to use his shoulders to clear high fences. A dressage horse needs his shoulders free to be able to attain self-carriage and perform required movements. It is of the utmost importance that saddle placement is correct in order to ensure peak performance in any of these, and in many other, equestrian sports.

some saddle brands tend to run wide while other brands run narrow, and some horses fit one brand well, but do not fit a second brand at all.

Ideally, the tree should be long enough, front to back, to span the entire length of the horse's rib cage, but should curve up slightly at the cantle to avoid the corners poking into the lumbar muscles (fig. 5.7). The rider's weight will then be supported by the strongest part of the horse's back—the center. Because the lumbar or loin area is the weakest part of the back, the tree should not be so long that it places any weight

Position Check

Place the saddle on your horse's back without a girth, and walk him around for a few minutes (have an assistant walk beside him to catch the saddle in case it slips). If the saddle actually falls off or slips without naturally settling into place, it probably does not fit. (For exceptions, see chapter 8, p. 113.) The well-fitting saddle should shift itself to the correct place—sitting snugly in position even without a girth. Some people who have found that "perfect fit" can complete 100-mile endurance rides with a fairly loose girth, even going up and down hills, with the saddle still remaining in place. (Of course, do not go out and ride with a loose girth just to test your saddle!)

on it. It is quite common to see a saddle that is too short, ending right in the center of the back, especially on a larger horse. This causes the horse to carry the saddle solely on that small part of his back—obviously undesirable.

Once the saddle is built, it is difficult to measure the distance across the points of the tree because of the amount of flocking in the panels. You have to rely on the manufacturer's measurement. Tree width is measured across the tips of the points of the tree. However, there is no standardization of point shapes—trees can have short or average points, long straight points, or flared points, each giving a different measurement and fit (figs. 5.8 A – F). Therefore, a medium tree in one brand, and a wide tree in another brand, may both fit a medium-sized horse. The way a tree fits also depends on how thick the flocking is in the panels and how the panels are attached to the saddle. If two saddles have the same size tree but the panels were put on differently, they will each fit your horse differently. So, never buy a saddle based on the way a similar saddle fits; always try the one you are actually going to buy.

Currently, many generic narrow, medium, or wide-tree saddles may not actually fit any horse well. If mass production saddle makers designed their generic saddles to fit certain breeds, it would be much easier to find saddles that fit your type of horse. For example, a generic saddle designed for a Thoroughbred would fit a large percentage of Thoroughbreds, as there tend to be similar back characteristics within breeds (see chapter 8). Custom saddlers could then concentrate on fitting the more challenging individual horses.

Trees with *long points* reach farther down on the side of the horse, which some horses like and others find uncomfortable (fig. 5.8 B). The trees with *flared points* do not follow the shape of the withers since the muscle is flat, so small pressure points are created (figs. 5.8 E & F). Check the points of the tree by sliding your hand down the sides of the withers (figs. 5.9 A – C). If you are not sure where the tree ends, look under the flap for

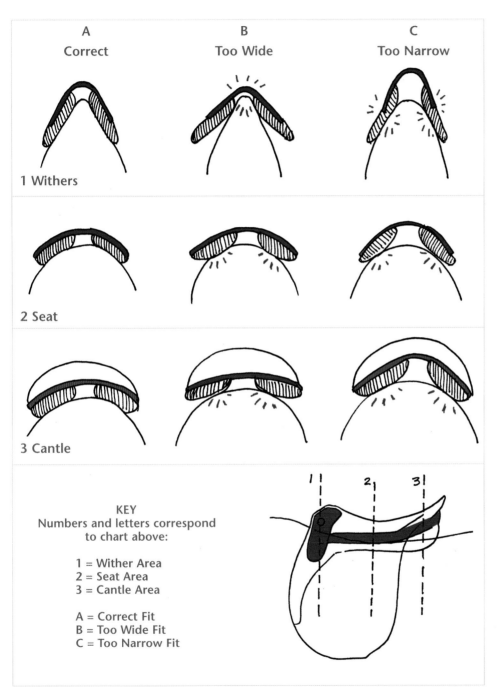

| A Correct | B Too Wide | C Too Narrow |

1 Withers

2 Seat

3 Cantle

KEY
Numbers and letters correspond
to chart above:

1 = Wither Area
2 = Seat Area
3 = Cantle Area

A = Correct Fit
B = Too Wide Fit
C = Too Narrow Fit

Tree Fit

5.6 A – C This series shows how the tree, in red, needs to parallel the horse's back. Row 1 shows tree fit in the wither area, Row 2 in the seat area, and Row 3 in the cantle area. (The saddle panels—denoted by cross-hatching—also need to follow the shape of the horse's back, see figs. 5.15 A – F.)

Column A shows correct fit. The tree follows the contours of the horse's back in each of the three areas.

Column B shows a too wide tree. The outer edges are away from the horse's body, and the inner edges take all the pressure close to the horse's spine.

Column C is a too narrow tree. The horse feels all the pressure from the saddle and rider on the outer edges of the tree, and the inner edges are above the horse's back.

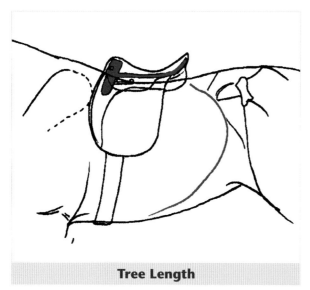

Tree Length

5.7 This tree, in red, is the correct length for the horse. If you follow the red line of the horse's last rib to his back, you can see that the tree and saddle end where the ribs end. To check where the tree should end on your horse, feel for the hard bone of the last rib at the point where the flank begins, then draw a chalk line (like the red line in this illustration) along the rib until it ends near your horse's spine.

the point pocket. You should feel even contact under your hand, with no area tighter than any other. If you feel it is tighter at the top and looser at the bottom, the tree may be too wide, and if vice versa, it may be too narrow.

Determining tree fit across the withers can be a bit tricky. Levelness of the saddle seat can help determine if the tree fits there (see *A Level Seat*, p. 66). You can also check the panels for contact (see sidebar, p. 70). You've probably

heard the "rule" about making sure there are three fingers of clearance between the pommel and the withers. Unfortunately, this is a false generalization. The ideal is to have the withers *and* the whole bony part of the spine *completely* free of contact with the saddle, so sufficient clearance—whatever it takes to achieve this—is the goal. Figure 5.2 A (p. 54), shows a cross-

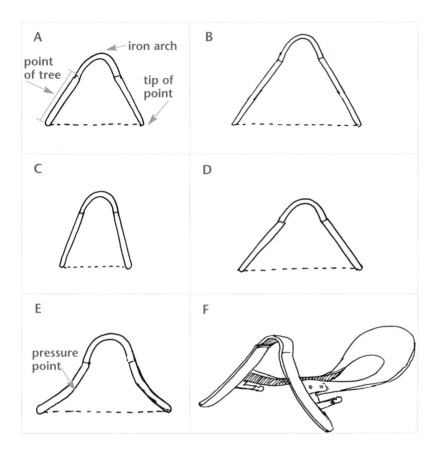

A

iron arch

point of tree

tip of point

B

C

D

E

pressure point

F

Tree Points

5.8 A – F Depending on the manufacturer, tree points can be different shapes and sizes. These illustrations show the front of the tree and possible measurements from point to point, indicated by the dotted lines. The tree in A has points of an average length and medium width, B has long points and a medium width, C is a tree with average length points and a narrow width, and D has average points but a more open angle, as would be appropriate for a wide horse. Figures E and F show a tree with points that flare outward, which often cause pressure points because of the localized contact area.

section of the muscles, vertebra, and the *spinous process bone* of the withers that your saddle needs to clear. On a high-withered horse, the pommel may only clear the spine by a finger or two, while on a low-withered horse, the clearance could be as much as four or five fingers-worth.

Place your hand well inside the gullet to check for pressure 4 or more inches in. Reach to the back of your horse's withers (fig. 5.9 B). If your horse has long withers, you will probably be unable to check all the way to the end of them.

(For help with long withers or other wither-fitting problems, see chapter 8, p. 113.) Move the saddle around a little to see if you feel pressure; if your hand gets pinched, your horse's withers will also. If one side of the withers pinches more than the other, the horse may be unable to turn or bend to one side.

You can also check wither clearance by asking a friend to look down the gullet while you are mounted to see if daylight shows through. If your horse has a prominent backbone, it may

Checking Tree Clearance

5.9 A – C Check your tree's fit by sliding your hand between the saddle and your horse's withers, as shown in A. You should feel even contact all the way down the point of the tree to the point pocket.

Check wither clearance by reaching inside the pommel and sliding your hand to the back of the withers, as shown in B. You should be able to do so without the top or sides of your hand being pinched.

You can also check tree clearance when mounted. While walking and trotting, reach one hand into the gullet as in C. Try while sitting and while standing in your stirrups. Your hand should fit between the saddle and withers without any pinching or uncomfortable tightness.

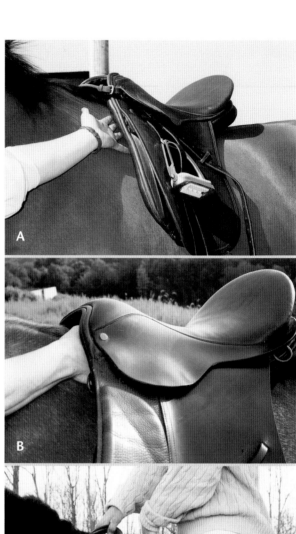

not be possible to see through. In these cases, slowly and carefully pass a flexible riding crop lengthwise through the gullet. It should go through and move around easily. Remember to use caution when using this technique, as some horses may be sensitive and react to the motion of the crop.

Another good method is to feel inside the pommel while standing in your stirrups at the walk and trot (fig. 5.9 C). Feel both the top and sides of the withers, as a saddle may often clear the top of the withers but will hit the sides as you go around corners or shift your weight. Sprinkling some talcum powder on the back of the withers before riding can also be helpful, as telltale white marks will appear on the saddle wherever you don't have sufficient clearance.

To decide if the tree is *too narrow* for your horse's wither area, stand at his side and look at the side of the saddle. A saddle with a tree that is the proper width will appear level from front to back, and the panels will display even contact with the horse's back (fig. 5.10 A). A saddle with a too-narrow tree will sit high in the front, the seat will slope down, and the panels will not touch the horse's back in the center, which is called *bridging* (fig. 5.10 B). The rider's weight will not be distributed evenly on the horse's back, but on only four points—one on each side of the withers and one on each side of the back at the rear of the saddle. These pressure points are painful, and the narrow tree will cause muscle atrophy along the withers, resulting in worsening saddle fit. (See also *A Level Seat* and *Panel Fit*, p. 66.)

Conversely, if the tree is *too wide* for the horse, the saddle will tip forward and the tree may press on the withers (fig. 5.10 C). Push down on the pommel of the saddle and watch the cantle. If it rises, the tree is too wide or there is excessive curve to the bottom of the panels (see also fig. 5.14.)

If your horse's back muscles are under-developed because of poor training, or atrophied from previous problems with saddle fit, be sure that the new tree has enough extra width at the withers to allow his muscles to fill out. The tree should be only *slightly* wide in this case, so that when you feel along the withers, the bottoms of the points of the tree feel a little bit looser than the tops. Do not be tempted to allow too much

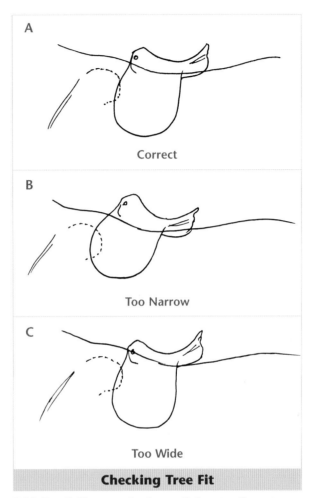

A

Correct

B

Too Narrow

C

Too Wide

Checking Tree Fit

5.10 A – C You can check tree fit by standing at your horse's side. Figure A shows a tree that fits on the horse's back. Panel contact is even and the seat is level. In B, is a tree that is too narrow for the horse. The pommel is high, the seat slopes down toward the cantle, and the panels are not in contact with the horse's back in the center of the saddle. The tree in C is too wide. The saddle has tipped forward onto the withers and the back end of the tree and the panels are raised up off the horse's back.

Jumping and Dressage Issues

Instead of following the contour of the withers, many close contact saddle trees flare outward, away from the withers (see figs. 5.8 E & F). Since the horse's withers are relatively flat where the points of the tree sit, the flare causes a very small and painful pressure point on each side. Most horses cannot tolerate this discomfort and in response, shorten their stride, hollow their backs, and jump poorly.

Close contact saddles have shorter points than any other tree style. They do not spread the rider's weight over a large enough area, so the horse is jabbed in the withers upon each landing. In fact, the points can sometimes be so short they do not hold the saddle in place, allowing the tree to rotate forward and down into the muscle on both sides of the withers (fig. 5.11). As the saddle rotates down, the cantle lifts, placing all of the rider's weight on an extremely small area of the withers, frequently resulting in severe muscle atrophy there.

To check your saddle for point length, measure from the bottom edge of the stirrup bar to the tip of the point (see fig 3.1, p. 24). A short point is approximately 1 to 1¼ inches from the bar to the end of the point, while a normal length point is at least 2 inches, and maybe longer. If the saddle you are considering purchasing has short points, eliminate it as a possibility. If you already own the saddle and it works for you otherwise, try using the rear billets to help hold the back of the saddle down and keep the points from digging in (see fig. 5.23 B). *Do not* shift the saddle further forward in an attempt to correct this problem. Many hunter/jumper riders instinctively do this to try to keep the saddle from tipping down in the front, but they are worsening

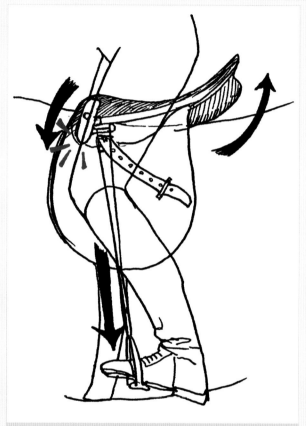

Short Points

5.11 This close contact saddle has short points, which do not hold the saddle stable at the withers. When any weight is placed in the stirrups, the saddle tips forward and downward. The horse feels extreme amounts of pressure on a very small area of the withers, especially when landing after a fence.

the problem by restricting the horse's shoulders (see figs. 5.4 A – D). Remember, your horse needs complete freedom in his shoulders to get both of you safely over obstacles. Anything impinging the withers or shoulders can hinder his ability to jump.

Some dressage saddle trees are constructed broadly across the iron arch of the head and the points, ostensibly to free up the shoulder (figs. 5.12 A & B). The saddle has to make contact somewhere, however. By having too little pressure distributed across the front of the tree, the areas around the stirrup bars end up carrying most of the weight of the saddle and rider. Added pressure in this area impedes the withers from lifting as the horse attempts to round his back, and as a result, the horse tends to conform to the shape of the saddle—dropping his back into a more swayed shape. These open-fronted, or so-called "frog-mouthed," saddles also tend to slide forward, necessitating a *foregirth*. If your horse has flat, smooth shoulders, the saddle may almost slide up onto his neck when you ask for more collected movements. (See chapter 8, for more about fitting saddles that slip forward.)

If you suspect your dressage saddle has a frog-mouthed shape, test by sliding your hand under the saddle while it is on the horse (see fig. 5.17). The frog-mouthed saddle exerts light pressure along the front of the tree and toward the rear of the panels, and heavier pressure near the stirrup bars. The saddle will be very loose when you feel under the points of the tree, and if you put downward pressure on the pommel, the saddle will tip down, then return to level when you put pressure on the cantle.

Frog-Mouthed Saddle

5.12 A & B Figure A shows a tree that is wide across the front of the head and the points. Dressage saddles often have this feature to help "free up the horse's shoulders," but the narrower part of the tree near the stirrup bars must then bear extra weight, creating the pressure points you see in B.

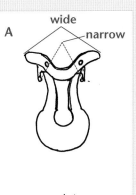

Another problem with dressage saddles, especially those with deep seats, is a tree that curves up at the cantle, carrying the panels away from the horse's back (see *Panel Fit,* p. 66). This curve concentrates the rider's weight in the center of the saddle instead of spreading it along the entire length. This kind of tree, sometimes referred to as a "banana-shaped" tree, allows the saddle to rock from front-to-back with each stride, and the horse becomes sore in the center of the saddle, often just behind the withers area (see fig. 5.14).

room for muscles to develop. The unsupported ends of the points of the tree will allow the saddle to go down in front, and the forward tipping of the saddle will concentrate the rider's weight at the front part of the withers at the top of those unsupported points (fig. 5.6 B). The increased pressure on each side of the withers will cause pain and possibly more atrophy. If you attempt to combat this issue with pads that keep the front of the saddle from tipping down, the horse will feel tightness at the top of the points. (See also *Temporary Problem Solving*, p. 149.)

A Level Seat

An important factor in good saddle fit is a *level seat*. To best balance the rider, the center of the seat should be approximately at the center of the saddle (see fig. 3.8 A, p. 33). When the lowest part of the saddle and the lowest part of the horse's back are aligned, the rider will be balanced in the center of the saddle and able to move in harmony with the horse. This is the *balance point*.

To determine the balance point, find the lowest point on the horse's back behind the withers by placing a small level (often called a *line level* and obtainable in hardware stores) along the center of the spine and moving it back and forth until the bubble is in the center of the level (fig. 5.13 A). Mark the balance point on your horse's back with chalk or talcum powder, then place the saddle in the correct place. Now, using the level, find and gently mark with the chalk or talcum powder the lowest point on the saddle. After making sure the mark on the horse's back transferred to the bottom of the saddle, remove the saddle and compare the two marks. It helps to have an assistant place a finger on the mark on the bottom of the saddle, while you hold the mark on the top, and then see how close your fingers are to each other. The lowest point of the seat of the saddle should correspond fairly closely to lowest point of the back (fig. 5.13 B).

The *marble test* can also help you locate the balance point. Visualize rolling a marble, or a golf or tennis ball, down from the pommel toward the cantle, and imagine where it would stop. Alternatively, you can actually roll any tubular object, such as a smooth round writing pen or a pill bottle, down from the pommel (fig. 5.13 C). It should come to a stop approximately in the center of the saddle.

Panel Fit

The *panels* are the parts of the saddle that most directly impact the horse. As you know, they need to feel comfortable to the horse and conform to his shape as well as distribute your weight over as large an area as possible. The panels may extend over the horse's rib cage because the ribs support the back, but they should not interfere with the shoulders, loins, or gluteal muscles, as those areas are not designed to carry weight. Horses can have flat or curved backs. The panel shape should match the horse's curves so

"…we must place the rider's center of gravity exactly over the centre of the bearing surface of the saddle which, being loaded, transmits the pressure equally to the rest of the surface."

Francis Dwyer

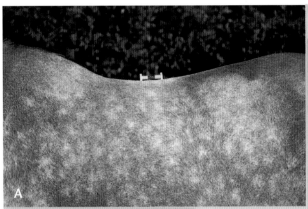

Finding the Balance Point

5.13 A – C Place a small line level at the lowest point of your horse's back, as shown in A, then move the level back and forth until the bubble is in the center. Mark this point on your horse's back with chalk or talcum powder. Place the saddle in the correct position with the level centered at its lowest point, as in B, and mark this spot. Compare the mark on the underside of the saddle with the mark on the seat. They should be very close.

Another way to find the balance point is to actually roll a tubular object like a pill bottle from the pommel, as shown in C. Where it eventually comes to a rest is approximately the center of the saddle.

the saddle will remain stable and be comfortable.

Visually check panel fit by first observing the saddle from the side. There should not be any noticeable air space between the panels and the horse's back. The panels should curve up slightly at the cantle and allow room for the back muscles to move without hitting the back edge of the panel. If you see air space in the center of the saddle, under the flaps, the saddle is *bridging*. If you can see daylight under the back of a saddle, there is excessive curve to the bottom of the saddle—causing the saddle to rock back-and-forth on the fulcrum of the curve—known as *banana-shaped* or *rocker* panels (fig. 5.14).

Stand behind your horse, look toward his ears, and see how the panels at the cantle area meet his

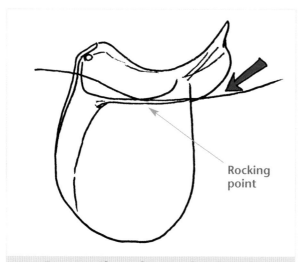

Banana-Shaped or Rocker Panels

Rocking point

5.14 This saddle's panels are too curved. You can tell by the gap at the rear of the saddle indicated by the red arrow. The saddle will rock back-and-forth in the middle.

"As regards size or extent of surface (area covered)... the greater this is with a given weight, the less will be the pressure on any given point, and consequently the less risk of a sore back, provided always that the pressure be equally distributed over the whole surface. To make a saddle a yard long, and put the weight altogether at one of its extremities, is not the way to attain this very desirable object...."

Francis Dwyer

back (figs. 5.15 A – F). The angle of the panels needs to mirror the angle of the horse's back because otherwise the weight of the rider will not be distributed over a large enough surface area. While in the withers area, the angle of the panels generally follows the shape of the tree, in the rear of the saddle, the angle can either follow the tree or be influenced by the saddler's preference in panel style. Unfortunately, this may not conform to the horse's shape.

The entire length of the panel needs to contact the horse's back for proper rider-weight distribution. A lack of panel contact in the center of the saddle, called *bridging*, is a common saddle problem. Bridging causes the rider's weight to be distributed on only four points, which, as mentioned previously, can cause serious pain (fig. 5.16 A).

One common cause of bridging is a lack of flocking in the center area of the panels, which can occur in a new saddle as well as a used one. If everything else about the saddle fits well, then *reflocking* can be considered to remedy the situation (see *Panel Construction*, p. 29). However, if bridging is caused by a too narrow tree, you may not be able to fix this problem (see figs. 5.6 A – C).

Check your saddle for bridging and other pressure points by sliding your hand up under the side of the saddle (fig. 5.17). Keep your palm flat against the back muscles, using your right hand to check the left side of the saddle, and vice versa. Slide your hand under the panel as far forward as you can (lift the saddle slightly if you need to), then slowly slide your hand all the way back to the cantle. Feel the amount of contact on your hand, and repeat several times to see if you get the same feelings, in the same places, each time.

Ideally, you should feel *even* contact all the way along the panels, with a gentle lessening at the cantle where the saddle curves up away from the back muscle. The areas where you feel *more* contact on your hand are likely to cause pressure points on the horse, and the areas under the panels where you feel *less* contact will not bear the rider's weight, creating gaps in contact that cause

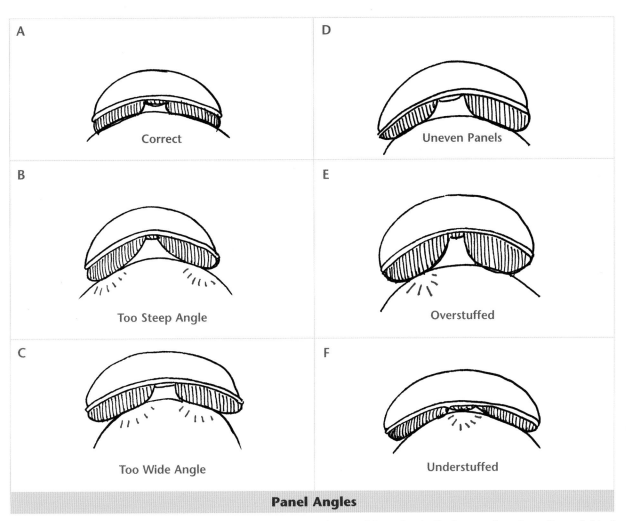

A	D
Correct	Uneven Panels
B	E
Too Steep Angle	Overstuffed
C	F
Too Wide Angle	Understuffed

Panel Angles

5.15 **A – F** The angles (and contours) created by the underside of the panels should match the contours of the horse's back in order to allow maximum rider-weight distribution. To view these, stand behind your horse. The panels in A lie parallel and as much of the surface area contacts the back as possible. The panels in B have too steep an angle; only their outer edges contact the back and the rider's weight is distributed across very narrow strips of panel. In C, the panel angle is too wide and only the inner edges bear the weight of the rider, putting pressure too close to the spine. The uneven panels in D will unbalance the rider and put excessive pressure on one side of the horse's back. The overstuffed or too thin panels in E will have limited areas of contact and weight distribution. Panels that are understuffed or too thin, as in F, will allow the tree to hit the horse's spine.

Panel Contact Evaluation Using Feel or Talcum Powder

To check "feel," see fig. 5.17. To check powder, study your horse's back muscles.

- You feel even contact (powder is evenly visible): the panels are conforming to your horse's back.
- You feel more contact on your hand (powder is less visible) at the front of the panels under the points of the tree: the saddle is too wide, or too narrow (see Tree Fit, p. 55).
- You feel less contact on your hand (powder is visible) in the center: the saddle is bridging.
- You feel more contact on your hand in the center of the panels (powder is less visible), and less contact at each end of them (powder is visible): the panels and tree are too curved for your horse.
- You feel increased contact on your hand (powder is less visible) at the back of the panels: the saddle is too narrow and is sitting down at cantle, or has less flocking at the rear.
- You feel lumps or small areas of high contact on your hand (powder is less visible): there are irregularities in the flocking or the panels shape (see Panel Fit, p. 66).
- You feel more contact on your knuckles or hand than on your fingers (powder is less visible on the outer edges of the panels): the panel angles are too steep and do not match your horse's back (see fig. 5.15 B).
- You feel more contact on your fingers than on your hand (powder is less visible closer to the spine): the angle of the panels is too wide for your horse (see fig. 5.15 C).

the horse to feel pain in some places and uneven pressure overall. You may also feel lumps in the panels or differentiations in each side. Noticing these kinds of particularities takes some concentration and a bit of practice, but this manual method is quite accurate, as has been proven when compared to readings taken with the newest in computerized technology (see p. 162).

If you are evaluating a used saddle, or one that you already own, sprinkle talcum powder on your horse's back and ride for a few minutes to help you see where the pressure points are. Carefully remove the saddle and look at the pow-

der distribution on the bottom of the panels and your horse's back. If the powder is evenly distributed, you have even panel contact. Areas where the talcum powder has disappeared from the back muscles indicates too much pressure from the saddle, and areas where the powder remains untouched indicates a gap (see sidebar, above).

Not only do the panels distribute the rider's weight over the horse's rib cage, they help prevent the tree from coming into direct contact with the horse's back. The height of your horse's withers determines the ideal thickness of the panels. A horse with low, flat withers can be rid-

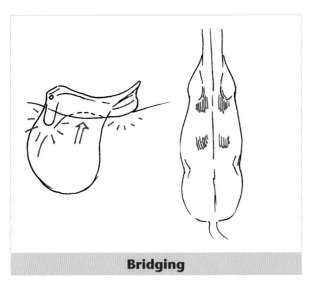

Bridging

5.16 A & B This saddle bridges, meaning it does not make contact with the horse's back in the center, as shown. Bridging causes the saddle to contact the back at four separate points, rather than distributing the rider's weight over a large area.

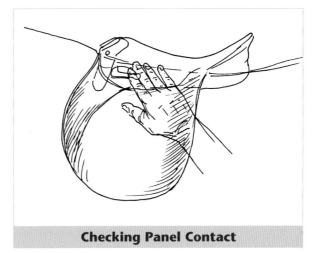

Checking Panel Contact

5.17 Slide your hand up under each panel to check its contact with your horse's back. Slide it forward as far as you can, then slowly move it back toward the cantle, always noting how much pressure you feel on top of your hand. Be sure to keep your hand under the panel, as it is easy to allow it to drift down under the saddle flap. The pressure should feel even along the entire length of the panel. If you feel deviations in the weight on your hand, your horse's back feels them, as well (see sidebar, p. 70). Be sure to do this on both sides of the saddle.

den in a saddle with thinner panels, while a horse with high withers requires much thicker panels—the thicker panels lift the tree over the withers while keeping the seat level (see *High Withers*, p. 119). A saddle with panels that are too thin will interfere with the withers and spine and will create pressure points near the loins (fig. 5.19 and also see 5.15 F).

Some saddles rock from front-to-back due to poor panel or tree shape (see fig. 5.14 and sidebar, p. 65). *Gussets* are pieces of leather that can be sewn into the outside back corners of panels

to increase their thickness or to fill in when they curve too sharply at the cantle. I often see gussets that are poorly shaped, however, and these are more harmful than helpful. The panel should gently rise up away from the back so that nothing digs into the muscles there, but many gussets square the edges of the panels, resulting in corners that dig into the back or loins. The seams

Allowing a Slight Bridge

Depending on how much your horse rounds his back during exercise, you may actually want to fit the panels with a *slight* bridge. This is especially true for many dressage horses. The slight bridge allows the horse a bit of freedom to round his back into the panel without feeling too much pressure (fig. 5.18).

5.18 A slight bridge in the saddle allows this horse to comfortably round his back.

Determining exactly how much bridge is appropriate can be a bit tricky. As a general guide, the ideal amount should feel as if the saddle is just a bit lighter in the center, but there should not be enough room to move your fingers around. To check how much your horse raises his back and how it affects the saddle, try this exercise with your *ungirthed* saddle in place. Ask the horse for a very small belly lift (see p. 5) with one hand, and feel under one panel with the other (or ask another person assist you). If the amount of bridge is correct, when his back is raised about half of an inch, the back muscles will fill the area of lighter contact, and you will feel even contact along the entire panel. This extra fitting measure ensures that your horse can comfortably round his back.

should always be on the *side* of the panel, but many gussets are placed so that the seams are on the *underside* and lie against the horse's back. This line of stitching can create a pressure point.

The close-contact jumping saddle has been popular in the hunter/jumper world for a long time, and riders are accustomed to having very little saddle underneath them. The thin panels of these saddles do not protect the horse from the tree, and the saddle often sits directly on the spine, especially at the back of the withers. To counteract these problems and keep their horses performing, riders add multiple pads, essentially sacrificing the "close contact" they desired. A

The Horse's Pain-Free Back and Saddle-Fit Book

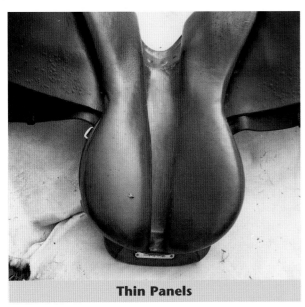

Thin Panels

5.19 Panels that are too thin or understuffed fail to keep the tree from interfering with the horse's spine.

rider will feel her horse much more effectively if she uses a saddle with panels of the proper thickness in relation to the height of the withers, rather than adding several pads to compensate for thin panels. A saddle with appropriately thick panels is also more stable than one balancing on a pile of extra pads because the panels move with the saddle as a unit, which can be very helpful when jumping.

The Gullet

The spine has no protective muscle covering and is not designed to carry weight directly. Imagine someone lightly kicking your shin bone—it will not take much impact to make you wince. If the same kick landed on your thigh muscle, it would not hurt as badly. Even moderate saddle pressure on the bony part of the spine is painful, and a horse will hollow his back to protect himself. When the saddle sits on the muscled part of his back, leaving the spine clear, he can absorb much more pressure and impact. The *gullet*, therefore, must be wide enough to keep the spine free and allow the horse's back to flex up and down, as well as slightly sideways, during movement (fig. 5.20 A—see also p. 44). For these reasons, it is better to have a gullet that is too wide than one that is too narrow. A narrow gullet can prevent a horse from bending as you turn because there is no room for the spinal curve inside it (figs. 5.20 B & C). One of the contributors to this book, Andy Foster, says he would like a penny for every time he's watched a horse work perfectly down the long side of the arena, only to throw his head up in the air when he comes into the corner—a clear sign of spine discomfort that many riders fail to recognize.

There should be at least one inch of clearance on each side of the spine before the panels begin, though in the case of a pony or a fine-boned horse, three-quarters of an inch or less is adequate. High-withered horses are generally

> "...the under surface of the saddle should be as nearly as possible the same relation to that part of the horse's back it is intended to occupy as a mould does to the cast that it is taken from, always saving and excepting that strip lying over the horse's backbone, which must remain altogether out of contact."
>
> Francis Dwyer

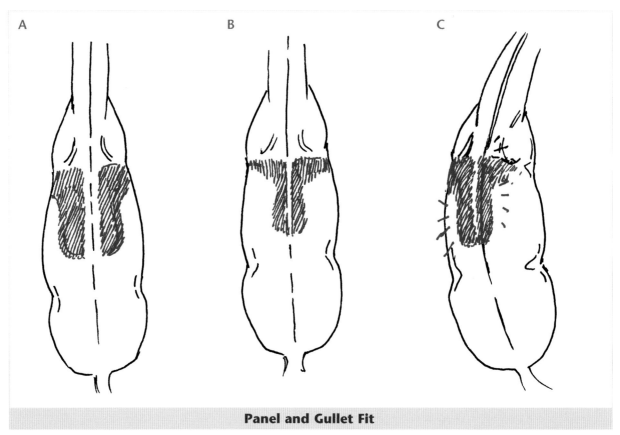

A   B   C

Panel and Gullet Fit

5.20 **A – C** Figure A shows the imprint of a saddle with wide, comfortable panels and a wide gullet, which allow the spine plenty of room to bend when the horse turns. In B, you see a saddle with narrow panels and a narrow gullet, which do not allow much room for the spine when the horse is traveling in a straight line, let alone when he bends, as shown in C.

more susceptible to pinching because their backbone sticks up into the gullet (fig. 5.21 A). The common practice of fitting high-withered horses with narrow gullets in order to hold the saddle up off the top of the spine should be avoided because the spine then becomes held in a vice-like grip between the panels (see *High Withers,* p. 119). A round-backed horse with thick back muscles and low withers might be able to tolerate a narrow gullet better because the spine itself is protected by his muscles (fig 5.21 B).

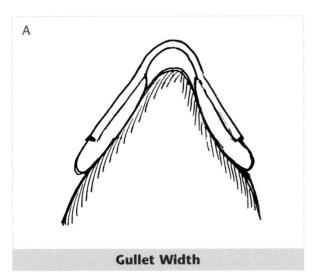

Gullet Width

5.21 A & B High withers that stick up into a narrow gullet, as in A, are extremely susceptible to being pinched. A horse with a very round back, as in B, can tolerate a narrow gullet more easily because his spine is level with or below his back muscles.

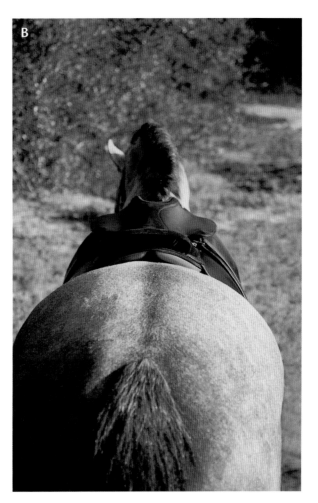

Stirrup Bars

Each time you stand in the stirrups, all of your weight is concentrated on the *stirrup bars*. On some saddles, the stirrup bars are *recessed*, or set in closer to the horse, so there is less chance that the rider will feel the buckles of the stirrup leathers under the thighs. However, placed like this, the stirrup bars can press into your horse's back through the panels, creating pressure points. Pressure from a stirrup bar is often an uncorrectable problem. Check for concentrated pressure under the bar by placing the saddle on your horse without a girth. Slide your hand

under the saddle and feel for pressure (see fig. 5.17). Remember, any increased pressure you can feel without weight in the saddle will be accentuated many times over when the rider is added. If you find a tight spot, put your finger against the saddle and ask an assistant to remove the saddle while you keep your finger in place. Note the spot you are holding in relation to the struc-

Feel What the Horse Feels

Try this exercise with a partner. Get on all fours and have your partner press her flat hand along your back muscles. This will mimic a well-made panel that would invite you to press back against it. Then, have your partner press into your back muscles with her knuckles, mimicking pressure points. This does not feel very pleasant. Next, ask her to press her knuckles briefly—and carefully—along your backbone. As the "horse," you will probably drop your back, and maybe push it to one side, in order to avoid her knuckles. Now you can imagine what your horse might feel like with a gullet that fails to protect his spine from saddle contact.

tures of the saddle. If your finger is near the stirrup bar, it very well may be the culprit. Stirrup-bar pressure can also be checked by riding a dirty horse with a clean, white saddle pad. Look for a dirt spot on the pad corresponding to the stirrup bar area (see fig. 9.7, p. 142).

Billets and Girthing

If you are satisfied with the saddle's fit at this point, it is time to add the girth to the equation. Tighten your girth slowly, carefully rechecking the saddle fit, as you may see changes occur. It will not be as easy to slip your hand underneath the panels or across the withers, but the contact should feel even in these areas. Pay close attention to the levelness of the seat, and notice whether the saddle now tips more toward the pommel or cantle. If the balance point moves forward and the back of the panels rise, the tree may be too wide, while if the balance point moves toward the cantle and panels are now digging into the muscles, the tree may be too narrow.

Billets can be short or long. With *short billets*, the girth's buckles are positioned under the rider's leg and may be uncomfortable and bulky. *Long billets*, on the other hand, are visible for six to twelve inches below the level of the flap, so the girth buckles are not under the rider's leg, resulting in comfort and closer contact with the horse.

Most saddles have three billets. They are riveted to allow the girth to hang perpendicularly to the ground and into the narrowest part of the rib cage near the elbow known as the *girth line* or *heart girth* (figs. 5.22 A – D). To identify the girth line, stand back and look for an upward curve or dip behind the elbow. On an average horse, the dip occurs about 4 inches behind the elbow. When a horse's girth line is several inches ahead or behind the average, a change in the billet selection on the saddle is required.

As a horse is ridden, the girth will always move according to the girth line. The saddle will then shift either forward or backward, following the girth. To determine whether the billets are placed appropriately for your horse's girth line, tack up and be sure to correctly position the sad-

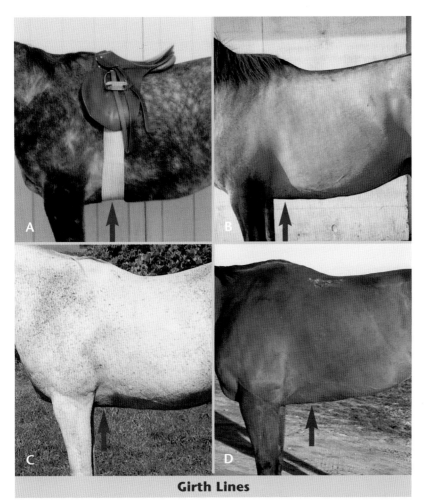

Girth Lines

dle. Put the girth on as you normally do (without worrying about the girthline), and then ride for at least twenty minutes (without a breastplate or crupper). If the billets are appropriately positioned for your horse, the ends of the girth should still appear perpendicular to the ground, and the saddle should still be in the correct place.

If the girth slants *forward* (the bottom of the girth is closer to the elbow than the top), or the saddle has slid forward onto the shoulder blades, then the billets are too far back on the saddle for your horse (fig. 5.23 A). To correct this situation, if you have three billets, you can use the two front billets to try to keep the saddle in place or have a saddler move the billets forward. If the girth angles *backward* (the bottom of the girth is farther from the elbows than the top), or the saddle slides backward, then the billets are too far forward for your horse (fig. 5.23 B). Use the two rear billets to keep the saddle forward or have a saddler reattach the billets farther back on the saddle.

5.22 A – D The girth on the saddle in A drops down perpendicularly to the ground at the narrowest part of the rib cage. It's called the girth line. You can find this point on your horse by looking for the slight upward curve in the lower line of the stomach, usually located about 4 inches behind his elbow. The horse in B has a normal girth line. In C, the girth line is very forward and close to the elbow, and photo D shows a horse with a girth line that is farther back than normal.

Forward and Back Girth Lines

5.23 A & B After riding, the girth in A has slid forward to find a girth line, which causes the saddle to slide forward as well. When this happens, use the front two billets only, if your saddle allows, or have a saddler move the billets forward on the saddle. In B, the opposite has happened, and the girth has slipped behind the vertical. This problem can be fixed by only using the two rear billets—rather than the two front billets as in this photo—to help push the saddle forward or by your saddler.

Some saddles have four or more billet straps that allow you to move the girth position easily, and saddles with adjustable billet positions make fitting a greater variety of horses with nothing more than a simple change of girth location suddenly possible.

One such adjustable system, seen on some newer dressage saddles and many endurance saddles, is a *V-system*, which allows you to change the position of the billets. This two-strap system has a *point strap*, or one billet placed far forward, and a *rear strap*, which serves to stabilize the back of the saddle. The rear strap may be attached to a "V," which allows it to slide toward the front or back of the saddle (fig. 5.24 A). A horse with a forward girth line will particularly benefit from this type of system. (Other, similar systems can be seen in figures 5.24 B and C.) With the V-shaped system, the front billet should drop perpendicularly into the girth line, and the rear billet should slant forward, with even tension in both billets keeping the saddle stable (figs. 5.24 C & D).

Girths are made in many different materials, shapes, and lengths. The type of saddle you are using, and the shape of your horse, determines the kind of girth you need. Saddles with short billets require a long girth, and vice versa. Girth material should be inviting to the touch, not rigid or lumpy. *Leather* girths need to be kept clean and soft to prevent cracks that lead to sores. *Cloth* girths are inexpensive and, as long as they are wide enough for comfort, work just fine. *String* girths easily mold to the shape of the horse, allow for air flow, and though *nylon string* girths have been known to cause skin irritation, *Mohair* rarely causes any reaction. *Cotton* string girths can shrink, so after you wash them, slightly stretch them between two nails on a fence or the side of your barn until they are dry. Girths are also made from other materials including *neoprene*, *synthetic fleece*, and various sorts of *synthetic cloth*. Girth hardware should be made of a metal that does not rust, such as stainless steel, or brass and nickel alloys, because rust on buckles is rough and can cause sores or damage the leather on your saddle.

When choosing a girth for your horse, have the same considerations you would when choosing a belt for yourself. If it is too tight and has no give to it, after a short time, it will become unbearably uncomfortable. Preferably, your girth will have elastic on both ends so your horse's rib cage can move evenly and he can breathe freely. A girth with elastic on one side is acceptable but may allow the saddle to twist unevenly on the back. A non-elastic girth may be uncomfortable, can become loose when your horse exhales, and may be overtightened to compensate.

By attaching the girth on the same billets, and approximately the same billet holes, on each side, you will avoid twisting your saddle. The girth should be tightened just enough to hold the saddle in place, and you should be able to slip two large, or three smaller, fingers between the girth and the horse's ribs. Girths that are fastened too tightly cause sore muscles, especially along the bottom of the girth line on the sternum—I've seen horses that suffer chronic pain from scar tissue that has formed in this area. Overtightening the girth also restricts breathing. If your saddle fits correctly, you will not need to overtighten the girth in order to keep it in place. If you feel the need to tighten your girth to an extreme point, check the saddle fit rather than strangling your horse.

In general, a *wide* girth is more comfortable and distributes pressures over a larger area than a narrow girth. A horse with a girth line well behind the elbow should have a wide girth. However, there are several situations where you may need a *narrow* or *shaped* girth (fig. 5.25). If the girth is sliding forward regularly, you may have a horse with a forward girth line, and a shaped girth will allow room for the elbows to move back during the stride. A horse with a for-

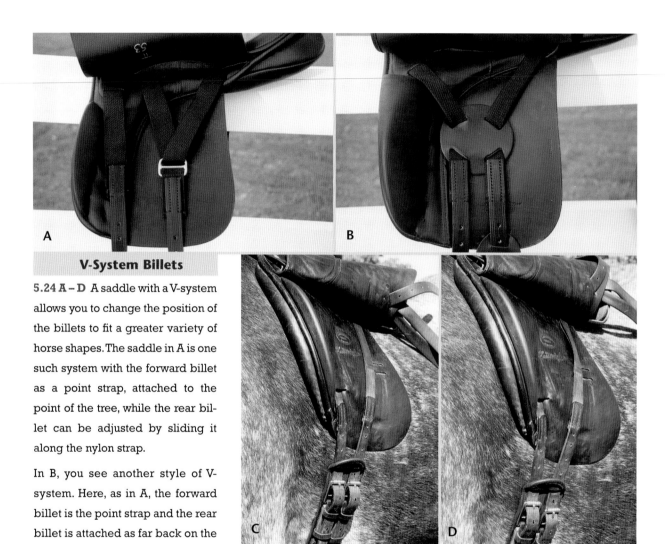

V-System Billets

5.24 A–D A saddle with a V-system allows you to change the position of the billets to fit a greater variety of horse shapes. The saddle in A is one such system with the forward billet as a point strap, attached to the point of the tree, while the rear billet can be adjusted by sliding it along the nylon strap.

In B, you see another style of V-system. Here, as in A, the forward billet is the point strap and the rear billet is attached as far back on the tree as possible, but the leather circle can be moved to alter the billet location for different horses.

Photo C shows a third style correctly adjusted with the same amount of tension on both front and rear billets.

Photo D shows the same saddle with the rear billet incorrectly adjusted. When the rear billet is loose like this, the cantle has no support, all the tension is on the front billet, and the purpose of the "V" is defeated.

Shaped Girth

5.25 This horse has a forward girth line and therefore benefits from a girth that angles toward his front legs underneath his body. This style of girth gives the elbow freedom, yet keeps the saddle back in its correct location.

ward girth line may also benefit from a girth that is angled forward at the sternum. A horse with a well-sprung rib cage (a really wide barrel) that pushes the girth forward toward the elbows, is also a candidate for a narrow or shaped girth.

If you use a *short* girth (as you would with most dressage saddles), be sure it is long enough so that the buckles do not interfere with your horse's elbows. When the girth is too short, the buckles, keepers, and buckle guards can strike this sensitive area with each stride (fig. 5.26 A). Also, the long, unpadded billets pressing against the side of the horse can cause narrow, intense lines of pressure against the horse's rib cage. Ideally, a short girth's buckles will rest about two inches below the saddle flaps, out of the way of both the rider's leg and the horse's elbow (fig. 5.26 B). Be sure there is enough room to tighten the girth properly without pinching the horse's side between the girth and the flap.

In high-speed sports such as eventing and steeplechasing, a rider may want a second girth for added safety. This is placed over the top of the saddle and is called an *overgirth* (fig. 5.27). It should be made from a strong, elastic material so the horse can breathe well while galloping.

Appearances Can Be Deceiving

When you are purchasing a wide girth, do not be fooled by appearances. Many girths are constructed from nice, wide pieces of leather, cloth, or fleece, but have narrow strips of leather or cloth down the center of the girth with the buckles attached there. These narrow strips bear all the pressure when the girth is tightened, in effect, acting like a narrow girth. Other girths are so wide their buckles and the billets on most saddles won't line up.

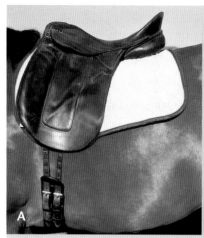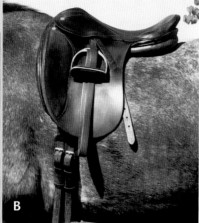

Short Girth Adjustment

Overgirth

5.26 A & B In A, the short girth is adjusted with the buckles too low on the horse's side. As his elbows move back with each stride, they will hit the buckles. The short girth in B is adjusted correctly with the buckles out of the way of both the rider's leg and the horse's elbow.

5.27 For added safety in some high speed sports, a second girth is placed over the top of the saddle like this.

CHECKLIST

Riderless Saddle Fit Evaluation			
Saddle Feature	**Factors to Consider**		
Position	■ Stability	*Seat*	■ Levelness
	■ Girth line alignment		■ Centered balance point
	■ Shoulder clearance	*Gullet*	■ Width / spine clearance
Tree	■ Width		■ Symmetry
	■ Angle	*Stirrup bars*	■ Pressure points
	■ Length	*Billets*	■ Girth line alignment
Panels	■ Even contact		■ Leather condition
	■ Symmetry	*Girth*	■ Girth line alignment
	■ Thickness / spine clearance		■ Correct length, width

The Horse's Pain-Free Back and Saddle-Fit Book

6 Saddle Fit for Horse and Rider: Ridden Exam

with Andy Foster

You have now assessed your current saddle, or a prospective purchase, for soundness and basic fit on your horse, and it is time to consider what happens to the saddle when your horse is in motion, how *you* fit in it, and how your riding changes its position and fit on your horse.

Ideally, a saddle provides support, security, safety, and comfort to the rider, and promotes communication between the rider and horse. It must not interfere with the horse's movement and needs to be balanced and fit the horse well. The saddle must also be appropriate for your sport and, in most cases, aesthetically pleasing. A tall order perhaps, but vital to the well-being and progress of both horse and rider.

Begin by viewing the saddle when your horse is in motion. With the saddle placed cor-

rectly on your horse's back, secured by an appropriately tightened girth, and without a pad (remember to use a thin cloth to protect a new saddle), walk, trot, and canter your horse so you can see what the saddle does in different gaits. Ideally, it will remain stable and in the correct position. You should not see any extra daylight appearing at intervals under the pommel or cantle. If it passes this test, you are ready to evaluate whether the saddle fits you, as a rider.

The challenge of finding a saddle that balances you, improving your performance and partnership with your horse, is a worthwhile pursuit. There is an intricate synergy between your effectiveness as a rider and the saddle you ride in. Most people have yet to sit in a saddle that fits them correctly. Therefore, some factors may be difficult to assess at first. One way to learn what *feels right* is to sit in a variety of saddles and see which ones feel the most comfortable. Test ride a number of saddles, paying close attention to the difference in your horse's way of going when you are riding in balance, versus when you are fighting the saddle. Riders consistently discover that they ride more effectively and feel more secure when they ride in a saddle that fits them properly and is correct for their sport. Even experienced riders who have ridden for twenty or thirty years remark that they feel more stable and able to progress when riding in a saddle that works with—not against—them. Instructors will often comment that the first time a student rides in a saddle that fits correctly, she can advance *two years* in one lesson.

Seat Bone to Stirrup Bar Relationship

The first variable in fitting a saddle to a rider is determining an effective position for the rider. Perhaps the most important factor in achieving a dynamic, balanced position is the relationship between the stirrup bars on your saddle, the location of your seat bones on the seat, and the length of your stirrup leathers (figs. 6.1 A – C). The most stable leg position is when the pelvis is in neutral, the hip joint is in line with the ankle, and the stirrup leather hangs perpendicularly to the ground. This alignment also applies to jumping, though because the stirrups are shorter, it is in a more forward position.

"If the stirrups be wrong, all the rest being right will be of little avail."

Francis Dwyer

In this correct position, the stirrups increase your stability and provide you with secure places to put your feet. A column of support for your upper body is created between your foot and your seat, providing you a solid base so you can remain balanced as your horse moves (fig. 6.2 A & B). The top of the column is formed by the distance between the hip joint and the stirrup bar, which should be the equivalent of the distance between the balance point of your foot on the stirrup and the center of your ankle—the bottom of the column. If the stirrup bars are positioned incorrectly for you, either too far forward or too far back, the stirrups become a hindrance. The leathers will not hang perpendicularly to the ground, and each leather and stirrup will act like a pendulum, swinging every time you place weight on it.

If you try to adapt to incorrectly placed stirrup bars, you will have to compromise your ideal position in the saddle. A variety of faulty rider positions are due to attempting to deal with this problem.

- The rider's foot may not rest on the stirrup in the optimum position where all the joints of the leg can function properly, so her leg becomes stiff, and she is not able to keep her heel down.

- The rider may find that she has to use a great amount of muscular effort in order to maintain a correct leg position. This will diminish the effectiveness of her leg aids.

- The rider may be constantly thrown out of balance and behind the motion of the horse. This will be seen particularly over fences and is caused by the pendulum action of the stirrup leathers.

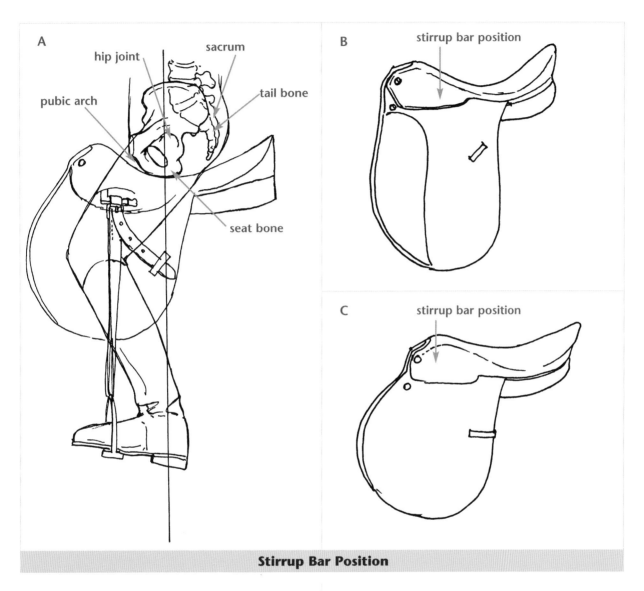

A

pubic arch
hip joint
sacrum
tail bone
seat bone

B
stirrup bar position

C
stirrup bar position

Stirrup Bar Position

6.1 A – C Figure A shows a side view of the rider's seat bone and hip location, and the saddle's stirrup bar position. The rider is in a correct stable position with the ankle below the hip joint and the stirrup leather hanging perpendicularly to the ground. The stirrup bar is in the correct place for dressage in B. And in C, it is placed forward to accommodate shorter stirrup leathers. (If you need to ride in an all purpose saddle, select one with a stirrup bar that is closest to the style of riding you do the most.)

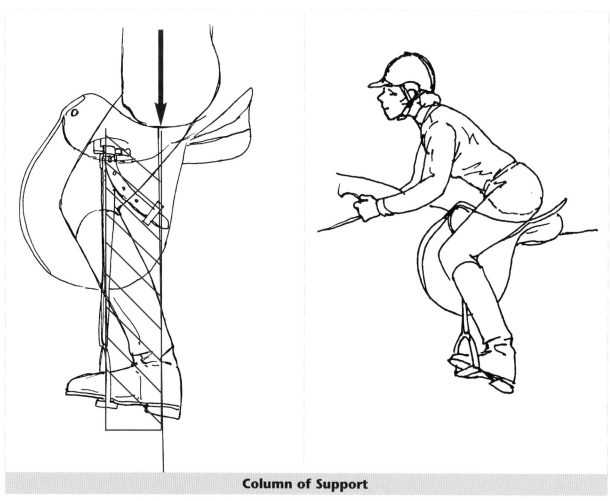

Column of Support

6.2 A & B The correct stirrup bar position allows the rider to have a column of support from the hip down to the stirrup, as shown in A. Though the rider in B has shorter stirrups for jumping, the stirrup bar is correctly placed forward so the ankle remains under the hip joint, the lower leg remains stable, and the upper body remains independent.

Most riders do not realize that they are attempting to adapt to incorrectly placed stirrup bars. Instead, they blame their poor riding on their own lack of understanding or athletic ability. To illustrate what the correct seat bone to stirrup bar relationship feels like *off the horse*, stand on the ground in balance, with your knees slightly bent as if you were riding with long stir-

Incorrect Stirrup Bar Positions

6.3 A & B Because the stirrup bars are too far forward, the rider in A is in a "chair seat" position. Her legs are out in front of her and she will use her reins to stabilize herself. In B, the stirrup bars are too far back for jumping, causing the rider to grip with her inner thighs and knees, which in turn makes her ankles "float" out behind her hips. When the horse lands after the jump, she will tip forward and brace herself against his neck.

rups. You can move your upper body around easily and independently, a feeling you would like your saddle to provide you. Now keep your pelvis in the same position, and try to move your legs one inch out in front of you. You will now fall backward unless you hold onto something (on a horse, you would probably support yourself with your reins or by gripping the saddle with your legs). Feel the tension in your body as you struggle to find your balance. When the stirrup bars on your saddle drag your legs forward, putting you in this *chair seat position*, you feel the same way.

You are "behind the motion" of the horse and will tend to sit heavily on his back (fig. 6.3 A).

Now try to place your pelvis more forward than is correct, with your feet an inch behind you. Gravity tips you forward, just as if your stirrups were hung too far back on your saddle. This is most common in close contact jumping saddles. Over fences, this stirrup position will cause your lower legs to swing back behind you, forcing you to grip with your inner thighs and knees (fig. 6.3 B). This, in turn, restricts the horse's movement, creates a pivot point over your knee, and leaves you with an instability that is not only undesirable, but in jumping, unsafe.

Return to your balanced riding position on the ground, and pretend you are riding with shorter stirrups. Stand with more bend in your knees, squatting over your legs in the same position you assume for jumping. Note that as you squat lower, your feet must remain farther in front of you, your back must be flat, and your buttocks must thrust out and back to remain in balance. (If you round your back, tuck your pelvis too far under, or hollow your back, you will notice that you are not able to squat down very far.) So, the shorter the stirrup you ride, the further forward the stirrup bar needs to be in order to allow you to be in the correct jumping position and the stirrup leathers to remain perpendicular to the ground.

Stirrup bars are placed in the saddle early in construction. It is not possible to change their position in most saddles (there are a few exceptions) without completely tearing it apart, but you can make some minor adjustments.

It is possible to slide a rubber, plastic, or leather strap (a rubber rein-stop for a martingale, or a leather keeper works well) around the stirrup bar to act as a "stopper." Place it *in front* of the stirrup leather if the stirrup bar is too far forward for you, and *behind* the stirrup leather if the stirrup bar is too far back. Some saddles are actually made with adjustable stirrup bars; this is a fine feature for flat work, but for safety reasons, it is not recommended for jumping saddles.

The Equiband™ was devised to help correct stirrup bars that are too far forward by preventing the stirrups from swinging forward when you rise to the trot. It consists of a long, flat, rubber strap that goes from one stirrup to the other across the cantle (fig. 6.4). The band is tied to the inner side of each stirrup with a half hitch (the first part of the knot you use to tie your shoelace). It needs to be tied so that the stirrups are pulled back when the band is over the cantle of the saddle, and it is important to have 5 to 6 inches of extra band after each knot, so if you push hard in the stirrups, the band will loosen but not come untied. If it comes loose from a stirrup, it may frighten your horse. The primary goal of the Equiband™ is to develop muscle memory, so the rider will be able to override the incorrect position of the stirrup bars and ultimately, maintain the correct leg position without the band.

You may get the feeling of an incorrectly placed stirrup bar from a saddle that is not in balance—for instance, on a saddle that tips down at the pommel, you will feel as if you are falling forward and will want to brace against the stirrup in an effort to keep from falling onto the horse's neck, your lower leg constantly swinging back toward your horse's hindquarters. This is especially true in a jumping saddle. If the saddle tips down at the cantle, it feels as if the stirrup bar has been placed too far forward. You will struggle to get out of the saddle—especially in the rising trot—and when you attempt to keep your heels down, your leg will swing forward. You will feel as if you are banging on your horse's back and simply can't get your legs underneath

Equiband

6.4 If the stirrup bars on your saddle are too far forward, you can use the Equiband™ to hold your legs back under your hips. This will help you to train your muscles to keep them there, in the correct position.

you. So, be sure to carefully study the saddle position on the horse, both standing squarely and while in motion, before making snap judgments regarding the stirrup bars.

Seat Considerations

The sitting area of the saddle consists of two parts. The *seat* is the back half of the sitting area, and the *twist* is the front and the center. Both areas are important to consider. The *seat size* refers to the entire sitting area, from pommel to cantle. Ideally, seat size for a rider is determined first, by the length of the thigh bones, and second, by the size of the buttocks. Most saddle retailers, however, only consider the size of the rider's buttocks. Failure to consider the rider's length of thigh, especially for a long-legged rider, often results in a too-small saddle that inhibits performance potential.

When seat size is correct, you can sit in the center of the saddle with your seat bones pointing straight down. You will have the same amount of free space (2 to 4 inches) between you and the pommel as there is between you and the cantle, and your knee will reach the center of the knee roll (see p. 27). You should be comfortable enough in the seat so that you can ride without constantly readjusting your sitting position.

Riders in seats that are *too small* often find their knees below or beyond the center of their saddles' knee rolls. If the knee rolls are thick, they will push the rider's knees out away from the saddle, making the lower leg unstable and restricting the hip joint. When she attempts to keep her knee in the correct place on the flap, her thigh bone will push her buttocks toward the cantle, tip her pelvis forward and down, jam her lower back, and severely decrease the effectiveness of her seat (fig. 6.6 A). If the rider is long-legged, she may adopt a curved "C" position to compensate (fig. 6.6 B). In this position, she will pinch at the knee and curl up in the shoulders in an effort to fit herself into the saddle. When a rider is "crammed" into the saddle, she will either ride up onto the cantle, which is uncomfortable for the horse, or too close to the pommel and stirrup bars, which is uncomfortable for her.

When the seat is *too long*, the rider slides back toward the cantle and her legs go forward into the chair seat position (see fig. 6.3 A). A rider with a short thigh must constantly shift forward to keep her leg underneath her, which can be painful since she ends up sitting on the pommel. If a seat is *too wide*, the rider will tend to feel upper thigh and hip pain, and if the tree is wide for the horse, as well, the saddle may tip down in front, throwing her weight forward and causing her to brace against her stirrups (fig. 6.6 C & D).

Ideally, the *tree fits the horse* and the *seat fits you*, happily marrying the two shapes together. This simple concept, however, creates some major challenges. It means that the shape and size of each specific horse and rider should be considered when building the saddle, while most saddle manufacturers build for the "average" horse and rider. Your horse might need an 18-inch saddle to cover the length of his rib cage

Eliminating Stirrup Leather Bulk

If the bulkiness of the stirrup leather and buckle on your dressage saddle is uncomfortable under your thigh, you can place the buckle just above the stirrup iron. (On a jumping saddle, the forward position of the thigh usually negates the buckle problem.) Feed the tip of the leather through the stirrup bar on the saddle and pull the leather through so that the buckle is now at the bottom with the stirrup. Place the stirrup leather through the stirrup, do up the buckle to your normal hole, then tuck the end of the strap back through the buckle so it comes to the inside of the loop formed by the stirrup leather. Pull the strap tight. When you are finished, the bulky part of the buckle and leather should face in toward the horse. When you put your foot in the stirrup, the buckle will face forward at the front of your ankle, out of the way. You can wrap the bottom of the leather to keep it in place, or have a small leather sleeve made to hold the excess.

6.5 A – D To move the buckle from its uncomfortable residence under your thigh, feed the leather through the stirrup bar and pull until the buckle is even with the billet holes you use. Next, attach the stirrup and buckle the leather at the appropriate billet hole, as shown in B. Pull the loose end of the leather back through the buckle and loop, as in C, pulling it tight so the buckle is snug on top of the stirrup. Use a leather keeper to keep all portions of the leather in place and to have the neat finished product seen in D.

Sport-Specific Stirrup Bar Positions

It is fairly common to find stirrup bars on a jumping saddle placed *too far back* for safety. This compromises the rider's stability over fences, generally swinging your lower leg behind the vertical, causing your knee to grip and your unbalanced body to tip forward, or encouraging you to brace on the balls of your feet and duck your fences (see fig. 6.3 B). Some people compensate by placing the saddle too far forward on the horse's shoulders (see figs. 5.4 A–D, p. 56). This restricts the shoulder freedom your horse needs to clear fences.

You need an *extremely forward* stirrup-bar position in a cross-country saddle because the sport demands a very short stirrup. Unfortunately, this is often achieved with the use of a tree that has points slightly angled forward, which may interfere with the horse's shoulder movement. Even if the stirrup bars on your cross-country saddle feel right, you should check the tree points. Look under the flap, and find the place where the points are visible. See if they are perpendicular to the ground, or angled forward. If it appears that the points are touching the back of the shoulder blades, especially after riding for a while, you may need to consider another saddle.

Treeless saddles designed for endurance do not have bars to attach the stirrups (see p. 37). Instead, the stirrup attachment is sewn into the flap or skirt and is located closer to your knee. As a result, you may find your hip- or knee-joint movement is restricted. On these saddles, however, it is relatively easy for a saddler to move the stirrup attachment into the correct place.

(see *Tree Fit*, p. 55), while you need a 17-inch seat to fit your thigh. If you have a custom saddle built on the 18-inch tree required to fit the horse, the saddler can construct an inner seat to fit you, but if you are buying a ready-made saddle, you may need to compromise.

One solution is to choose a saddle that fits your horse, and then "adapt" the seat size for yourself. For example, if you have a saddle that fits your horse but is uncomfortably large for you, you can "build" a smaller seat with a *seat saver*—a padded piece of fleece or foam with "keepers" that hold it on top of the saddle. Place a wedge of foam or a rolled-up towel between the seat saver and the cantle (fig. 6.7). This works best with saddles that have a high cantle to hold the foam in place.

The *seat depth* depends entirely on personal preference and is often based on the security needs of the rider. The difference between a *deep seat* and a *shallow seat* is actually based solely on the height of the pommel and cantle—the other structures remain the same (fig. 6.8). The distance from the rider's seat bones to the horse's back is the same, whether the seat is deep or not. A shallow seat provides a rider more freedom to move with the horse and position herself as needed, while the deeper seat may lock her in one fixed position. Although some riders think a deeper seat provides more security, the stability provided by correct stirrup bar placement is what really makes a difference. When the stirrup bar placement is correct, the rider will feel secure in any seat.

Seat Size

6.6 A – D In A, the rider is in a saddle that is too small. Her thigh is pushed toward the cantle, which forces her to sit with more of her weight in the rear of the saddle, and in this position, her seat aids will be largely ineffective. Photo B shows a long-legged rider in a seat that is too small. Her thigh is cramped between the knee roll and the cantle so she must compensate by pinching her knee and curling her shoulders forward. The saddle in C is too wide for her hips. It is tipping the rider forward, causing her to brace against her arms and stirrups, and hollow her back. And, the discomfort she will feel in her hips, as shown in D, will inhibit her ability to give clear aids.

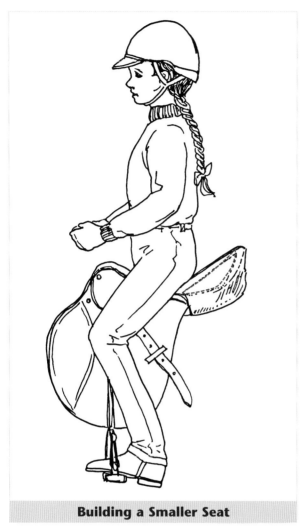

Building a Smaller Seat

6.7 If needed, you can "build" a smaller seat into your saddle. Cut a wedge of foam and adjust it along the cantle so that it fills in the gap behind you, helping you to sit in the center of the saddle. Put a sheepskin seat saver over your saddle to hold the foam in place.

Correct *seat width* properly supports the crotch and prevents pain in the seat bones, hip joints, and thighs. The seat needs to be broad enough to allow your seat bones to rest comfortably on the flat part of the seat, inside the seams. If your seat bones are hanging off the saddle, the seat is *too narrow*. The trees used in most of the older, close contact saddles, for instance, are too narrow for many riders, particularly women. Equally uncomfortable are seats that are *too wide*, which inhibit your ability to use your legs correctly. A rider will feel as if her hips are being stretched out to the side, and she has to rock her pelvis backward or forward to try and accommodate the over wide seat. Unfortunately, there isn't an easy way to adjust seat width. An uncomfortable saddle is just difficult to ride in.

The *twist*—or waist—is the area of the saddle from the pommel to the center of the saddle where it widens into the seat (see *Seat and Twist Construction*, p. 32). Each brand and style of saddle offers different twist shapes, so you need to find a style that suits the anatomy of your pelvis and hips. The *width* and *length* of the twist is important in terms of both rider comfort and freedom to move properly in the saddle. You will be able to tell when the twist is correct by your level of comfort in the saddle (see 6.9 A – C).

The width of the twist needs to be rounded gently so that it is kind to the crotch area. The key to a comfortable twist is to have the support extend about 5 inches down along the inside of your thigh. If the twist is too narrow, it can be very painful, if not damaging, as your crotch will

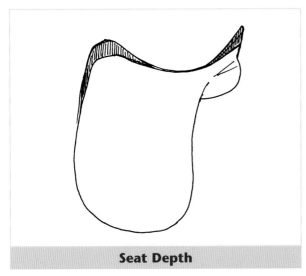

Seat Depth

6.8 The difference between a *deep seat* and a *shallow seat* is measured by pommel and cantle height as shown here by the shaded area. All other saddle structures remain the same, including the center of balance.

not be adequately supported. Crotch pain is a clear indication that the shape of the twist is inappropriate or the saddle is too small, and it is a significant cause of poor riding technique.

If the twist is *too wide*, your pelvis and hips will feel overly stretched and pained, like when you ride a really broad horse for a long period of time (see sidebar, p. 96). Many a rider suffers because she may have been told that a particular twist is the correct length and shape for her, and she may believe that she just has to "toughen up" in order to ride correctly. This is absolutely untrue; a saddle should feel comfortable to all parts of your seat.

If the *twist length* is not correct, you will expe-

rience discomfort in your saddle. If it is *too short,* or rises too quickly in front, your crotch will bump against the pommel, especially during the rising trot. Discover whether you need a twist with a quick rise, or one that is flatter, by sitting on a hard chair with your legs apart. Along the centerline of your jeans where the pubic arch is, feel the space from the chair to the bone of your pelvis (see fig. 6.1). If you can get more than two to three fingers in that space, you will need a saddle that rises quickly in front. If you can only get a finger in the space, you will need a saddle that has a flatter twist. If the twist on your current saddle is too short or rises too quickly, you will probably need a different saddle. If the twist is too long, you will feel unsupported by the seat, but you may be able increase your security with the seat-saver solution from page 94.

Pommel Considerations

The *pommel* of the saddle needs to be high enough to clear the withers adequately, and yet low enough not to interfere with your position. If you hit the pommel when you ride, check the saddle and make sure it is sitting level on the horse (see *A Level Seat,* p. 66). If it sits low behind, it will feel like a saddle with a high pommel when you post or jump. If your saddle is sitting level and you still hit the pommel, there are three possible reasons why you are having trouble. Your horse may not be using his back correctly, so you might not be receiving the thrust necessary to propel you out of the saddle. Or, you may be riding with your pelvis tilted forward

Altering a Narrow Twist

If you experience crotch pain, the likely reason is a narrow twist shape causing lack of thigh support. It is possible to improve support for the thigh by adding a skirt block to your saddle. Place a piece of foam under the skirt behind the stirrup bars (figs. 6.9 A – C). Move the foam until you experience immediate pain relief in the crotch area. For most uses, the skirt is tight enough to keep the block in place. If it slides around, Velcro or sew it into place, or have a saddler attach it permanently. You can protect the foam with a home-made leather or nylon cover.

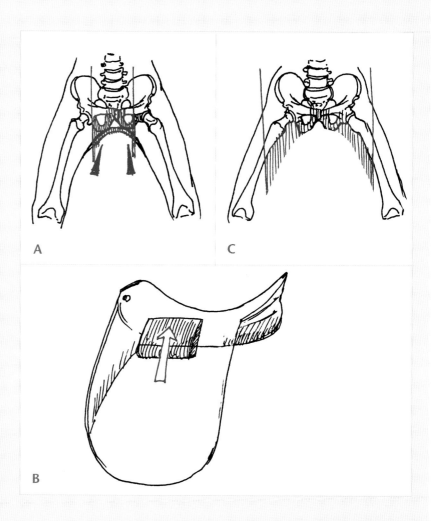

A

C

B

6.9 A – C The parallel red lines and crosshatched area in A show how the rider's base of support is only as wide as the seat bones in a saddle with a narrow twist. To widen the base of support, place some foam under the skirt, as shown in B. Notice, in C, how this alters the weight distribution so it's shared by the pelvic area and thighs.

The Horse's Pain-Free Back and Saddle-Fit Book

and down, so you are unable to receive the upward thrust from the horse. Lastly, it may be that your saddle is constructed in such a way that the pommel is too high for you—frequently seen on deep-seated dressage saddles.

Saddle Flaps

The *saddle flap* is the piece of leather that goes under the rider's leg to protect it from the billets (see fig. 3.4 A, p. 26). Unless a saddle was made with "adjustable flaps," their position cannot be changed. If you order a semi-custom or custom saddle, the flaps can be placed to suit your needs. Manufacturers make saddles for people with "generic-sized" legs, and short- and long-legged people suffer accordingly. A short-legged rider finds that her leg becomes ineffective when the flap is too long because her calf contact is with the flap rather than the horse's side. A rider with very long legs is equally frustrated because she winds up with hardly any flap underneath her lower leg, her knees are pushed out because they override the knee rolls, and the top of her boots catch on the bottom of the flaps.

When deciding on saddle flap style, consider your discipline and the approximate length of stirrup you will ride in, the shape and length of your thigh, and the shape of the horse. For aesthetic appeal, choose a saddle flap that is visible all around your leg when the stirrups are correctly adjusted. Your knee should come approximately to the center of the knee roll, and the flap should be wide enough to allow you to move your leg back without leaving the leather.

Sport-Specific Twist Length

The correct seat for jumping, as defined by Bertalan de Némethy in *Classic Show Jumping: The de Némethy Method*, is the three-point seat. De Némethy coached the U.S. show-jumping team for many years. The three-point seat distributes the rider's weight evenly between the two seat bones and the pubic arch to form a triangle of support. In order to comfortably achieve this correct rider position, you need a saddle with a twist that accommodates your pelvic shape (see fig. 3.8 A – C, p. 33). Generally, the twist in a saddle designed specifically for jumping is longer and narrower than that of other saddles. This allows you to bring your knees and thighs closer together for stability and to lift out of the saddle to clear the pommel during a jump. The narrower twist will not be uncomfortable if the shape is correct for you and the seat is wide enough to accommodate your seat bones. If the twist is too short or too wide, it will be more difficult to rise over the saddle in the proper, stable, forward position.

Three-day event riders prefer an even longer twist to allow plenty of room to adapt their position to the varied terrain and jumps—particularly drop fences.

Dressage riders, who are more stationary in the saddle, generally choose a shorter twist.

How much leather needs to be in front of, or behind, your leg is determined by the angle between your thigh and calf created by the length of your stirrups or the length of your thigh. The shorter your stirrup leathers or the longer your thigh, the more forward the flap needs to be (fig. 6.10).

Knee rolls and *thigh blocks and rolls* are padded, raised areas on or under the saddle flap to help stabilize your leg (see fig. 3.4 C, p. 26). Knee rolls are generally covered by suede to improve grip. If the rolls and blocks are in the correct place, they will not be a hindrance to your riding, and in fact, you should not even notice them.

The rider's thigh is relatively straight while the barrel of the horse is curved. Therefore, one purpose of the blocks is to support the thigh, allowing it to rest straight and evenly against the horse's side. The other purpose is to support the rider in certain movements such as jumping or in extended gaits. The placement of knee rolls, thigh blocks, and thigh rolls then depends on the shape of your thigh, the shape of your horse, and your horse's gaits and type of movement.

A slab-sided, narrow-at-the-shoulder Thoroughbred requires a thicker knee roll and thigh block to support the rider's lower thigh and knee because there is "no horse" under the knee. The rolls and blocks will give the knee a place to rest, thus helping maintain lower leg contact. A wide Friesian, on the other hand, already offers plenty of width under your knee, so a thinner knee roll is best. A rider on a Warmblood with a dramatic extended trot and a big canter uses the thigh blocks to help stabilize her

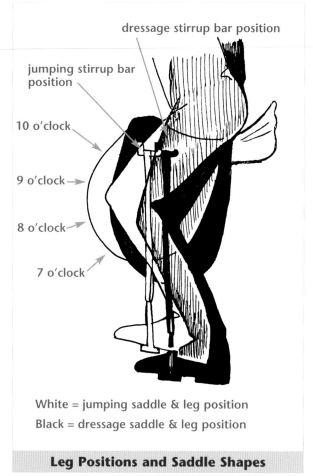

Leg Positions and Saddle Shapes

White = jumping saddle & leg position
Black = dressage saddle & leg position

6.10 In this drawing, the saddle flaps and corresponding leg positions of a dressage and jumping saddle are merged. In order to protect the rider's leg, when the rider's knee is at the 7 or 8 o'clock position, as for riding dressage, the saddle flap needs to be long but not extend far forward. When the knee is at the 9 or 10 o'clock position for jumping with short stirrups, the flap needs to extend more forward but not be as long.

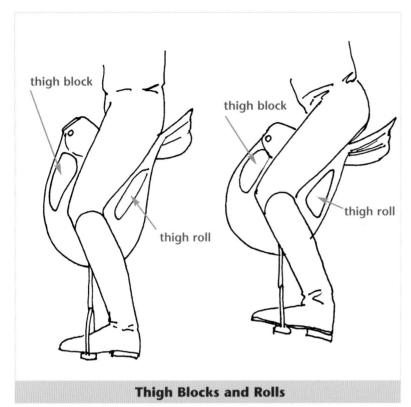

thigh block

thigh block

thigh roll

thigh roll

Thigh Blocks and Rolls

6.11 Thigh blocks and rolls are attached to the saddle parallel to the rider's thigh and should not interfere with the rider's ability to use her leg.

legs as her horse's stride reaches its maximum.

Ride in your saddle at all gaits to help decide if the position of the knee rolls and thigh blocks needs to be adjusted. The thigh block—or roll—should lie parallel to, just in front of or behind, your thigh (fig. 6.11). Your knee should rest in the center of the knee roll, and you should not feel as if your knee is being pushed away from the flap.

You can experiment with knee roll and thigh block and roll modifications without making

permanent changes by taping a piece of foam temporarily into position under, or on top of, the saddle flap. Protect the foam with a cover if you plan to use it as a long-term solution. Be aware that duct tape leaves marks on your saddle, and always test any tape on the *inside* of the saddle flap before using it.

What follows are some options for modifying the knee rolls and thigh blocks and rolls on your saddle to improve leg contact.

If you ride with long stirrups, your leg hangs over the wide part of the horse's barrel, and you have:

■ *thick thighs and a wide horse.* It will be difficult to get your lower leg snug against the horse's side. It may be helpful to choose a saddle with a slightly forward stirrup bar (see, p. 84). Choose a very thin knee roll, or do not have a knee roll at all.

■ *thin thighs and a wide horse.* You require little extra in the way of knee rolls or thigh blocks, unless your horse is an extravagant mover, in which case you should have more thigh block at the front.

■ *thick thighs and a narrow horse.* Your leg will naturally fall along the side of your horse's barrel.

- *thin thighs and a narrow horse.* You will not have a problem keeping your leg on your horse, unless he is an extravagant mover, in which case you should place more thigh block at the front of the saddle flap.

If you ride with short stirrups, your leg hangs over the narrowest part of the horse's back, and you have:
- *short, round thighs.* Adding more to your thigh blocks will probably not solve your problem. You may need stirrup bars that are a little farther forward than you are accustomed to.
- *long thighs.* Your knees probably go over the knee roll, so remove the knee roll, and if you feel that you need support for your thigh, add a small thigh block.

If you ride with long or short stirrups and you have:
- *very long, thin legs.* When you put your knee on the horse, your ankle comes away from the horse's side, and when you put your ankle on the horse, your knee comes away. You should add a knee roll so that your knee is supported when your ankle is on the horse.
- *very tight hips.* Your hips will not allow you to comfortably drop your legs down the horse's sides, and you will be served best without a thigh block or knee roll.

CHECKLIST

Rider Fit Evaluation	
Saddle Feature	**Factors to Consider**
Saddle balance	■ Security ■ Contact ■ Stability
Stirrup bars/ stirrups	■ Placement ■ Alignment under the hip
Seat	■ Length ■ Width ■ Twist shape ■ Levelness ■ Comfort
Pommel	■ Size and shape
Saddle flaps	■ Length ■ Width ■ Knee roll/thigh block characteristics
Rider alignment	■ Vertical alignment ■ Front-to-back balance ■ Side-to-side balance

Synergy:
Rider Balance
and Saddle Fit

with Wendy Murdoch

If the saddle you're evaluating seems to be in fair to excellent condition, fits your horse, and fits you, then it's time to test it in a riding situation. A harmonious horse and rider partnership is most attainable when the saddle, horse, and rider merge together in comfort and support while in motion. It is important to recognize the saddle as the communication device in this situation, and learn to read the messages it gives you.

If you are evaluating a new saddle, protect it with a very thin cloth or saddle pad as you did when you evaluated basic fit in chapter 4. Wrap the stirrup leathers in plastic wrap, old socks, or another smooth material to avoid marking the flaps. Unfortunately, there is no way to avoid marks in the billets, so before you ride, make sure the retailer will accept a saddle returned with billet marks.

Enlist a knowledgeable observer to watch and videotape your ride, if at all possible (see sidebar, p. 102). During your ride, if you are not sure whether a problem—such as your leg drifting forward—is due to the saddle or your own bad habits, trade places with the observer. If your horse is reasonably symmetrical, you are both fairly well balanced, and you both experience the same problem, then the saddle is probably the culprit.

Right from the Start

Few of us carefully consider the simple act of mounting. If you pull the saddle to the side, you not only risk twisting the tree, you also hurt your horse's withers and spine. There's a better way to begin your ride. *Use a mounting block*. People shun using a mounting block because it is "elementary"

Moving Pictures

A video is great way to observe how a saddle affects your riding. Be sure the videographer shoots footage from all angles. Ride straight lines and circles to see if the saddle shifts while the horse is moving, and make audible comments about what you are feeling while you ride. Watch your test ride several times, if necessary, to evaluate whether the saddle interferes with your riding, your horse, or your ability to communicate with each other.

If you board at a large stable or have a number of friends who ride, borrow several different saddles of different sizes and videotape your ride in each one. Observe whether your horse feels or moves any differently, or whether your position is affected at all, by any of them in particular. You will get an excellent sense of how saddle fit affects your horse's performance as well as your riding.

or, not "cool," but using a mounting block is one of the kindest things you can do for your horse. When you are out in the field with no stump or mounting block in sight and you have to mount from the ground, do so in a way that causes the least amount of damage to your horse and saddle (figs. 7.1 A & B).

Assess Mounted Saddle Fit for the Horse

Once you've mounted properly from a block and warmed your horse up for about 20 minutes, you can begin your working assessment of the saddle's fit with a rider added. Ask your observer to note whether the saddle stayed in place or shifted to a new position during this period. If the saddle moved from its original place, dismount and reposition it correctly, then ride again. See if it continues to shift. If the saddle slides forward or backward, check to be sure the girth is in the correct place (see p. 76). If the saddle shifts from side-to-side, the tree may be too narrow. (This is common with fairly wide, flat-withered horses.)

Ride on a straight line, away from your observer, while she watches to see whether the saddle remains squarely on your horse's back during motion. Ideally, the saddle moves the same on each side: it should not slip off to one side and remain there, or consistently move across the horse's back one way more than the other. If the cantle shifts to one side, check the horse's shoulder conformation and, of course, be sure your stirrups are even (fig. 7.2, and see also chapter 8). Also, recheck for manufacturing defects—such as an uneven panel—that you may have missed during the initial examination (see chapter 4). If the saddle still seems to be even and level, the cause of the saddle slipping to one side might be you. Many riders are uneven, or ride in a way that shifts the saddle to one side. It is important to learn how to distinguish rider issues from saddle issues.

Mounting

7.1 A & B In A, the rider is mounting from the ground correctly. She is standing very close to her horse to begin. She has placed her left hand on his neck—where she can hold a bit of mane—and her right hand on the opposite side of the saddle near the location of the right-hand stirrup bar. She then gives a little "hop" as she begins the mounting motion to further ease the pressure on her horse's back and saddle. In B she is mounting incorrectly. She is standing too far away from her horse and has grabbed the pommel with one hand and the cantle with the other, pulling the saddle to one side, and catching her horse's withers as she drags herself on board.

Saddle Shifting to One Side

7.2 After riding for 20 minutes, this rider's saddle has shifted to the left.

Next, ride a circle, about half the size of your arena, and ask the observer to watch the cantle. Ideally, the back of the saddle should move up and down very little—especially at the trot—to avoid bruising the horse's back or creating a friction rub. If the saddle does rock forward, lifting at the back, there are several possible causes.

- The saddle may be too wide (see p. 63).
- The panels may be too curved, forcing the saddle to rock over a central point (see *Panel Fit,* p. 66).
- The points of the tree may be too short (see *Jumper and Dressage Issues,* p. 64).

The even side-to-side movement seen on a straight line should change when traveling on a circle to the left: the saddle should move slightly farther to the right than to the left (toward the outside of the circle). When you reverse direction, the saddle should move exactly the same amount to the left as it did to the right (fig. 7.3). This is one of the reasons you need a wide gullet: even on a circle as the saddle moves toward the outside, the horse's spine must remain clear so there is no pressure on it (see *The Gullet,* p. 73). For various reasons, some horses work more fluidly in one direction than they do in the other. If you know your horse moves stiffly in one direction, you can expect the saddle to move differently on the stiff side.

Assess Mounted Saddle Fit for the Rider

There are many riders who do not know what "riding in balance" feels like. They have never experienced the freedom of movement that a well-fitting saddle provides to both rider and horse. These riders simply grow accustomed to the pain their saddle creates, or unconsciously assume defensive postures to avoid the pain. They wind up crooked and rigid, which interferes with their timing, balance, and, ultimately, the performance of their horses. Children are especially adept at unconsciously

Cantle Movement

7.3 Note how the cantle of the saddle moves slightly to the left of center as the rider circles to the right.

The balance of the saddle on the horse is critical for correct rider position. This includes the levelness of the tree from front-to-back, the symmetry of the saddle from side-to-side, the position of the stirrup bars, and the shape of the entire seat. When the saddle is correct, you can remain in balance over your feet, just as in the exercise discussed on page 86. You no longer need to use grip to stay in place. Gravity works with you, not against you. If the saddle fits the rider well but is out of balance on the horse's back—slopes forward on a horse with a high croup, for example—the rider will be neither comfortable nor able to ride effectively.

Many avid riders never truly feel safe on the back of a horse. Certainly, if you are inexperienced or have had an accident, this is understandable, but the majority of riders with fear issues are actually simply unbalanced in the saddle. When this is the case, your inner ear (your instinctive equilibrium monitor) warns you that you are out of balance and could fall, and since you do not know why you are unbalanced, you may feel insecure or frightened as a result.

Test your balance by sitting in your saddle and slowly tipping forward and backward. Is there a place where sitting is effortless? Ideally, you should be aligned so that gravity flows straight through you from your head to your feet. If you cannot find this *sweet spot*, perhaps your saddle is the reason why.

The *classical position*—where a vertical line can pass down through the rider's ear, shoulder, hip, and ankle—is the ideal rider alignment.

compensating for poor saddle fit. As with many other things, riding habits and patterns that start when you are a child can affect your entire career—for better or, too often, for worse.

Classical Position

7.4 A & B In A, a dressage rider displays the classical position: a vertical line could be passed from her ear through her shoulder and hip, to her ankle. The hunt seat rider in B is in the classical jumping position. While she has folded her torso forward, her hip is still in line with her ankle, allowing her feet to provide a solid base of support.

When riding in a forward position (galloping or jumping) your angles are more closed. Your torso remains balanced over your feet and your hip is still aligned with your ankle. This position is effective because the angles provide a biomechanical advantage that allows you to move with your horse and remain in alignment with gravity. The motion of the horse can then be absorbed by those joints best designed for shock absorption—the hip, knee, and ankle—placing less stress on the stabilizing structure of the body—the spine. While riding styles may differ somewhat from each other, each one has its roots in this classical position (figs. 7.4 A & B).

Classical alignment activates the stabilizing muscles of the torso (stomach and back muscles) that are designed to support the upper body. This allows the limbs freedom of movement so the rider can have independent use of her aids. Any deviation from the classical alignment restricts the rider's movement and the horse's ability to move fluidly beneath her.

Shake one of your hands in the air. Now tightly curl one finger while shaking your hand. Notice how tightening one finger affects the entire hand, reduces free motion throughout the fingers and wrist, and even restricts your breathing. Transfer this concept to the saddle. If the

The Horse's Pain-Free Back and Saddle-Fit Book

saddle restricts your hips or lower back, it affects your entire body. The restriction of one area of movement not only interferes with your balance, it also affects the timing and fluidity of every other movement. When your timing or ability to follow is off, then the horse's movement is hampered. Over time, structural and muscular damage to the rider, and ultimately, the horse, becomes increasingly likely.

Ask a friend or assistant to take a profile photograph of you riding your horse, and then take the developed picture and draw a straight vertical line up and down through your hip to see if your ear, shoulder, hip, and ankle line up correctly. If not, either your body position, or your saddle, is causing a misalignment.

Side-to-side imbalance can result from crooked saddle structures, the rider, or the horse—or a combination of these. Sometimes there's a "chicken-and-egg" situation: for example, a crooked horse affects the rider, or a crooked rider affects the saddle, which affects the horse.

Refer back to the exercise you did on page 86. Repeat this test, but this time, put one foot just a half-inch in front of the other. Move your upper body around to check for mobility. Notice which muscles tighten. With your legs placed unevenly, can you still find a spot where it is effortless to stand? Now move one foot 2 inches in front of the other one. Notice the increased tightening of your muscles to remain in balance. This demonstrates how riding crookedly, whether it is caused by you, your horse, your saddle or any combination, can dramatically affect your riding and balance.

Unless your instructor is aware of the intricacies of saddle fit and how a crooked saddle can sabotage your riding, you could spend countless hours, days, and even years—not to mention dollars—trying to correct a problem that has mistakenly been attributed to you. Unevenly attached stirrup bars, warped trees, uneven seats and panels, uneven flaps and knee rolls, and uneven billets, can all cause you to sit crookedly in the saddle (figs. 7.5 A & B). Side-to-side imbalances can be caused by something as simple as uneven stirrups, which create uneven forces and damage to both your saddle and your horse's back. Many people are unaware that they ride with uneven stirrups and have become so adapted to riding with them, they find it painful to ride with them adjusted correctly. Others believe their legs are uneven, when in reality, muscle tension holds their bodies out of alignment.

On the other hand, if *your* position is uneven, and you ride in the same saddle for several years, the saddle will adapt to your position and *become* crooked. It is not uncommon to find saddles with trees weakened on one side as a result of years of uneven riding. The effect that riding crookedly or riding in a crooked saddle can have on your horse can be demonstrated by asking a friend to get on her hands and knees and crawl slowly forward. Place the palms of your hands (to simulate your seat bones) side-by-side on her long back muscles, exerting even pressure. Now increase pressure with one hand. Watch what happens to the "horse." Weight your "seat bones" evenly again, and repeat the

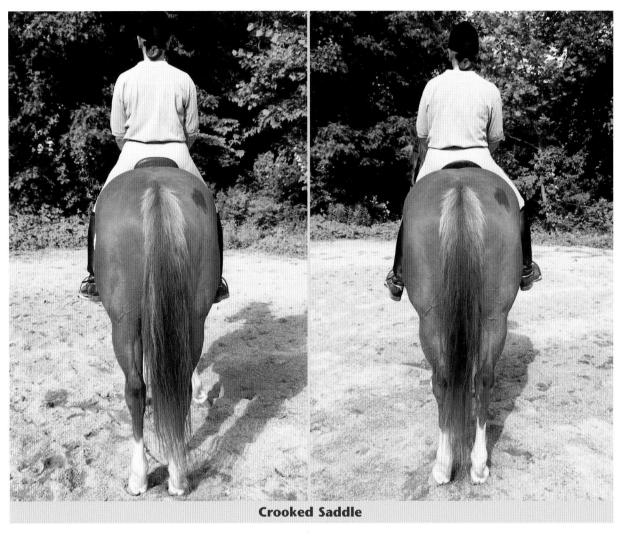

Crooked Saddle

7.5 A & B The rider in A sits evenly on her horse's back because the saddle is symmetrical. In B, she is sitting on the same horse in a saddle made with crooked panels and an asymmetrical tree, and her position has changed dramatically. Her pelvis has dropped down to the left, which has forced her upper body to compensate—dropping down to the right. Her stirrups appear to be completely different lengths, but the leathers were identical in length and adjustment before she mounted. The twisted saddle has positioned her right leg further forward, making her left leg look—and feel—as if its stirrup leather is adjusted to a longer length.

exercise. Notice how different positions and weights cause your "horse" to shift her balance.

Likewise, when *your horse* is physically uneven, the saddle cannot sit squarely on his back. Many riders are accused of riding unevenly, or misdiagnose bad saddle fit, when the problem is really the horse's conformation (see chapter 8). In many cases, once a horse is treated for sore muscles or poor shoeing, the saddle—and rider as well—will be carried evenly without modification.

It is important that your saddle does not aggravate old—or present new—balance issues, that it is effective as a means of security and communication, and that it is comfortable. Read through the following questions and answer them during, and after, your ride. Enlist a friend to read them aloud as you are videotaped so you can record how you feel as well as how you look.

When you begin, be sure the saddle is level on your horse. Mount properly from a block, and sit in the saddle at the halt. Ask your assistant to hold your horse and read the questions out loud, if that is helpful.

Step 1

With your feet in the stirrups, tilt your pelvis forward and backward until you are in a position where you feel your seat bones are pointing straight down (see fig 6.1 A, p. 85 to help find your seat bones).

- Do you feel as if the twist of the saddle is cutting you in half, causing crotch pain (see figs. 6.9 A – C, p. 96)?

The Weighting Game

If your horse and your saddle are straight and balanced and you are still having problems with crookedness, perhaps the third element in the equation should be considered: you. Try this experiment. Put two pairs of bathroom scales down on a level, solid floor, and put a foot on each scale. Bend your knees in a riding stance, looking forward, not down. When you feel level, ask a friend to read the weight on the scales so you do not alter your position. You may be quite amazed at the different weights between the scales! Even out the weight on each scale by adding or reducing pressure on each leg until the readings are the same. Remember this balance so you can reproduce the feeling when you are riding.

- Do you feel as if your hip joints are being stretched across the saddle (see fig. 6.6 D, p. 93)?
- Do you feel contact with the saddle at your pubic arch as well as both seat bones? Is this painful?
- Do you feel pain in your lower back?
- Do you feel pain in your hips?
- Does the saddle make you hollow your back?
- Does it feel as if the cantle of the saddle is pushing your pelvis forward and down, making it difficult to keep your seat bones pointing down?

Step 2

Take your feet out of the stirrups.

- Do your legs hang in a different position than they did when your feet were in the stirrups?
- Do you have to reach forward with your legs to find the stirrups? (Note: in a jumping saddle, it is appropriate for your feet to go forward to find the stirrups.)

Step 3

Without stirrups, ask your horse to walk (you may want an assistant to lead you).

- Is it difficult for you to maintain a level pelvis once you start to move?
- Does your back abnormally hollow or round?
- Does your pubic arch hit the saddle and does the position of your pelvis alter in response?

Step 4

Put your feet back in the stirrups and begin putting your horse through his paces. Ask your ground person to observe your leg position and balance.

- Do you fidget when you first get on trying to find the "sweet spot"? Do you shift around in the saddle, readjusting your position every few minutes?
- Is it difficult to keep your leg correctly positioned?
- Do you feel unstable or unsure of your balance, especially when working at speed?
- Do you experience crotch pain?
- Other than the usual exercise-induced muscle soreness, would you experience pain after riding in your saddle for an hour?

Children and Saddle Fit

Children are malleable. In other words, they adapt to their environment. Given bad saddles, they will simply develop unconscious body positions to cope, and typically, they will not complain—they don't usually have enough experience for comparison anyway. Like some adults, they so enjoy just being on the horse, they will put up with discomfort. As a parent or instructor, consider the body patterns being created that can affect a child's riding career. Make an effort to appropriately fit both child and pony with a saddle in good condition. The most important quality in a child's saddle is that it must sit level. For many, if not most, children, their saddles sit lower in the back because the trees are too narrow for their wide—or fat—ponies. When the saddle slopes downhill like this, the child learns to ride in a chair seat position. I feel the best solution is to simplify the equation and start children bareback, or on bareback pads, so they can find their balance uninhibited by foreign influence—provided you have a pony or horse you can trust. A safe mount is really important regardless of whether the child has a saddle or not!

- Do you push yourself back onto the rise of the cantle?
- When your foot is in the stirrup, does the stirrup leather hang straight down or at an angle (see fig. 6.1, p. 85)?
- Are you pushing too hard on or bracing against the stirrup?
- Are you sitting squarely in the saddle in the classical position (see figs. 7.4 A & B), or are your legs and body out of alignment?
- Does your lower leg flick back over every jump, or do you feel as if you are being pitched forward on your face over fences?

Step 5

Ask your ground person to evaluate or photograph you from behind.

- Are you sitting straight or leaning off to one side?
- Do your stirrups look even?

Rider Balance and Saddle Fit	
Saddle/Rider	**Factors to Consider**
Saddle position	■ Evenness side-to-side and front-to-back ■ Maintains position in motion
Rider balance	■ Vertical line from ear, to shoulder, to hip, to ankle ■ Weight distributed evenly
Seat	■ Levelness ■ Balance point ("sweetspot")
Twist	■ Comfort level
Stirrups/ stirrup bars	■ Evenness ■ Placement ■ Stirrup leathers perpendicular to ground
Rider comfort	■ Hips ■ Lower back ■ Seat bones ■ Pubic arch ■ Legs

Confounding Variables: Fitting Saddles to Every Horse

Although the basics of saddle-fitting are fairly straightforward, the "confounding variables" complicate the process. Most horses and riders have at least one physical trait that does not match the "average" saddle. What is average, anyway? It's a number based on the sum of the total possibilities. Average has little to do with actual individuals. We will explore some of the more challenging and tricky physical traits that can make saddle-fitting daunting, as well as various options for overcoming these hurdles to achieve better fit.

One major complicating factor is that *horses change shape*. Muscles change rapidly at times, particularly in response to a seasonal shift in performance level, type of work, or nutrition. Competitive horses might begin the year unfit or grass-fat, lose weight and be in good condi-

tion by mid-season, then be a bit on the thin side late in a hard season or during the winter. Endurance horses can lose weight during a long ride (50 to 100 miles) and significantly change shape in one day!

The key to fitting horses through these changes is to recognize that the better the original design of the saddle, the fewer adaptive changes it will need to adjust to your horse's development. A saddle that is symmetrical, with broad, flat, thick panels, a sufficiently wide gullet, and a tree with angles that fit the horse's withers (see *Tree Fit*, p. 55), is the best choice for flexible saddle fit in accordance to your horse's shifting musculature. An even better solution is to have a couple of different saddles available to match your horse's various needs throughout his working seasons, depending on how dramatically his shape tends to change. (For other options, see *Temporary Problem Solving*, p. 149.)

If you have just bought a horse that is changing his "job," be aware that his shape will probably change, so it is best if you do not buy your dream saddle yet. Instead, use a second-hand or borrowed saddle, or find something you can easily afford that matches his current shape, and plan to exchange it in a few months as he develops into his new line of work. Allow three to six months for conditioning, depending on how out-of-shape or poorly muscled he is. It is really advantageous to be able to trade saddles as your horse develops his back, since a correctly fitting saddle will allow his back muscles to develop most quickly. You might change saddles as many as three times before you are ready to search for a permanent saddle.

Similarly, it is difficult to know exactly when to fit *young horses* because they can change so rapidly, and it is of the utmost importance to start them without pain. It is amazing how many "trainers" start their young horses in poorly fitting saddles—for instance, with broken trees—because they don't want their "good" saddles damaged during the initial backing period. Many behavior problems experienced during the first months under saddle are, therefore, probably caused by poor saddle fit!

If you must acquire a saddle before your young horse is in regular work, find a used saddle that fits him properly. It can be sold later. It would be best to wait until your horse is at least three years old and has been in regular work for

---

Custom Solutions

If your horse is extremely hard to fit, or if you have a hard-to-fit shape, the most satisfactory solution for both of you may be a custom saddle (see *Custom Saddles*, p. 185). You could avoid years of buying and selling saddles that never quite fit you or your horse, countless hours of fruitless lessons, and some expensive veterinary bills for treating saddle-induced problems by just purchasing a custom saddle to begin with.

---

90 days or so before you measure him for his permanent saddle. If you notice your youngster is experiencing a growth spurt, wait until the body parts that are growing at different rates slow down. If you are going to have a local saddler build or fit your saddle, ask him to evaluate your horse before you begin training, then again after 30 days, and again after 90 days. This gives him a good idea of your horse's rate of growth and development before he begins his work.

Challenging Conformation Variations

Sometimes the way a horse is built makes it particularly difficult to find a saddle that fits him and his rider. Many of these common physical saddle-fitting challenges are hereditary or breed related, while others can be acquired over time.

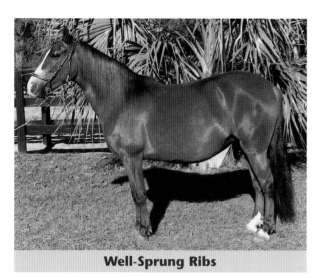

Well-Sprung Ribs

8.1 This Paso Fino has well-sprung ribs and a girth line that is very close to the elbow, which tends to pull the saddle onto the shoulders.

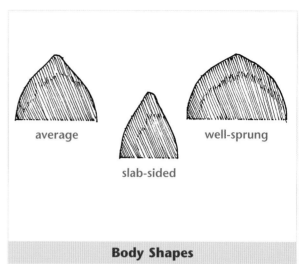

Body Shapes

average

slab-sided

well-sprung

8.2 These cross sections show the difference between an average-bodied and slab-sided horse, and one with well-sprung ribs. The flare of an average-bodied horse's rib cage serves to "catch" the girth and hold the saddle correctly in place. The shape of a slab-sided horse allows the girth and saddle to slide back, and well-sprung ribs tend to push them forward.

Well-Sprung Ribs

As we have discussed, some horses have a girth line (the narrowest part of the rib cage) that is located immediately behind, or very close to, the horse's elbows (see p. 76). The too-forward girth line tends to pull the saddle onto the shoulders. Although this conformation can appear in all breeds, it is especially common in breeds with *well-sprung ribs* such as Warmbloods, Quarter Horses, Paso Finos, Arabs, types of ponies, and mules (fig. 8.1).

The general solution to this problem is to attach the girth to the front billets of the saddle or use a point billet with a V-shaped system (see p. 78). Attaching the girth near the front pushes the saddle back to the correct spot. A girth that curves forward at the sternum can also be used

(see fig. 5.25, p. 81). Remember, tightening the girth beyond what is comfortable for the horse will *not* keep the saddle from sliding forward.

Slab-Sided

There are horses with a conformation type that allow even a correctly fitting saddle to slide back. These horses often have very little contour to their ribs, known as *slab-sidedness* (fig. 8.2). The girth line on a slab-sided horse is located farther back than is normal and is often accompanied by a narrow or steeply angled back. Slab-sidedness can appear in any breed, but is most commonly seen in Thoroughbreds.

A saddle that slides back puts the rider's weight on the horse's loins—the weakest part of the back. The problem can be remedied by attaching the girth to the rear billets on the saddle, moving the billets farther back, or using a V-shaped billet system (see p. 78). If the saddle fits in every other way, and the billets are properly adjusted, a breastplate can help as well (see *Breastplates*, p. 132).

Narrow or Steeply Angled Back

As mentioned, slab-sided horses often have a *narrow back* as well, though the two characteristics do not necessarily go hand-in-hand. A horse with a narrow back generally has an apparent spine protruding higher than the back muscles, and the back muscles slope down at steep angles (figs. 8.3 A – C. Note: If your horse has a narrow back *and* high withers, please consult *High Withers*, p. 119, first.)

Narrow backs can be found in any breed but are most commonly seen in Arabians, Thoroughbreds, Paso Finos, Icelandics, Tennessee Walkers, and American Saddlebreds. They are also prevalent in upper-level eventing and endurance horses with very little extra fat or muscle because of long distance training, or in

Narrow Backs

8.3 A – C The horse in A has a narrow back with little muscle along the spine, especially near the withers. The view of the horse in B shows how the spine can protrude along a narrow back, and in C, you can clearly see how muscle can atrophy along the withers just behind the shoulder blade.

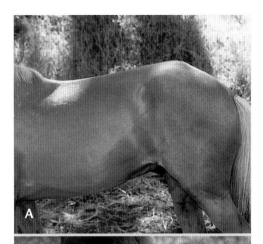
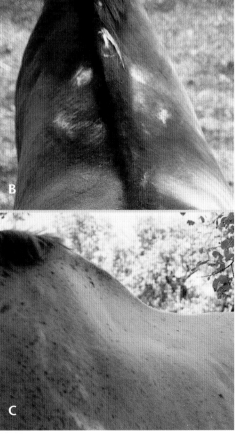

horses that have worn poorly fitting saddles and now have atrophied or wasted muscle along their toplines (fig. 8.3 C).

Some horses with narrow backs are fairly flat under the cantle area of the saddle, while others show more angulation there. Most commonly, Connemaras, Arabians, and Lusitanos have steeply angled backs. When a horse with this conformation raises his back, there is considerable upward movement at the top of the rib cage (toward the outer edges of the saddle panels). It is, therefore, important to use a saddle with narrow panels, or panels that are thinner at the outer edges, which will allow the ribs to lift. Otherwise, a linear area of pressure is created under the outer edges of the panels.

The key to fitting a narrow horse, or one with a steeply angled back, is to make sure that the saddle sits on the back muscles, and not close to, or actually on, the spine. Look for a narrow tree with panels that follow the angle of the withers and slope down along the entire length of the saddle (fig. 8.4, and see *Panel Fit*, p. 66). A saddle with panels that are too "flat" will concentrate pressure right next to the spine.

The width of the gullet is also very important. If it is too wide, the saddle will touch the spine or carry the rider's weight out over the ribs rather than correctly over the back muscles (fig. 8.5 A). A too-narrow gullet can also be a problem. The spine of the narrow back is more prominent and sticks up into the gullet space, and without the usual round back muscles to displace it, the gullet will rest directly on the spine (fig.

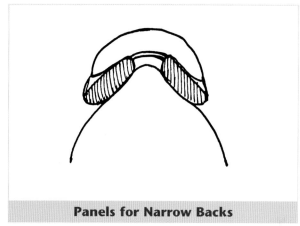

Panels for Narrow Backs

8.4 The panels on this saddle slope steeply and follow the angle of the narrow back. This allows a rider's weight to be equally and evenly supported by both panels.

8.5 B). If you can easily see your horse's backbone, especially if it rises well above the back muscles, find a saddle with thick panels that lift the saddle enough to maintain spinal clearance (see *Panel Fit*, p. 66).

Wide Back and Flat Withers

Some horses are born with *very wide, flat backs* and *flat withers* (figs. 8.6 A & B). They are very comfortable to ride bareback, though you may easily slide off without withers to anchor you! For the same reason, fitting saddles to these horses can be a challenge. If overweight, horses of any breed become wide, although many Quarter Horses, Morgans, pony breeds, Spanish breeds, draft crosses, and mules are naturally so.

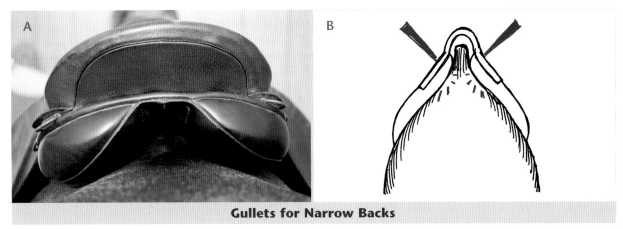

Gullets for Narrow Backs

8.5 A & B In A, see how a saddle with a very *wide* gullet places the panels far away from the spine of a narrow-backed horse. This puts the rider's weight on the sloping edge of the horse's rib cage. On the other hand, a *too-narrow* gullet can end up pinching a narrow horse's spine, as shown in B.

A Friesian, in particular, has a very low wither area and broad, round back—like a beer barrel—which is extremely difficult to fit. The tree angle must flare out across the withers rather than down, and unfortunately, very few sufficiently wide saddle trees are manufactured.

To compound this fitting challenge, flat backs and minimal withers naturally allow the saddle to slide sideways. If your sport involves quick turns, you will want to do everything you can to prevent the saddle from slipping, and many riders over tighten the girth to try to keep the saddle in place. This does not improve the comfort of the horse or the balance of the rider, nor does it solve the stability problem. Instead, search for a saddle with a very wide tree and thin panels that allow the saddle to sit as closely as possible to the horse's back

(fig. 8.7). Thick panels will sit the saddle too high above the back and will be less stable.

Extra wide trees are difficult to find, especially in jumping and cross-country saddles. A few manufacturers offer a wide model of a close contact saddle. (Interestingly, most of the wide brands are found in the inexpensive lines.) There is a selection of all-purpose and dressage saddles in extra-wide, though an extra-wide dressage saddle is often constructed with a wide mouth at the front of the tree, which narrows near the area of the stirrup bars and creates a pressure point, *(see sidebar, p. 65).*

Once you are *sure* the saddle fits your wide-backed horse, various saddle pad options can be useful for improving stability (see chapter 9). Avoid thick pads, since they will narrow the tree

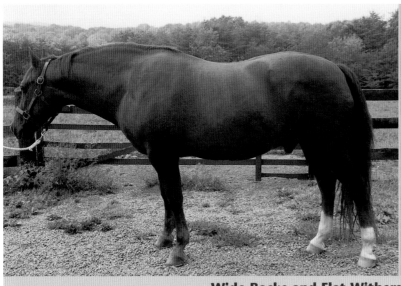
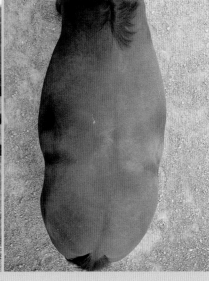

Wide Backs and Flat Withers

8.6 A & B The horse in A has a naturally broad, wide back, as well as some extra weight, which can make him extremely difficult to saddle. Compare the aerial view of the wide back in B to the narrow back shown in 8.3 B, and you can see how different the horses' saddles need to be.

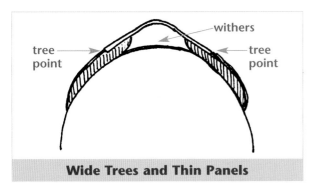

Wide Trees and Thin Panels

8.7 The tree of this saddle has a very open angle from point to point, allowing it to lie parallel to the withers of a wide, flat horse. Its panels (shaded) are very thin, which keeps the saddle close to the horse and more stable on a wide back.

fit and make the saddle less stable. A thin, wool fleece pad can help stabilize the saddle (natural wool fleece is less slippery than synthetic fleece), as can a chamois cloth. Thin, wool felt pads become very grippy after some of your horse's hair has worked into the material. And, when you use wool felt exclusively on one horse, it will mold to his back, further improving the saddle's stability. Look for other thin pads made with a non-slip material surface to help keep your well-fitted saddle in place.

High Withers

High withers can occur in any breed, and any type

of conformation, though some horses' withers (most commonly Thoroughbreds, Thoroughbred crosses, and Quarter Horses), just *appear* to be high. Often the muscle on either side of the withers has atrophied, or the horse drops his back in response to pain, and his withers appear prominent as a result (see fig. 8.3 C). For fitting purposes, it is important to notice the difference between *temporary* and *conformational* high-witheredness (fig. 8.8 A).

When fitting a high-withered horse, contributor Andy Foster advises you to *pretend the withers are not there*. No matter how prominent the withers are, concentrate on matching the angles of the tree points to the shape of the back muscles on either side of them (see *Tree Fit*, p. 55). Then, build thick panels to lift the saddle up and away from the spine and the withers (see *Panel Fit*, p. 66 and *The Gullet*, p. 73).

A tree with a cut-back pommel is designed to protect high withers from pressure, but the concept does not always work. If your horse has high, *short* withers, a cut-back might work well, but if your horse's withers are high and *average* or *long*, the cut-back pommel can touch the back of them (see *Long Withers*, p. 122). When considering such a tree, feel at least 4 inches behind the front of the pommel (where the cut-back ends) to be certain it is clear of the bone.

If your saddle works well in most ways, but it is too close to your horse's high withers, you can make a *high-wither pad* to solve the problem (figs. 8.8 B & C). This pad modification lifts the saddle, frees the withers, and keeps the rider bal-

anced. Using it for a while may encourage some horses' backs to fill out enough so that eventually, the problem is alleviated. For other horses, this pad can be an excellent permanent solution, especially for those with extremely high withers.

Use closed-cell foam because it holds its shape well, half an inch to an inch thick, depending on the height of your horse's withers (see p. 147). Cut a slot in the foam from the front of the pad to the back of the withers—no more than 1½ inches wide or the foam will slide. Seal the back of the slot with duct tape to help keep the pad from splitting (but be watchful for increased pressure on the horse's spine from the tape since it has no give to it).

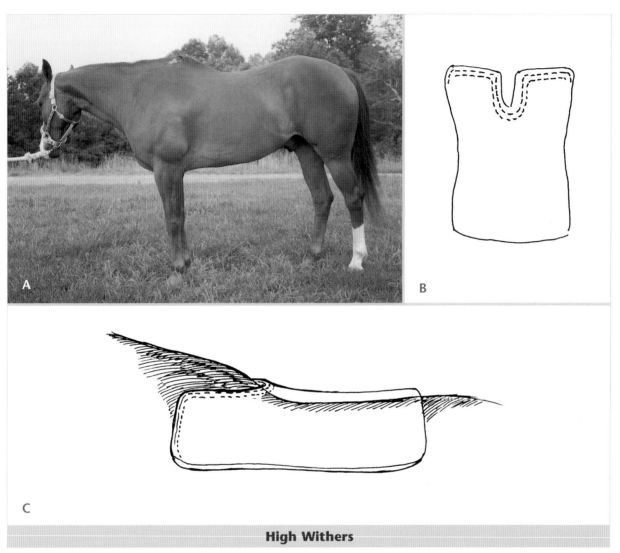

High Withers

8.8 A – C The horse in A has naturally high withers, and it can be challenging to find a saddle to fit him properly. In such a case, a special pad made of closed-cell foam can lift the saddle, which helps to free the horse's withers. Also, cut a 1½ inch wide, wither-length slot, as shown in B. Reinforce the area you have cut with a material like duct tape. Place the pad on your horse's back so the withers stick up through the slot, as in C. The sides of the pad should extend forward on each side of the withers. The will help to lift the saddle overall, as well as fill hollow areas on the sides of the withers.

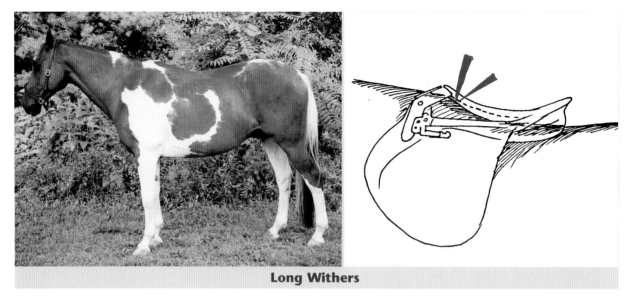

Long Withers

8.9 A & B The horse in A has very long withers. A horse with this conformation often has problems with pressure points right behind the head of the tree, as indicated in B. He will need a saddle with thick panels to make sure the gullet clears the spine.

Long Withers

Long withers are most commonly seen in Thoroughbreds, Saddlebreds, and Tennessee Walkers and do not need to be especially high to create a saddle-fitting problem (figs. 8.9 A & B). Finding the pressure points on a long-withered horse can be difficult, as ideally, you need to get your hand back to the problem area inside the gullet (usually out of reach, unfortunately). The best method for checking this far under the saddle is to use a riding crop (see p. 62). You can also "read" the saddle pad by looking for a dark spot on the midline of the pad (see fig. 9.7, p. 142). And, white hairs or a scarred area at the back of the withers are physical indications of a current or previous saddle-fitting problem.

The key to fitting a long-withered horse is to have thick enough panels so that the gullet clears the spine. You can also add a pad about half an inch thick to help your saddle clear the back of the withers (see p. 120).

Thickly Muscled Withers

Some horses have a slightly dropped back with *thick muscles on each side of their withers* (fig. 8.10). This muscle is called the *spinalis thoracis*, and it lies under the *trapezius*, which is the muscle directly under the points of the tree. A wide

• The Horse's Pain-Free Back and Saddle-Fit Book •

spinalis thoracis muscle can occur in all breeds and back shapes. When prominent, it presents a saddle-fitting problem because as the panels press against it, the horse becomes reluctant to lift his back or turn in tight circles. As the muscle continues to get sore, your horse's back may drop or become more swayed after a ride, and even more so over the course of several months.

If you raise your horse's back with a belly lift, the *spinalis thoracis* muscle disappears, and the sides of the withers flatten, making saddle fit easier (see p. 5). A consistent program of belly lifts can reestablish tone in your horse's stomach muscles and help alleviate this fitting problem. Another solution is to find a saddle with a very wide gullet in the front third of the saddle to clear the muscle.

Large Shoulders

Gaited horses and Quarter Horses, in particular, tend to have large shoulders that actually *push* the saddle back (fig. 8.11). In this situation, the girth needs to be attached *further forward* to help achieve correct vertical alignment with the girth line, rather than attached *further back* as you do with a saddle that *slides* back. The girth then holds the saddle in place, and the big shoulder prevents the saddle from sliding forward and hitting the back of the shoulder blades.

Uneven Shoulders

Uneven shoulders can be inherited, or they may appear while a horse is very young, usually caused by stiffness in the lower neck, chest, and

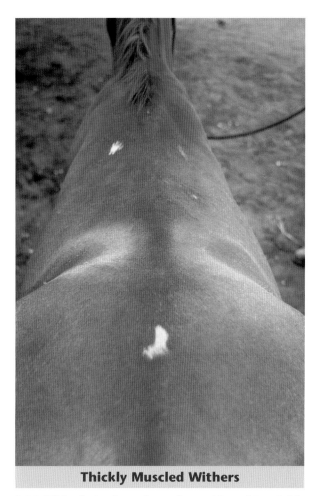

Thickly Muscled Withers

8.10 White hairs have formed on either side of this horse's withers where the *spinalis thoracis* muscle protrudes. It is important that this horse's saddle has a wide gullet to help keep pressure off this area.

withers. It has been shown that people with tension in their shoulders and neck tend to hold one shoulder higher than the other, and so do horses.

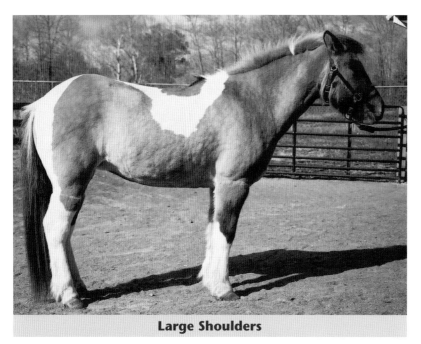

Large Shoulders

8.11 This Icelandic horse has very large shoulders, which tend to "push" saddles back and out of position.

to hold him while you place a stool or sturdy bucket behind his hindquarters. Talk to your horse and let him know where you are as you climb onto the stool, facing his ears. Now, you can look down at him from above for a "bird's-eye view" of his back, shoulders, and neck (figs. 8.13 A – C). Safety is paramount, so avoid this exercise if your horse kicks or spooks when approached from behind.

As you look down upon your horse's back, check for side-to-side symmetry. (Make sure your assistant keeps your horse's neck straight.) See if his shoulders appear to be the same size and shape. Look at the junction of the withers and the shoulders, and compare where each shoulder starts. In many cases, one side will start to bulge out from the withers in a different location than the other. Move your eyes along the back muscles and check to see if one side slopes off at more of an angle or bulges up more than the other. Is there any unevenness in the shape of his barrel or the middle of the back muscles where the center of the saddle sits?

Almost 80 percent of the time, a horse's *right* shoulder is flatter, closer to his body, and more forward than his *left* shoulder. The left shoulder tends to bulge away from the body and is set farther back (fig. 8.12). The heel on the left side is usually lower than the right, which sometimes has a heel so high it appears to be a clubbed foot. The reason for this percentage is unknown, though it may be related to the same genetics that cause right- and left-handedness in people.

You can see if your horse's shoulders are symmetrical by standing him squarely on a level, hard surface, preferably pavement. Ask a friend

To help determine whether your horse's shoulders are even, stand him squarely and, with chalk, draw a vertical line from the back of the each shoulder blade to the top of the spine (fig.

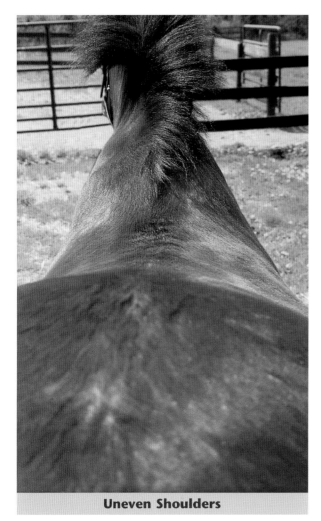

Uneven Shoulders

8.12 This horse's left shoulder is larger and appears to be set further back than his right, which looks flatter and smaller. His saddle will tend to twist and slip forward on the right, tipping his rider that way as well.

meet. If the two lines do not meet, his shoulders are uneven. Most horses will be slightly uneven, which is not a problem, but if there is 1 to 3 inches of space between the two chalk marks, the saddle will probably slip to one side.

When a horse has uneven shoulders, the saddle tends to "stop" at the bulging shoulder, but continues sliding forward toward the smaller, flatter shoulder. Although it is possible to adapt a saddle to accommodate uneven shoulders, it usually requires a custom saddle or an adjustable panel, and certainly an extremely knowledgeable saddler. If the saddle has a foam panel that can be adjusted, have the panel on the bulging, large shoulder "scooped out" so the shoulder can bulge into the space created (figs. 8.14 A & B). This modification allows the saddle to settle into the same place on both shoulders. Unfortunately, this correction is more difficult than it sounds, and most saddles do not lend themselves to this approach. Saddles with wool flocking, for example, may be reflocked to create a gap for the bulging shoulder, but the flocking will soon settle back and the problem will return.

You also may try using thin pads to improve the situation, as you can with uneven back muscles, but for most horses with uneven shoulders, putting a pad on the side with the flatter shoulder does not correct the problem. Instead, it usually drags the saddle further toward the same side, making the situation worse.

If you are riding a horse with asymmetrical shoulders, it is usually more difficult for him to turn smoothly toward the lower, more forward-

8.13 C). Be sure the lines are perpendicular to the ground and his front feet are square. Now, look down at the top of the spine where the two lines

set shoulder (the right, in my first example). In most of these cases, the muscle tension must be relieved and corrective shoeing must be applied before your horse's body can be reconditioned. Note that after treatment, the shoulders may still appear uneven, but functionally, the horse will move and carry the saddle normally.

Uneven Back Muscles

Uneven back muscles, seen in all breeds, commonly result from uneven shoulders, which cause the back to develop differently on each side. Poor posture and pain can also contribute to an uneven back, as can an unbalanced rider (see chapter 1). Examine your horse for uneven back muscles as you would when looking for uneven shoulders. Look down at your horse from your bird's-eye view, and if the back muscles appear uneven, chiropractic or muscle treatment should be sought before making any major saddle changes.

If your horse appears to have reasonably symmetrical shoulders but uneven back muscles, adding a thin pad or shim to the underdeveloped side of the back can be useful (see *Temporary Problem Solving*, p. 149). After you add the shim, ride for 20 minutes, then ask a friend to check from behind to see whether the saddle is now even from side-to-side. Riders often grow accustomed to riding slightly unevenly, so you may feel uncomfortable once the saddle is corrected. After about three weeks, however, you will begin to feel right in the new position.

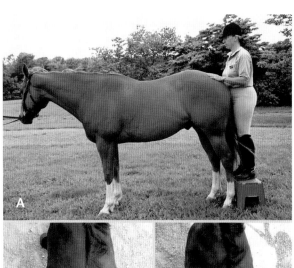
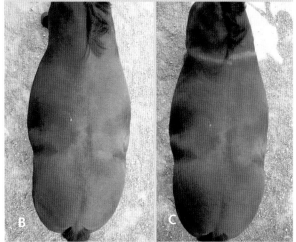

Checking for Uneven Shoulders

8.13 A – C You can best check you horse for shoulder symmetry by having an assistant stand him squarely on even ground while you stand on a bucket close to his hind end, as in A. Place your hands gently on his hindquarters so he knows you are there, and have your helper keep the horse's neck straight. You will now have a "bird's eye view" of your horse's back, similar to the view in B. To determine if your horse's shoulders are even, draw a chalk mark from the back of each shoulder blade to the top of the spine, as in C.

The Horse's Pain-Free Back and Saddle-Fit Book

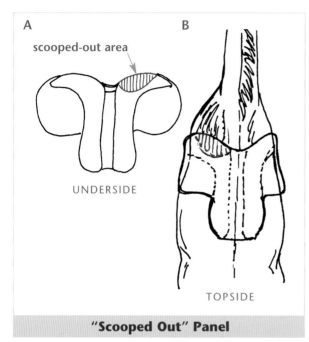

A   B

scooped-out area

UNDERSIDE

TOPSIDE

"Scooped Out" Panel

8.14 A & B You can adjust a saddle to accommodate a horse with a bulging left shoulder by having the panel on the left side "scooped out" by a saddler, as shown by the red area in A. When you place the saddle on the horse's back, the horse's left shoulder will now spread into the space that has been provided by the altered panel, as shown in B.

Uneven Hips

A saddle can also slip off to one side because your horse has *uneven hips*. Stand behind your horse and study his hindquarters; note if one side appears to be higher than the other. A high hip can push the saddle down toward the opposite shoulder, causing the rider to feel uneven. A high hip is usually caused by an injury and can be corrected with chiropractic treatment, though some horses were injured at such a young age, they will never become level.

If you cannot correct your horse's hips through treatment, you may need to have a saddler flock your saddle slightly unevenly to correct the balance. Check it every three months to see if your horse has changed shape. To encourage even muscle development, you should only use the uneven saddle as a *temporary* measure.

Swayed Back

Any significant downward curvature between the withers and the loins is considered a *swayed back* (figs. 8.15 A & B). Foals, yearlings, and two-year-olds rarely have swayed backs, and some breeds naturally have flatter backs—in particular, Morgans, Quarter Horses, Connemaras, and mules—so use them as a source of comparison. Also note that if your horse is young or one of these breeds and has any downward curve in his back, he may have a swayed back. In the vast majority of cases, a horse drops his back as a form of evasion because he is in pain. Truly congenitally swayed backs are usually severe and difficult to miss because they actually look deformed.

When working with a sway-backed horse, first check for any back pain that may need treatment. Focus on relieving that pain and consider borrowing a saddle, in case your horse changes shape. As he heals, back changes can be rapid.

Swayed-back saddle issues may not be as difficult to solve as you think. Sometimes, merely shift-

Swayed Back

8.15 A & B The horse in A has a typical swayed back that has been caused by back pain or age and can be helped with treatment. The horse in B, however, was born with a swayed back. When you try to lift his back with a belly lift, he can only move it slightly.

ing the saddle a little farther back than normal frees the shoulder and allows you to sit fairly balanced without any extra pads. (Be careful that the saddle does not put pressure on the loins.) Select a saddle with panels that have enough curve to fit your horse's shape, and avoid saddles with long, flat panels, which will never fit his conformation.

If the saddle slopes downhill toward the cantle, you may be tempted to add shims under the cantle to balance yourself (see *Temporary Problem Solving*, p. 149). However, the most common problem encountered when fitting a sway-backed horse is *bridging* (see *Panel Fit*, p. 66). The center of the saddle bridges the dip in the horse's back, and adding pads at the cantle will lift both the rear and the center of the saddle, thus creat-

ing even *more* bridging. Unless the tree shape fits extremely well, lifting the cantle can also drive the points of the tree into the withers (see *Tree Fit*, p. 55). If you wish to try to use shims to balance the saddle, add the material to both the rear and center of the saddle, leaving the front third of the saddle free of padding. Be careful, as the extra padding may make you feel less stable, even though you are better balanced.

Roached Back

A horse with a spine that is raised or curved upward in the lumbar area is considered to have a *roached back* (fig. 8.16). Roached backs are, in many cases, congenital. However, some horses with back pain may arch their backs upward.

The Horse's Pain-Free Back and Saddle-Fit Book

A saddle on a roach-backed horse generally tilts forward, concentrating the rider's weight at the front of the saddle and driving the points of the tree into the area just behind the shoulder blades. This unbalanced saddle position can create pressure points, limiting both the horse's performance and the rider's effectiveness. Saddle-fitting issues in these cases can be dealt with similarly to horses with high croups.

Croup-High

Many horses are *croup-high*—that is, their hindquarters are higher than their withers. Quarter Horse and Quarter Horse-crosses are often seen with this conformation (fig. 8.17 A). Arabians, also, may have a sharp rise through the loins to the hindquarters.

High hindquarters push the rider's weight forward and downward, and each time the rider puts weight in the stirrups, the saddle tends to flip up at the back, as it does when a tree is too wide (see *Tree Fit*, p. 55). This concentration of weight creates pressure points toward the front of the saddle.

A saddle with a lot of upward curve in the cantle area can help fit a croup-high horse. It can sit level on the front two-thirds of your horse's back, and then curve up away as his loins rise to his hindquarters (fig. 8.17 B). The panels should be round at the back corners to avoid edges that drive into the loins. The general shape of the panel curves need to match the shape of your horse's back.

You can also lift the saddle by using a *closed-cell foam pad* that is thicker at the front than it is

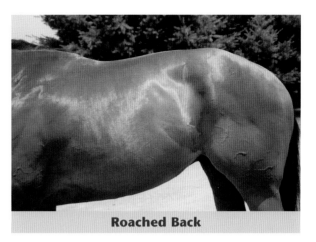

Roached Back

8.16 This horse was born with a roached back. It is difficult to find a saddle that can accommodate the position of his spine.

at the back (see p. 147). The pad should change smoothly from the thick front to the thinner rear, thereby preventing any uneven pressure points. For some mature, croup-high horses, a custom saddle may ultimately be the only way to balance the rider's weight correctly.

Problematic Breeds and Types

Some specific breeds or types of horses are just naturally built in ways that complicate the process of saddle-fitting. In some cases, the conformational equation seems too difficult to figure out. The secret is really to address each fitting issue individually before attacking the problem as a whole. Three of the most commonly mis-fit members of the equine family are ponies, Arabians, and mules.

Growing Pains

Most young horses experience several growth spurts. During this time, their hindquarters will often be higher than their forehand. Growth spurts typically occur when they are between one-and-a-half and two-and-a-half years old, and again some-time in their third year. Hunter and jumper classes where three and four-year-olds com-pete for breeder recognition, money, and prestige are getting more popular, prompt-ing riders to push young horses to jump at a time when they are still croup-high. The increased pressure that occurs at the front of saddle during this time is particularly detri-mental to young horses, since their develop-ing front legs can be damaged. Consequent wither pain promotes bad behavior, which is then punished or "over-trained," often ruin-ing a promising young horse.

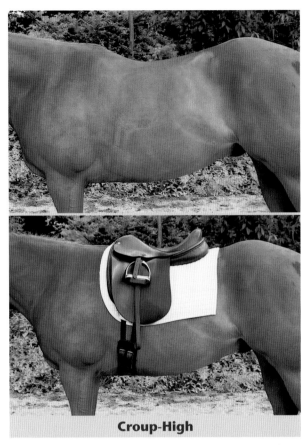

Croup-High

8.17 A & B The horse in A has a back that rises from the withers, through the loins, to the hindquarters. In B, his high croup is accommodated by a saddle with a lot of curve in the panels at the back. The curve follows the ascent of his back and does not interfere with his loins.

Ponies

Many ponies are quite wide across the withers, and unfortunately, pony saddles are usually made on fairly narrow trees. Ponies can get as sore as horses and usually express their pain by becoming unruly. What you might assume to be bad man-ners could just be a pony telling you he hurts.

It is thought to be easier for a child to sit on a narrow, little saddle rather than a wide one, but a too-narrow saddle sits high in the front, unbal-ancing the rider by placing her legs out in a chair seat position. The ideal saddle needs to incorpo-rate both a *wide tree* for the pony and a *narrow twist* for the child. However, very few, if any, manufacturers make pony saddles this way, so make do with a tree that is wide enough to fit the pony. Even though this is not the perfect solution, the child will adjust to a too-wide twist more easily than the pony will to a too-narrow tree.

Arabians

Arabians can be more difficult to fit than many other breeds (fig. 8.18). They tend to have prominent shoulders and short-coupled backs that rise sharply through the loins. To further complicate things, Arabs tend to have narrow or "A"-shaped withers (usually about 6 to 9 inches back from the shoulder) with a muscle that slopes steeply away from the spine. They also have a well-sprung—or wide—rib cage. This combination causes a saddle to pull down in front and lift in the back when the girth is tightened. In addition to their short, wide rib cage, their backs generally dip down or are somewhat swayed. This results in a lack of space for a saddle to be correctly placed. Saddles with shorter trees may work, but then a rider who has long legs or needs a larger seat has a problem. To help this situation, Arabs need saddles with panels that curve up at the back to follow the loin-line and avoid jabbing this sensitive part of the back. For best fit, the girth usually needs a V-system or forward billet attachment.

Mules

Mules are challenging to saddle-fit because they are wide through the barrel, with narrow shoulders, a forward girth line, low withers, and a smooth transition from the rib cage to the shoul-

Arabians

8.18 A complex conformational blend makes the Arabian horse one of the most difficult breeds to fit with a saddle.

ders (fig. 8.19). The back muscles slope quickly from the spine, almost as if the spine were in a smooth A-shape similar to a narrow-backed horse, except mules are not generally very narrow.

Even a well-fitting saddle tends to slip forward onto a mule's shoulders. Saddles also tend to slip from side-to-side because of the low withers. Breastplates and cruppers can be used to keep the saddle in place, and may need to be adjusted more tightly than one typically would on a horse (see p. 132). A thin, non-slip pad may help, too (see chapter 9).

Saddle Fit Accessories

There are countless items on the market that offer to help alleviate saddle troubles. While generally safe to use in addition to basic tack essentials—like a girth or a set of reins—it is important that such accessories are not used to *hold* poorly fitting saddles in place. Instead, they should be used to *help* a well fitting saddle stay correctly in place in specific situations or in the cases of certain conformations. Accessories should always be conscientiously adjusted for proper and comfortable fit. Here, I have briefly discussed a few of the most common.

Breastplates

A *breastplate* can help keep a saddle in place while going up steep hills, performing high speed maneuvers, and jumping over large obstacles (figs. 8.20 A & B). However, if your saddle will *only* stay in place with a breastplate, it most likely does not fit. Using a breastplate to "lock" the saddle forward places continuous pressure on a horse's chest and shoulders and restricts fluid movement of the front legs. This "solution" causes a shortened stride and can lead to problems such as unsoundness, stiffness, or foot pain. A breastplate should be adjusted so it only comes into play during extremes of movement and interferes as little as possible with shoulder motion.

Breastplates come in two styles: *hunter* and *jumper*. The hunter style is used for trail horses as well as for hunting and in hunter shows. Properly adjusted, it allows plenty of freedom for the shoulder to move. It should be loose at all gaits while your horse is working on level ground. In more extreme sports, such as foxhunting over rough ter-

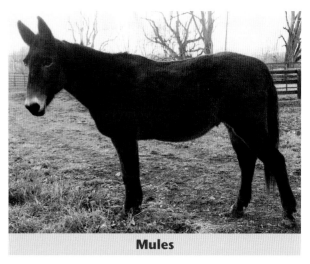

Mules

8.19 Mules can be very complicated to fit because they possess several different characteristics that all cause saddles to slide forward.

rain or eventing at the upper levels, it can be worn loosely to prevent the saddle from sliding under the horse's belly if the girth or billets break.

The correctly adjusted jumper breastplate should not restrict the motion of the shoulders and is designed to act only when the horse reaches the peak of his bascule. At this point in the jumping effort, the forces on the saddle are both downward and backward toward the tail as gravity pulls on the rider's weight. The jumper breastplate will prevent the saddle from slipping back as a result of these forces.

Cruppers

A *crupper* can be a useful accessory to prevent the saddle from slipping and the girth from chafing

The Horse's Pain-Free Back and Saddle-Fit Book

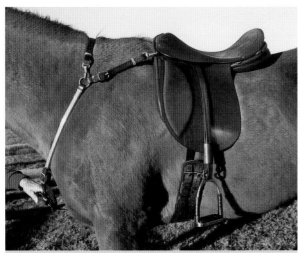

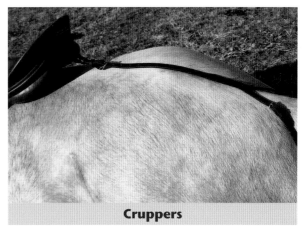

Cruppers

8.21 A crupper helps to keep a saddle from slipping forward when riding down steep hills.

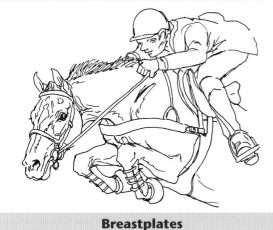

Breastplates

8.20 A & B A correctly adjusted hunter breastplate, shown in A, should be loose enough so it does not put any pressure on the shoulders until you are going up a steep hill or jumping a big fence. A jumper breastplate, like the one in B, should only become snug at the top of the horse's bascule.

the back of the elbows when going down steep hills (fig. 8.21). However, a crupper should *not* be relied on to hold the saddle in place except in extreme cases. If you discover that you need one for everyday riding, your saddle does not fit your horse properly. (The exception might be in the case of a mule, see p. 131.) Correctly fitted, a crupper should be loose when riding on flat or mild hills. When traversing a steeper hill, the strap should tighten as it keeps the saddle in place.

Foregirths

Dressage horses with forward girth lines are often saddled with *foregirths* holding the saddle in the correct position (fig. 8.22). Foregirths—non-elasticized leather straps that often feature a metal "tree," or wither-shaped piece—are placed at the front of the saddle to prevent the saddle from slipping forward. However, pressure from the foregirth can restrict the motion of the rib cage and shoulders and limit the stride just as if the saddle were placed too far forward. In addition, because foregirths are tightened securely and have no elastic, the chest is very restricted, and lifting and expanding the chest is an integral part of achieving true collection. Therefore, foregirths are really one of the most counterproductive and unkind devices used today. Contributor Andy Foster feels that 90 to 95 percent of foregirth use is unnecessary. Instead, a dressage saddle that slides forward can generally be corrected by changing the placement of the billets and girth to a more forward position. If the saddle continues to slide forward, it may have a different fitting problem and may need to be replaced altogether. *Only the occasional horse with extremely poor conformation needs a foregirth.* A crupper may be a kinder solution.

Of course, the most common saddle-fit accessory of all is the saddle pad. I discuss pads and their various forms, materials, and uses in the next chapter.

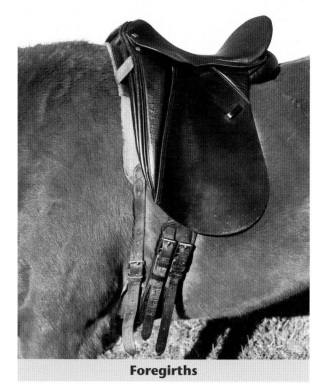

Foregirths

8.22 A foregirth was designed to keep the saddle from slipping forward. This is a very restrictive saddle accessory, as it does not have any "give" to it and is adjusted tightly around the rib cage and the back of the shoulders. It is not recommended for most horses.

9 Sensible Use of Saddle Pads

In the popular fairy tale *The Princess and the Pea*, a princess' royal skin is so sensitive, when she lies down to sleep, she can feel a single pea placed under a large pile of mattresses. Like the princess, your horse can feel pressure points from the saddle through any amount of pad material. It would be wonderful—and easy— if your favorite saddle could fit every horse with a simple change of saddle pad. Unfortunately, this is not the case, and in fact, often the pad makes the saddle fit *worse*.

The original purpose of a saddle pad was to protect the bottom of a saddle from sweat and dirt. Its job has expanded dramatically in modern riding. Now, a pad is used to create a cushion between the hard saddle and the soft muscles of the horse's back. It helps fill in gaps when a saddle needs reflocking. It is used as a temporary tool to balance a rider. A pad can improve the comfort of both horse and rider. What is often ignored, however, is that in all cases, a pad should be used with a saddle that *already* basically fits. Pads will *not* correct a major saddle-fitting problem, contrary to many advertising claims. Your ideal should really be to find a saddle that fits well when using a simple, straightforward, thin pad, thereby allowing you the closest connection to your horse. If necessary, intelligent use of pads may help when a saddle is close to fitting, but *not quite* perfect, or when you know your horse's body is in the process of changing dramatically.

The addition of a pad with the intent to correct a saddle-fitting issue frequently causes a sudden, dramatic improvement in your horse's performance. This is, however, a temporary fix

Under a saddle, the horse's back is like a foot in a shoe. If you add a heavy wool sock to the inside of a snug shoe, your foot becomes compressed, as does your horse's back muscle if you use a too-thick pad. If you add a rider and put the horse in motion—sometimes very fast motion like running, stopping suddenly, or jumping—you can imagine the discomfort or pain the horse is now feeling in his too-snug saddle.

Research with a computerized saddle-pressure measuring device (see p. 162) has shown that, in many cases, a pad actually *increases* the amount of pressure the horse experiences in the location of a pressure point. Pressure points can also become significantly larger and more painful, under a pad. The computer also shows that sometimes a pad can indeed improve the fit of a saddle.

Pads come in many varieties, with new materials, styles, and therapeutic properties available every year. They can be made from dozens of materials, including foam, felt, wool, cotton, air cells, fiberglass, and other synthetics.

Before using a pad, ask yourself what you want to accomplish, in terms of overall saddle fit, with your selection. Do you want to keep the bottom of your saddle clean? If so, all you need is a thin, non-therapeutic pad. Do you just want to look appropriate for your chosen riding discipline? Select a thin pad correctly styled for your needs. Do you have a specific fitting problem you are trying to solve? Study different types of pads and pad materials, and talk to tack shop sales people and other riders. Do you just want to add

that may last for a few days or for a number of months. Placing a pad under the saddle causes the saddle to sit differently, relieving the existing pressure points, but in most cases, they shift to a new location (fig. 9.1). Your horse will go well until the relocated pressure points again create pain, now in a new area, and then the behavior or lameness problems will return. Often, the first temporary "success" encourages a rider to search for another, different pad, and, because the horse goes well again for a little while, most people continue this routine, never realizing that the real pea under the mattress is the saddle!

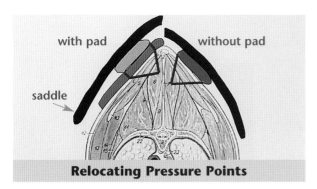

Relocating Pressure Points

9.1 On the right side, this cross section shows where a pressure point is located (green line) without a saddle pad. When a pad is added (red line) the pressure point sits at a different spot on the horse's back muscle (yellow line). The pressure is not removed, just relocated.

a soft interface between your saddle and horse? Be advised that a well-flocked or good foam panel is perfectly comfortable the way it is. Does your saddle have really hard panels and you'd like to soften the feel for your horse? Have a look at therapeutic and non-therapeutic pads to see which might be the best. Do you need to balance your saddle from front-to-back or side-to-side? A saddle pad might worsen your problem rather than help solve it.

Evaluating Saddle Fit with a Pad

If you decide you want to use a pad, carefully evaluate your saddle fit without the pad, first. A pad can improve fit under one saddle and worsen fit under another, so be willing to try different pads until you find one that works. If you use a thin pad just to keep your saddle clean, it should

not alter the saddle fit at all. Any other pads may change pressure points or saddle fit, so re-evaluate the fit before you mount.

A saddle pad should be centered, large enough to fit under the entire saddle, and shouldn't slip off to one side. I frequently see pads that are not big enough or are placed unevenly, creating a ridge next to the horse's back (figs. 9.2 A & B). When the edge of the pad is underneath the panel, painful pressure results—worse than a wrinkle in your sock! At least an inch of pad should extend beyond the outside border of your saddle. If you have an exceptionally large saddle, you may need to get a custom-made pad. On the other hand, little harm is done if the pad is too large for the saddle, unless it is so long or stiff that it rubs on the loins. (A common practice to avoid is the use of a Navajo-style pad with the front part folded back. The extra thickness creates more pressure at the front of the saddle and a ridge where the fold ends, and lifts the pommel slightly, creating a gap or bridge—see *Panel Fit*, p. 66.)

When selecting any pad, it is very important to choose one *shaped to the withers* rather than *flat and square* (figs. 9.3 A & B). If the pad stretches tightly over the bone of the withers, the pressure may cause bruises or sores, even when the rider pulls the pad up into the gullet (see sidebar, p. 139). This is similar to the pain you might feel when you put your boots on and your sock is pulled too tightly over your toes.

One reliable way to check whether your pad has altered the fit of your saddle is to check the

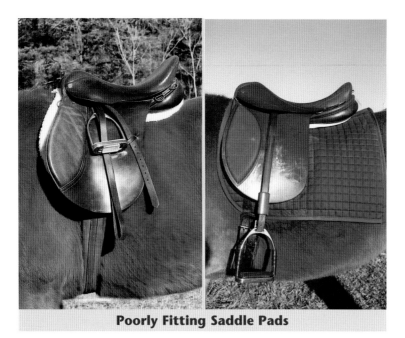

Poorly Fitting Saddle Pads

9.2 A & B The shaped pad in A is too small for this saddle, and a painful ridge of pressure is formed where the back of the panels is right at the edge of the pad. It is likely that similar pinching is happening underneath the saddle flap, as well. While the green quilted pad in B fits well, the small white pad added for extra cushioning is too small. The backs of the panels are hanging over the edge creating a ridge of pressure similar to what you see in A.

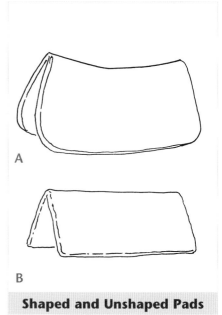

Shaped and Unshaped Pads

9.3 A & B A shaped pad, like figure A, conforms to the shape of the horse's withers, but an unshaped pad, like B, does not follow the natural contour of the withers, creating a pressure point at the peak of the bone.

levelness of the seat (see *Level Seat*, p. 66) Use the same process you learned in chapter 4 to help determine if your pad alters this for the better or worse. Always ride for about 20 minutes to allow the pad and saddle to settle into place before you make any evaluation. Certain pad materials will compress significantly after this time, altering the way they affect saddle fit. Dismount and stand back to observe your saddle. Is the center

of the seat still the lowest spot? If the saddle has remained correctly balanced, it is possible the pad will work under this particular saddle (figs. 9.5 A – D).

Reading your saddle pad after you ride is another method of discovering important information about your saddle and pad fit. For this exercise, if your saddle pad is white, begin with a slightly dirty horse. If you are evaluating a dark-

Keeping Saddle Pads Off the Withers

Part of your tacking-up process should include adjusting your saddle pad so that it is not stretched uncomfortably across your horse's withers. Once your saddle is settled correctly in place, lift the front of your pad into the gullet, creating a space similar to that which the pommel provides when the horse is saddled without a pad (fig. 9.4 A).

It can be difficult to keep saddle pads properly tucked up in saddle gullets, espe-cially in the case of endurance horses on long rides. If your pad persistently slips down across your horse's withers, you can secure it with a Velcro™ or leather loop attached to the pad and the nearest D-ring. Or, you can attach a small, U-shaped bracket to the underside of the pommel and loop a strap from the center of the pad to it, but make very sure that there is enough clearance between the bracket and your horse's withers (fig. 9.4 B).

9.4 A & B Keep pressure off your horse's withers by lifting your saddle pad into the gullet, as in A. You can help to keep the pad from slipping out of this position by attaching it to a bracket in the gullet, as shown in B, and described above.

colored pad, place a piece of thin, white sheet between the pad and your horse's skin—this will not interfere with the fit of the saddle and will help you read the patterns more easily.

Ride your horse for at least 15 to 20 minutes, until he has broken into only a *light* sweat—a completely sweat-soaked pad won't provide a clear picture. Remove the saddle and pad. Turn the pad over and examine it in good light. You may want to temporarily mark the left and right sides of the pad, because when you turn it over, they will be reversed.

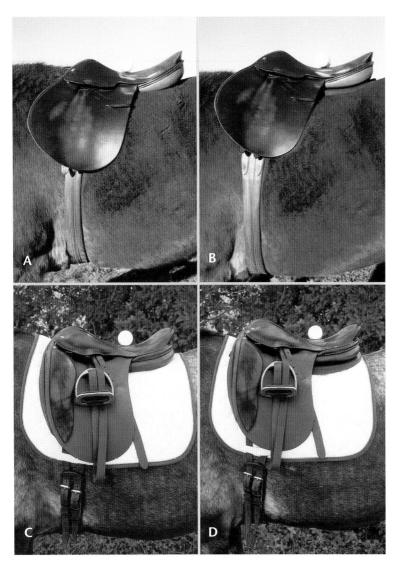

How Pads Change Balance

9.5 A – D In photo A, this jumping saddle is sitting level without a saddle pad. The pill bottle has come to a rest in the center of the saddle. In B, a pad has been added that is too thick for this saddle and this horse. The front of the saddle sits up too high, and you can see that the pill bottle shows how the center of the saddle has moved back. The dressage saddle in C fits the horse very well, and the thin cotton quilted pad has not changed the center of the seat. After adding a thick pad in D, however, the pill bottle has shifted toward the cantle, showing how the center of the seat has been changed.

To check the fit of a *thick* pad, obtain two pieces of clean, white, thin sheet or cloth. Use the first one to test the saddle fit alone, putting it under your saddle as if it were a pad and riding for at least twenty minutes. Remove it carefully and set it aside, then put the other, fresh, cloth next to the horse's skin. This time, add the pad you wish to test with your saddle. Again, ride for at least twenty minutes. Remove and compare the patterns on the two pieces of cloth. If you notice significantly more, or different, dark sweaty patches on the sheet you placed under the pad, then that particular pad probably increases the pressure on your horse's back.

If you see a nice, even pattern of dirt and sweat marks on pads of normal-to-thin thickness, usually the saddle is evenly touching the horse's back. As a general rule, if you see areas

Pads and Gullet Width

Thick pads often fill up the saddle gullet, narrowing the space available for the withers and the spine. Select a pad that is made with its own gullet or is thin in the middle, allowing for the spine (fig. 9.6). If your saddle has a wide gullet and your horse is small, however, you may be able to use a thick pad under your saddle without harm because there is enough space in the gullet for both pad and spine. You can also create a gullet in the pad yourself: cut a thick pad in half, and insert the two pieces into a thin pad with pockets on each side.

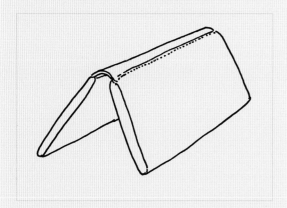

9.6 This is a pocket pad with thick padding inserted on each side of the spine. The center is thin—as you can see, it is similar to the gullet of a saddle. This type of pad will not interfere with the width of the saddle gullet.

that are dirtier, darker, or have more concentrated sweat, they indicate heavier pressure or more friction (fig. 9.7). Drier, lighter areas *generally* mean less pressure. Unfortunately, this is not an exact science. Pressure can hinder sweat glands, and it is possible for an area under *heavier* pressure to produce *less* sweat, leaving only a light sweat mark on the pad. So, remember to use your pad-reading as another piece of information, but not the final answer, to saddle- and saddle pad-fitting issues.

What follows are some of the commonly seen saddle pad patterns and their possible causes. If you notice:

- *Very dirty or sweaty areas at the front and rear of the saddle pad and lighter areas along the middle of the panels.* The saddle is putting more pressure on the front and rear of the saddle and bridging in the center. Causes for this pattern include too little flocking, a too narrow tree, panels that do not follow the shape of the horse's back, and a rider tipping forward or backward.

- *Dark areas in the middle part of the panels with light areas at their ends.* The saddle is rocking, probably because the bottom of the panels are too curved or overflocked.

- *Asymmetrical dark areas (fig. 9.7).* The saddle, the horse's back, the rider, or any combination of these is asymmetrical.

- *Dark areas concentrated at the back of the saddle with slight or no marks under the front of the saddle.* The saddle is tipped back and your weight is concentrated toward the cantle.

Reasons for this pattern include a too narrow tree, too little flocking at the back of the saddle, the seat center or balance point is too far back, or a rider in a chair seat position.

- *Dark areas concentrated under the points of the tree, and very light, dry areas toward the back half of the saddle.* The saddle is too wide or needs reflocking in the front area.

- *Light, dry areas under the points of the tree.* Usually, the saddle is *too wide* and is shutting off the sweat glands, however, a *very narrow* saddle can also give the same pattern. If you correct the fitting problem and the dry areas persist, the sweat glands may have been so damaged they no longer function.

- *Dark areas around the stirrup bar.* Usually signals a poorly designed saddle with the stirrup bars wrongly placed or recessed too far, or a gullet that narrows in that same area. They may also indicate that the horse has a thickly muscled area behind the withers that you need to consider when fitting (see p. 122).

- *Dark area at the top of the withers.* The pad is pulling down on the withers or your saddle is hitting them. If you have a horse with long withers (see p. 122) the dark mark may be 6 to 8 inches behind the front of the saddle, along the center of the pad.

- *Dark areas inside the gullet, either on or alongside the spine.* The pad was not properly lifted off the spine under your saddle, the saddle has a narrow or uneven gullet, or the saddle is sitting off to one side and touching the spine.

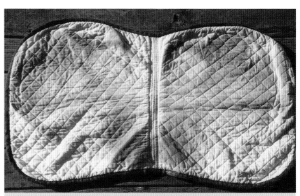

Reading Your Saddle Pad

9.7 When you read your saddle pad's underside, the left side of the saddle shows on the right side of the pad. Note, here, that the sweat and dirt marks on the two sides of the pad have different shapes: the right side appears to exert more pressure than the left. This indicates that the saddle is sitting unevenly, which could be caused by a twisted tree, uneven panels, uneven back musculature, an unbalanced rider, or a combination of all these. The darker marks mean areas of high pressure are concentrated toward the cantle area. There are also light marks in the center and near the front of the saddle, which tell you that the saddle is sitting heavier at the rear. This is because the saddle is too narrow, has panels poorly flocked and incorrectly shaped for the horse, or the rider is sitting in a chair seat position.

Adjusting Tree Width with Saddle Pads

If your saddle tree is slightly *too wide* for your horse's back, the addition of a thick pad may improve the fit, like wearing a heavy sock inside a shoe that is a bit too large (see *Tree Fit*, p. 55). The thicker sock prevents your foot from slopping around inside the shoe. However, a saddle that is *very* wide will continue to tip forward despite adding a thicker pad, and while it may be possible to add a shim to raise the front of the saddle, sometimes a saddle is just too wide for a pad to solve the problem.

If the tree is *too narrow*—the most common problem I see—a thick pad will actually intensify the problem. Over time, the increased pressure from the pad will cause the muscles along each side of the withers to atrophy or shrink. Often, pads sold to specifically cushion the withers, such as pommel pads and pads thicker in the front, can actually further compress the withers. A thick pad also lifts the front of a saddle with a narrow tree. This raises the location of the tree points, taking away some of the support they offer and narrowing the gullet. The tree then behaves as if it has short points, rotating forward and downward into the sides of the withers. If your tree is too narrow, a thick pad is never the best choice.

Besides the thickness of your saddle pad, you must also choose a material: natural or synthetic (man-made). Natural fibers rarely cause skin reactions, while some horses are sensitive to synthetic materials and may react with rashes, hives, or hair loss. Irritation is especially noticeable immediately after a pad is first introduced, even if it is not new and has been used on another horse. Some manufacturers claim synthetics are more durable than natural fibers, and this may be true with some materials. However, all pads will break down and need to be replaced eventu-

ally (see *Saddle Pad Care*, p. 155). Natural fibers used to be more difficult to clean than synthetics, but modern technology has made this less of an issue. In the end, if the pad works for you, your saddle, and your horse, it does not matter whether it is natural or synthetic.

Types of Saddle Pads

Non-Therapeutic Pads

Non-therapeutic pads do not make any special claims regarding their use or beneficial effects. They are often affordable and come in a variety of materials, both natural and synthetic.

A standard *quilted cotton pad* is made from a cotton cloth filled with a thin material, usually light foam or cotton batting (fig. 9.8 A). When compressed, the pad is less than an eighth of an inch thick, does not interfere with saddle fit, and rarely causes skin reactions. Thicker, cotton-quilted pads are also made. They may be a quarter of an inch thick or more and may interfere with saddle fit, but rarely cause any other problems. These are useful pads and are readily available in all colors and shapes.

Wool fleece pads are made either with the wool woven into cloth or left on the leather sheepskin. One-hundred percent wool fleece pads have some cushioning ability, and are known to have excellent air circulation properties. Due to its structure, wool whisks sweat away from the skin, making it especially useful for endurance horses. Wool fleece will stay warm even when wet—unlike cotton—which can be especially useful for horses ridden for long periods in a cold rain. Wool seems to help minimize pressure points, as has been documented by a computerized saddle pad (see p. 162).

Wool fleece pads have long had a reputation for being hard to clean, but almost all of the fleeces woven on cloth can now be machine-washed, and new tanning methods are providing machine-washable leather fleece. Sweat and dirt brush out of fleece easily, so they do not have to be washed as frequently as most other pads. The main disadvantage to leather wool fleece pads is their expense, but they last for many years.

Synthetic fleece is the common and durable pad material that looks like wool but is made from a variety of synthetic materials. In general, synthetic fleece does not breathe as well as natural fleece, though there are some new types that claim to allow better air circulation than the natural ones. They may be sold in single or double thicknesses—single thickness is best because you do not want the material to interfere with saddle fit. Some synthetic fleeces will wrinkle or shift under the saddle, so if you choose this type of pad, read it carefully after you ride to make sure it is staying in place.

Wool felt pads are versatile because they form to the shape of the horse's back and generally do not interfere with the fit of the saddle. These pads usually are three-eighths to a half an inch thick. Felt made from 100 percent wool is best, though 70 percent wool, 30 percent synthetic blends are also acceptable. A pure-wool, felt pad can actually wear out more quickly than felt made from a synthetic blend. This fiber is soft against the horse's back, whisks sweat away from the skin, is hypoallergenic, and breathes well.

Felt has a reputation for being difficult to clean, but many new felt pads are made to hose off and dry in the sun. It is also easy to brush or shake the dry dirt and sweat off of them. Some wool felt pads can be purchased with a machine-washable cover, just be sure this cover doesn't make the pad too thick for your saddle.

A piece of *full-grain butt leather* (a particular cut of heavy leather) makes an excellent saddle pad because over time, it molds to the horse's back shape. This pad originated in the Spanish and Portuguese riding schools and is used today by many classical dressage riders. It is a very useful pad that I encourage other disciplines to try. The leather is relatively stiff, which actually prevents smaller pressure points from reaching the back because the entire pad maintains its shape, actually "blocking" the pressure points. When a regular pad becomes stiff, it rarely maintains a shape that protects the back and, instead, usually ends up rubbing.

If you can find a saddler to make you a leather pad, it is critical that he shape it properly for the withers and curves it up at the cantle so that it does not rub. The pad does not need to be custom fitted as long as its topline is properly shaped. Be sure the center seam over the spine is smooth. These pads only need minimal cleaning because the sweat and dirt easily brush off. The sweat is beneficial because it makes the leather stiffer, which actually better protects the horse's back.

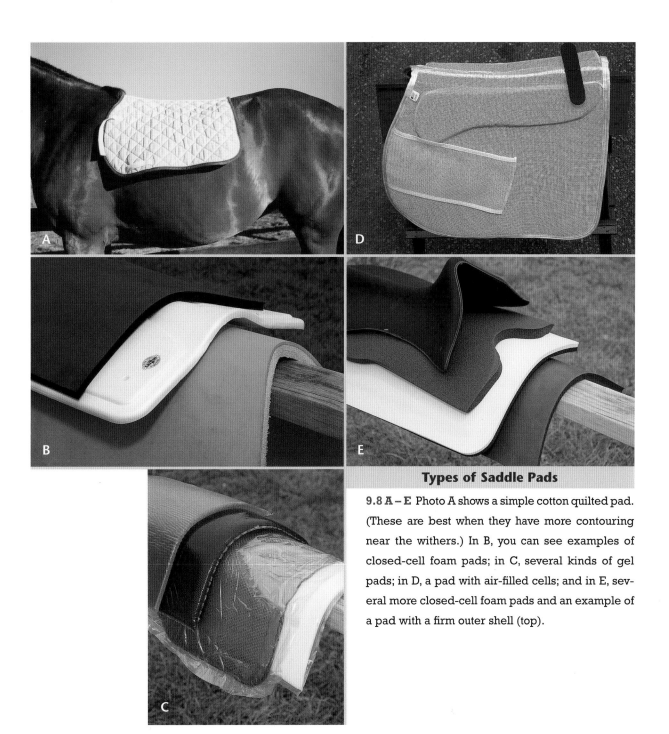

Types of Saddle Pads

9.8 A – E Photo A shows a simple cotton quilted pad. (These are best when they have more contouring near the withers.) In B, you can see examples of closed-cell foam pads; in C, several kinds of gel pads; in D, a pad with air-filled cells; and in E, several more closed-cell foam pads and an example of a pad with a firm outer shell (top).

Therapeutic Pads

Therapeutic pads are designed and marketed to be problem-solvers that deal with saddle fit, back pain, shock absorption, cushioning, and pressure distribution. These pads often incorporate materials developed to help prevent bedsores and cushion various parts of human bodies. Some of these materials were designed for NASA and the space program. The shape and function of the horse and saddle, however, is very different from a human confined to a wheelchair, lying flat in a bed, or sitting in a rocket ship, and as you have learned, many saddle-fitting problems cannot be solved by a saddle pad, therapeutic or not.

Some therapeutic pads claim to absorb shock. The difference between *pressure* and *shock* is that pressure is static, and shock is similar to the reverberation you feel after you hit a nail with a hammer. The saddle absorbs a great deal of shock: sit down, set a saddle on your thigh, and pound on the seat a few times. You really will not feel much vibration. There may be situations when you need a pad that offers some shock-absorbing qualities, for instance, if you tend to bounce on your horse's back when you sit the trot. Shock absorption *may* occur with certain pad materials, but the problem is, we cannot measure it. We can, however, measure pressure. In general, it is pressure that creates the majority of problems, as sore areas are caused by constant, sustained pressure in one location. Pressure is what the horse feels with every step if the saddle and pad fit are wrong.

An *open-cell foam* pad is similar to a sponge: you can squeeze the air out of it. There are a number of different open-cell foams. The most common are the kinds used for making seat cushions, pillows, and egg-crates. Some varieties of foam are very soft, full of air, and easily compressed, while others are denser, have less air, and do not compress as much. Squeeze the pad between your fingers to see how thin the pad will become with your weight in the saddle. If an open-cell foam pad compresses down to a quarter inch under the weight of the rider and saddle, regardless how thick it was to begin with, it will interfere little with fit, and may even enhance the horse's comfort. A very thick—2 to 3 inch—piece of open-cell foam compresses down, but will still be about an inch thick under the saddle and can interfere with fit. The gullet is often completely filled by the thick foam, and the saddle is held away from the horse's back until you mount. The saddle is then unstable and the girth will probably be loose. I don't recommend using these thick, open-cell foam pads.

Closed-cell foam is the basis for many therapeutic pads on the market (fig. 9.8 B). The air in a closed-cell foam is contained inside the material and does not compress like open-cell foam, so the pad retains its shape until worn out. The texture of this foam varies from hard and dense, to very soft and supple, and is available from about ⅜ to 1 inch thick. One inch is too thick for most saddles.

Closed-cell foam is advantageous because it will remain a certain thickness under your saddle. For example, you can purchase some closed-cell foam pads that are thicker at the front than at the back, and use them to balance a saddle (see *Shim Solutions*, p. 153), and the pad will retain these beneficial features until it wears out. Because there is so little compression, closed-cell foam pads may be too thick to fit under your saddle. Be aware that these pads decrease the gullet width and space available for the spine, so choose one with a gullet (see fig. 9.6). These pads can leave the rider feeling unbalanced or "perched" on top of the horse, and although some riders and horses like the "bounce" provided by closed-cell foam, others find it uncomfortable.

This type of pad often claims to absorb and dissipate pressure, but because the air remains in a fixed location, when a pressure point pushes on the top of the pad, the foam actually transmits it through the pad to the horse's back. In fact, the pressure point can actually become *larger* than was the case prior to using the pad. This has been documented in numerous computer scans.

Gel pads are made from various semi-liquid materials or viscoelastic polymers (fig. 9.8 C). Some of the gels are fairly firm, while others are quite soft. These pads tend to be heavy, which is not a problem unless you are trying to make a lighter weight class in competition, and in some cases, can actually be useful if you must add weight.

When there are no specific pressure points in the panels, gel pads can form a soft interface between the saddle and horse. Their main advantage is that they are not very thick, so they fit better under most saddles than many closed-cell foam pads. Some riders and horses like the feel of gel. A rider can even cushion a hard saddle by using a gel pad on *top* of the saddle as a seat saver.

There are several disadvantages to the gel material. The pads often "bottom out" under pressure because the semi-liquid nature of gel moves away from a lump, so the horse ends up feeling the pressure point. Since the gel is pushed away from the pressure point, it gets thicker in the surrounding area, frequently making pressure points larger and more severe after about 20 minutes of riding.

A gel pad is seldom shaped for the withers, so it stretches across the top of them, creating another potential pressure point, and because of its semi-liquid nature, gel moves into and fills the gullet space more completely than any other material, putting excessive pressure on the spine. Gel is best used only in a pad constructed with a pocket on each side to hold two separate pieces of gel away from the spine (see fig. 9.11).

Air-filled cells of various sizes are currently being considered as possible solutions to saddle-fitting problems (9.8 D). Air can be useful in a saddle pad because it moves *away* from pressure. However, inside a single contained cell, air under pressure becomes hard, just like a football becomes hard when it is blown up tightly. If there is a pressure point on the saddle, the air has no place to move, except toward the horse's back.

A pad with a *firm, outer shell* is one of the most recent additions to the market (fig. 9.8 E). These pads are made from fiberglass—or another hard, plastic material—imbedded in a soft, cushioning material such as wool felt. This type of pad does not let pressure points through at all and is one of the few materials that can actually distribute pressure evenly along the surface of the pad. It shows some promise for use with a saddle that does not fit. If the pad fits properly, almost any saddle can be put on top of it without causing the horse discomfort. However, these pads *must* be fit correctly, and it is not always possible to find a professional who knows how to do so. Plaster casts and back-measuring devices can be used to help you get the right fit, but it is not an easy task.

If a poorly fitting saddle is placed on top of a hard shell pad, the rider may, at first, feel totally out of balance, but with careful use of shims, this type of pad can be useful in settings such as therapeutic riding programs, mounted police work, and riding schools. Here, the shell can fit and protect the horse's back, and the saddle most appropriate for the student can be used.

Innovative, new pad designs are being developed every year. Some of these become an excellent contribution to the saddle industry, while others are expensive disasters. Use caution when examining new pad ideas and apply all the concepts introduced in this book before buying anything. Many pad manufacturers are using computer saddle-pressure testing data to market their pads, but if these tests were conducted on a stationary horse, they have little value (see p. 162). Almost any pad will show a good scan—until you put the horse through all of his gaits. Also, the test results must be collected after the horse has been ridden for a while—at least 20 minutes—to evaluate whether the pad material changes or compresses during the course of an average ride.

Pads that Should Never be Used

Pommel pads are frequently used, and I wish they could be banned. The reason people usually add a pommel pad is because the saddle is sitting close to the withers. A pommel pad cannot possibly solve the problem; it can only add to it! Pommel pads not only put excessive pressure on the withers, but the rear edge of the pad creates a pressure point under the stirrup bar area. A bridge begins in the center of the saddle where the pad ends. If your horse has high withers, or your saddle is too wide, refer to the beginning of this chapter and chapter 8, *Confounding Variables*, for the corrections that *can* be made to improve the situation.

Riser, *bounce*, *lollipop*, *bump*, or other similar pads elevate the cantle of the saddle, and are some of the worst types of pads to use (figs. 9.9 A – D). They are often used with a saddle that slopes down toward the cantle, usually one that is already too narrow or placed too far forward. Adding a riser pad, while certainly lifting the back of the saddle, pushes the points of the tree into the withers (or the shoulder blades if the saddle is placed too far forward). To make matters worse, a large bridge area is created under the center of the saddle and the gullet is filled by the pad's stem, increasing pressure on the spine.

Another pad style that needs to be discarded is sometimes called a *wither pad*. It has a long slot cut out for the withers, beginning an inch or two back from the front of the pad and extending six to eight inches down the centerline. The concept is to relieve pressure on the withers by creating an open space for them, similar to the high-wither pad I described on page 120. This pad, however, is commonly made from a thick material—usually felt with a fleece cover on the underside—that wraps through the wither slot to the top. This thick roll of pad material presses along the edges of the withers, and when you add a saddle, especially one with a narrow gullet, serious pressure points develop.

Temporary Problem Solving

Shims are thin pads that can be placed under various parts of a saddle to *temporarily* change the balance or fit. If your present saddle is not balanced, a shim can be a very valuable tool that allows you to experience riding in a correctly balanced saddle. Shims are also great as a temporary solution for a horse with developing and changing musculature.

"Temporary" is the key concept here. Decide how long to keep a shim in place by checking to see if you are not solving one problem by creating another. If this is the case, you should not use the shim for more than a few weeks. If there does not appear to be any adverse effects, you may be able to use the shim for a long time, even for many months. Shims can also provide appropriate permanent solutions for:

- professionals who ride many horses.
- high-withered or high-crouped horses.
- riding schools or camps where there are a limited number of saddles to fit an ever-changing population of horses (see chapter 12).
- seasonal changes in your horse's shape.

Any time you use a shim to correct or alter a fit, be sure to check and recheck your saddle and shim regularly. If you are using the shim to correct a saddle fit problem, the horse's muscles should recover, and will therefore change shape again. You might need to change your shim configuration as often as every month. If old problems return or you start having new problems, the shim has outlasted its usefulness, and you need to discard it and find a new solution.

It is important to understand that changing the balance of a saddle with a shim may make

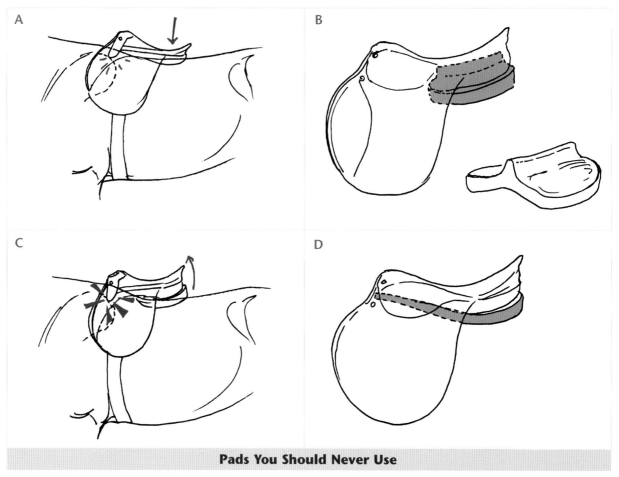

A

B

C

D

Pads You Should Never Use

9.9 A – D In A, the saddle is placed too far forward, causing the cantle to sit downhill. Unfortunately, some riders use bounce, riser, or bump pads (short, thick pieces of foam that sit under the back of the saddle) as seen in B. If such a pad is added, the points of the tree will be driven painfully into the horse's shoulder blades (C). In addition, a lollipop pad—also often used to raise the back of a saddle that sits downhil—extends a narrow piece of foam down the length of the saddle's gullet, and pressure is then placed directly on the horse's spine (D).

your problem worse, or simply fail to improve it. The shape of the horse's back is complex. Compare it to the bow of a boat or a fan blade. The saddle panels must smoothly follow the complex curve to fit well. If they do not, pressure points result. When you add a shim, you are essentially changing the shape of the bottom of the panel, so the combination of shim and panel must still follow the curve of the horse's back.

It is best to make a shim out of *open-cell foam* because it has a softer transition from the beveled (tapered) edges. *Closed-cell foams* can be used, but the edge of the shim needs to be very carefully beveled so as not to leave a ridge. To determine the thickness of the shim, factor in the size of the gap you are trying to fill. Consider the amount of compression the foam material will have: open-cell foams start thick but compress, so they work well when you want to fill smaller spaces. The closed-cell foams do not compress much and will work better if you are filling larger gaps or trying to use a saddle that is too wide.

Measure the saddle panel to determine the length of shim you need. For example, if you add a shim to a saddle that is a bit wide and is tipping down in front, you need to measure about a third to half of the way from the front toward the center of the bottom of the panels (figs. 9.10 A – D). Cut the shim several inches longer than you require, allowing room for error and adjustments. Next, place the material on the horse's back, under the saddle. Check to see if it's close to the size you need. Sit in the saddle to see if the problem you are trying to correct is fixed or worsened before refining the shim. Then bevel the edges of the foam using an electric carving or serrated kitchen knife. You want the edges to blend smoothly under the saddle, leaving no corners or lumps. As you

bevel, the foam may become too thin, and the reason for cutting the foam larger than the exact size will be apparent! If the edge is too thin, cut it off, and try again until you have the right shape and size.

Put the finished shim between your saddle pad and saddle, where in some cases, it will remain correctly positioned. In other cases, it will slide out of place, most likely at the time when it is most awkward to retrieve. The ideal way to keep the shim in place is to use a thin saddle pad with a pocket along each panel (fig. 9.11). Place your shim inside the pocket, and if it continues to slide around, secure it with one or two big stitches across the center of the pocket just in front of, or just behind, the shim.

If you are using a regular full pad and are adding a shim for refinement, it is best for the full pad to be made of open-cell foam because it will allow the edges of the shim to blend in well. The shim should be placed on top of the full-length pad. You can glue or sew the shim to your saddle pad, but if you need to make a change at a later date, it will be more difficult.

Some manufacturers make closed-cell foam pads with shims already built in that make either the front, center, or back of the pad thicker. These pads can actually work better than adding a shim of your own, especially if a fairly thick shim is required. Pads with shims built in should have a smooth transition from the thinner to the thicker part; those with ridges at the edge of the shim should be avoided.

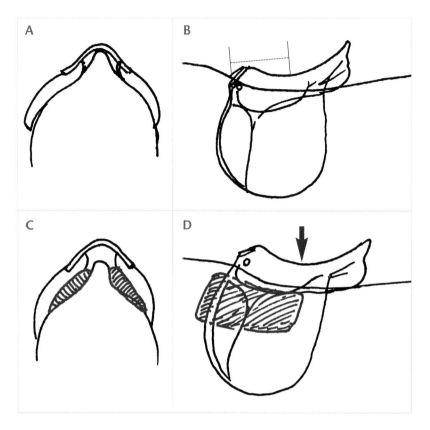

Use of a Shim

9.10 A – D The saddle in A and B is too wide so it tips down in the front, putting the balance point (or center of the seat) too far forward, driving the tree points into the sides of the withers, and on a horse with medium-to-high withers, causing the pommel to pinch the top of the bone. Shims can help alleviate this problem. Determine how long your shim should be by measuring a third to half the length of a panel from the front of the saddle, as shown by the red lines in B. Your shims (shaded) should be placed under each side of the saddle, and as you can see in C, they will effectively narrow a too wide saddle. The seat will now be level and the balance point in its center, as shown in D.

Shim Solutions

Your Saddle Has Thin Panels or Slopes to the Rear
Some saddles are made with panels that are too thin, and even though the tree seems to fit well, the saddle still slopes in one direction or another. If your saddle has thin panels at the *front*, see p. 153. For panels that are thin in the *center*, see next solution. If the panels are too thin at the *back* and the saddle slopes accordingly, have a skilled saddler add a gusset or temporarily problem-solve with a thin shim added to the rear third to half of the panel length (fig. 9.12 A). In

fact, if this is all it takes to balance your saddle, it could even serve well as a long-term solution. If the saddle requires very thick shims to compensate for the thin panels, however, I would advise you to begin looking for a saddler or a new saddle.

Your Saddle Bridges or You Have a Sway-backed Horse
Adding a shim to the center area of the panel can be helpful if:

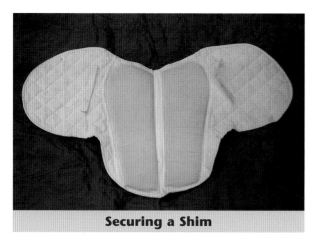

Securing a Shim

9.11 Use a thin quilted cotton pad with pockets to secure a shim. Add a few large stitches in front or behind your shim to keep it in place.

- your saddle has thin panels in the center, yet fits well otherwise.
- you have a mildly sway-backed horse, and your saddle bridges.
- you need to temporarily pad the center of your saddle until you can have it reflocked.

While the saddle is on your horse, carefully mark with chalk where the bridge starts and finishes, and keep in mind that the beveled edges of the shim must end where the bridge ends (fig. 9.12 B). These shims should be secured by stitching them into a pocket pad (see above).

You can also solve a bridging problem with a shim that fits on the underside of the saddle between the panel and the tree. Cut a piece of felt—or stiff, closed-cell foam—that's a little longer than the bridging area and slightly nar-

rower in width than the panels. Next, carefully bevel all edges as described on page 151. Turn your saddle upside down and work the shim in between the panel and the tree, taking care to center it where the bridging occurs. It will probably not be easy to get it in place. Be aware of how thick the shim you are adding is, as too much can create severe pressure points and a saddle that rocks over the bulge created by the shim. If you add so much that you stretch the leather, you can damage the shape of the panel. Regularly recheck the shim to be sure it stays in place.

On a significantly sway-backed horse, the cantle may sit very low (see *Swayed Back*, p. 127). Begin with a tree that fits well, then add a set of shims under the back of the saddle for balance. The center of the panels will be farther from the swayed back once you raise the cantle, so you will now have to fill the bridge in the middle of the saddle. You may end up with a lot of padding under the saddle, but your horse will be much more comfortable with support along his entire back, and in some cases, may even become *less* sway-backed. You will also feel better sitting on a solid, level surface.

Your Saddle Slopes to the Front, is too Wide, or Your Horse is Croup-High

Adding a shim to the front can be helpful if:
- your saddle is *slightly* too wide.
- the front of the panel is thin.
- the panel needs to be reflocked in the front.

Front shims will prevent the saddle from tipping down toward the pommel (fig. 9.12 C). They

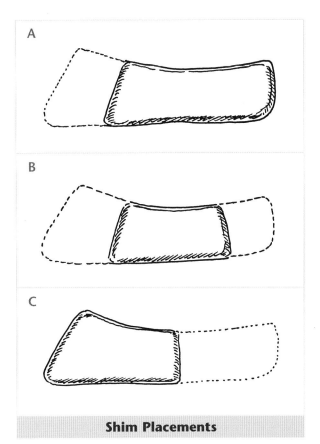

Shim Placements

9.12 A–C A shim that is placed beneath the rear third or half of a saddle, as in A, will help center the balance point. Figure B is a shim used with a saddle that bridges, or on a sway-backed horse. This shim must be centered carefully and the beveled edges must end exactly where the panels touch the horse. In C, a shim is used under the front third or half of the saddle when it is too wide.

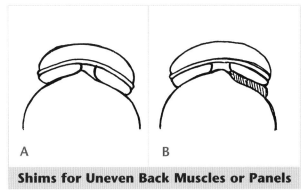

Shims for Uneven Back Muscles or Panels

9.13 A & B A horse with uneven back muscles like the one in A, will cause the saddle to tip to one side. This can also happen if the panels are unevenly flocked. In B, a shim (shaded) has been added, leveling the saddle.

are best made with closed-cell foam because most of the rider's weight is concentrated over the stirrup bar area, which is in the front.

While these shims work well with saddles that are *slightly* wide, those that are *significantly* too wide will be more difficult to balance this way because the points of the tree will push through the shim. Also, the wide tree does not follow the angle of the withers, which may push the shim out from under the saddle (see *Tree Fit*, p. 55). If you do try to shim a significantly wide saddle, only use closed-cell foam. If it can only be balanced with very thick shims, you should look for a replacement saddle.

Typically, you need to raise the front of the saddle on croup-high horses as well (see *Croup-High* p. 129). The difference is that you are hopefully beginning with a tree that fits and matches the angles of the withers. You may need to have a fairly thick shim—an inch or more—depending on how high you need to raise the pommel. Be careful that this alteration does not create a new pressure point at the back of the saddle. Also, if you need to raise the front significantly, you may feel insecure due to the thickness of the pad and the instability of the saddle. There are several special pads on the market today with built-in shims that are thicker in front for use under a wide saddle. This kind of pad can be useful, however, some of them are very thick, and add too much padding overall.

Your Saddle is Uneven from Side-to-Side

Balancing a saddle from side-to-side can be tricky. The majority of saddles slip to one side because the horse has uneven shoulders (see *Uneven Shoulders*, p. 123), and adding a shim can easily make the problem worse. Remember, the saddle will *slide forward* on the side with the smaller, flatter shoulder, twisting the saddle in that direction. If you add a shim to that side, rather than prevent the forward slip, the extra pad will often actually pull the saddle even further toward the flatter shoulder. Ultimately, a shim is *not* the answer to side-to-side problems caused by uneven shoulders. If your saddle slips to one side due to uneven back muscles or a tilted rib cage, a shim works well when added to the entire lower side of the back (figs. 9.13 A & B). Make the shim from thin, open-cell foam, and bevel the edges carefully.

Your Horse Displays Muscle Atrophy

Many horses have hollow pockets on either side of the withers caused by atrophied muscles. You can use shims to *temporarily* fill in these hollow areas, allow your saddle to fit more comfortably, and the atrophied muscles to redevelop. Make the shim the shape of the hollow area. It should look like the end of an orange that has been cut into thirds—flat on the saddle side and round on the horse side. You can trim back the rounded side accordingly as your horse fills out.

Saddle Pad Care

Pads should be washed or cleaned regularly to prevent the build-up of sweat and dirt, which creates lumps or bumps under the saddle and sore spots. Be aware that many horses are sensitive to laundry soaps and will get skin irritations, so use only mild, unscented detergent without fabric softener or other additives that might increase the likelihood of an allergic reaction. Be sure to rinse saddle pads well—if your horse has sensitive skin, rinse them several times. In general, follow manufacturer's instructions for best results.

Examine your pad every few months for signs of wear. As pads break down, the saddle and pad fit is changed, which can be the source of new pressure points. Some pads and shims can remain effective for several years, while others might last only one season. When you remove a pad from daily use, keep it around for future shim material, or donate it to your dog as a good bed.

Examine your saddle pad in good light. Look for small depressions, large compressed areas, or an imprint of the saddle on the surface of the pad. Check the overall thickness, especially toward the front where the points of the tree would sit. If the pad is noticeably thinner in any one location, it is wearing out. Any sign that the inner pad material is breaking down means it is time to replace the pad. Pad material can wear out even when protected by a fancy covering, so check the filling regularly.

Keep a notebook recording the locations of any breakdowns. They are likely caused by pressure points from your saddle, and if a new pad shows similar signs of wear in less than six months, you have a serious saddle-fitting problem that you need to address. If you notice signs of wear that are not from the saddle, evaluate your storage system. The edges of a saddle rack will compress areas of your pad if you store it under your saddle. This damage can be prevented by covering the outer edge of your racks with foam—pipe-insulation foam works well on metal racks—or by changing your pad-storing habits.

Sunlight accelerates the breakdown of foam, therefore, store all *foam pads* in a dark place. As foam ages, you may notice that it seems stiffer than a new pad of the same type. If you squeeze foam and it does not quickly recover its original shape, it is losing its "memory." When this occurs, the pad does not have the same cushioning properties, and will not be as protective as it once was. In reality, most foam begins to break down within a few weeks of manufacture, though it will generally work for six months to a year.

Wool felt pads can compress or wear thin at pressure points. The material in thin areas will appear rougher than normal. Felt bulging on the side of the pad that comes in contact with your horse signals wear caused by high pressure points pushing through the pad.

Synthetic felt pads can wear similarly to wool felt and very often may not show any visual signs of wear at all. However, they may become stiff, especially if there is a foam layer in them. Regardless, synthetic material usually lasts longer than wool felt.

The *cotton quilted pad* is thin to begin with, so wear usually shows as the cover material itself becomes thin, similar in appearance to the knees of your jeans wearing out. Unless the side in contact with the horse becomes rough and causes a friction rub, such wear is harmless.

When *synthetic fleece pads* wear out, the material becomes thinner and may look threadbare, like the cotton quilted pads. If the fleece is thick, examine your pad carefully, as you will be able to *feel* a thinning area before you can *see* it.

Wool fleece takes many years to wear out completely, but can become thin in areas of high pressure or friction. If you do not regularly clean your pad, the fleece will appear to be packed down and thin. Brush it, and the dirt should leave and the flat area should fluff back up. Later in life, poorly tanned fleece pads will lose their fleece in tufts leaving bare areas, which will present a problem as they increase in size.

10 Measuring Your Horse's Back

You can be aided in the saddle-fitting process by learning to *measure your horse's back*, a difficult task considering it is a three-dimensional shape that does not remain motionless. To be certain the measurements are both accurately taken and correctly interpreted, it helps if the person doing the measuring has some knowledge of equine anatomy and biomechanics as well as saddle-fitting. If the measurements are taken with a device placed or adjusted incorrectly, or the numbers are read inaccurately, the information will be of no use. A measuring device placed one inch too far forward could be one or two tree sizes wrong. A horse that is not standing squarely will not provide an accurate reading. All of these elements are important to consider, so the average person should use results from measuring equip-ment as a *rough* guide to help narrow a broad field of choices.

Measuring Back Shape

There are several manageable back-measuring techniques that can be useful to the lay person, including using a *flexible ruler*, a *Lauriche back measure*, and a *plaster or plastic cast*. Other methods are more difficult and less accurate. The commonly used method of bending coat hangers to the shape of a horse's back is inaccurate and should not be used.

Before using any measurement system, be sure the environment is quiet and your horse is standing on level, hard ground—not sand or gravel. He must stand squarely, with his head and neck in alignment and carried as is natural for his conformation. If your horse's head or

Measuring with a Flexible Ruler

10.1 A – G A flexible ruler is a cheap, easy method of measuring your horse's back. You can record the measurements by creating cardboard templates—useful tools for saddle shopping.

Step 1 Place and mould a flexible ruler across the back where the points of the tree lie just behind the horse's shoulder blades. Leave 2 inches above the top of the withers (1 inch if your horse has really high withers), and be sure the ruler even contacts the withers on each side (A).

Step 2 Put the ruler on a large piece of cardboard, and trace the inside of its curve. Mark the left and right sides, and label this template No. 1 (B).

Step 3 Repeat Steps One and Two, this time 4 inches behind the first measurement (C). Label this template No. 2.

Step 4 Repeat Steps One and Two, 4 inches behind your second measurement (D). Label this template No. 3.

Step 5 To get template No. 4, gauge the amount of curve to the horse's back by laying the ruler along the spine (E), and then tracing that curve on a piece of cardboard. Mark the withers' end, plus the locations of your three measurements taken 4 inches apart along the curve of the tracing.

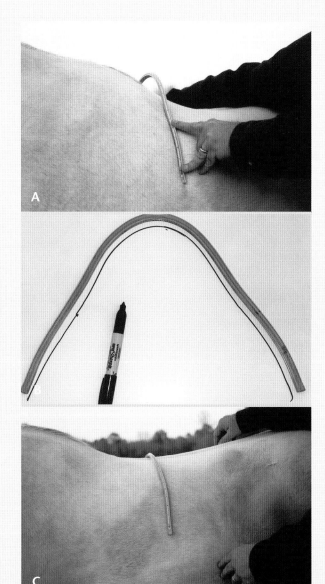

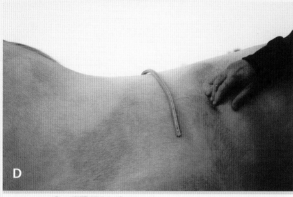

D

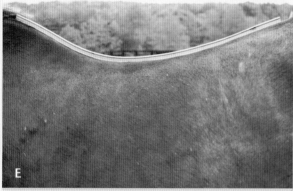

E

F

G

Step 6 Cut out the four templates (from Steps Two to Five). Check their sizing by placing the cardboard remains from each template on top of your horse's back (F). They should fit on the horse's back. (The convex edge of No. 4 should follow the curve of the horse's back.)

Step 7 To check a saddle for fit, hold the templates as shown in G. Hold No. 1 under the front of the saddle and No. 2 and 3 at 4-inch intervals back from the pommel. Put No. 4 under the saddle to see if the curve of the saddle matches the curve of the horse's back.

neck is held in an unnatural position—too high or too low—the resulting back position will be impossible to read accurately. The back should be raised slightly with a small belly lift (see *Belly Lifts,* p. 5) to imitate its potential movement during exercise.

A *flexible ruler* is a standard-size, plastic-coated, lead strip that can be obtained from a stationery store, quilting shop, or drafting supply outlet. It only allows you to measure one piece of the horse's back at a time, so it is not perfect, but it can provide useful information regarding the angles of the back where the tree and panels must fit (see sidebar, figs. 10.1 A – G).

Twenty years ago, Andy Foster began trying to find a way to measure the shape of a horse's back accurately. He wanted something that would allow him to recall the shape any time he wanted, even several months later. The result of this effort is a tool called the *Lauriche Back Measure* (10.2). The device consists of a set of calibrated vertical posts in a horizontal frame. When the posts are lowered onto the horse's back, a complete template of the horse's back shape is recorded. This device measures the entire area where the tree and panels contact the horse, from front-to-back and side-to-side. Two carpenter's levels are built into the system. (Be warned that any similar device *without* a set of carpenter's levels will not provide complete or accurate information.) Once the calibrated numbers are recorded, the Lauriche can replicate the measurements of an individual horse at any time.

Lauriche Back Measure

10.2 The Lauriche Back Measure has calibrated posts that can be individually adjusted to give a three-dimensional back measurement. This is the most accurate method of measuring for a saddle, however, it requires some skill and familiarity with the equipment.

In order to get an accurate measurement, the Lauriche requires patience, a great deal of knowledge about saddle-fitting, and careful attention to detail. The horse must stand squarely on solid ground and be supported by a small belly lift as the posts are carefully adjusted to the shape of his back, one at a time.

The main advantage of the this system is that the entire three-dimensional shape of a horse's back can be accurately measured and recreated by a saddler in the shop. The shape of the shoulders can be recorded, and you can set any saddle on top of the posts and look inside to see where pressure points are. If there is a saddle-fitting problem, you will see the posts sticking into the panels or gaps where there is a lack of contact. You can also compare measurements from year to year to see where your horse has changed shape.

A *plaster or plastic cast* of your horse's back can give you a permanent record of its shape. The plaster cast is made from strips of plaster, and a plastic cast is formed from heat-sensitive plastic. Either cast can be mailed to a saddler or carried into a tack shop where saddles can be set directly upon it. The process is time consuming, however, so your horse must be capable of standing quietly for a long period of time (figs. 10.3 A – C).

To make a plaster cast, use 6-inch wide, fast- or ultra-fast-drying plaster. You will need at least six rolls of the cast material, which can be purchased from your veterinarian. If your horse is fidgety, acquire a *very mild tranquilizer* from your veterinarian so he is quiet while you work—but be careful! Excessive tranquilization can relax the back muscles and the mold will not be accurate. Be sure your horse's coat is slightly dirty to help prevent the plaster from sticking to his hair.

Cut the plaster rolls into approximately 20-inch lengths for an average-size horse, 18 inches for a small horse, or 15 inches for a pony. Start by wetting the strips, then placing the pieces across the back, overlapping each other by about half an inch. Place the next layer going the long way. Repeat that pattern until you have used up about six rolls of plaster. This will make the cast between 1/8 and 1/4 inch thick. If you make it any thicker, you will lose the detail. Your horse

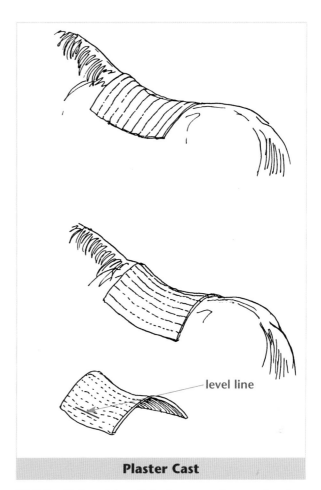

Plaster Cast

10.3 A – C Lay strips of plaster crosswise, overlapping each strip by half an inch, as in A. In B, the next layer is added lengthwise, again with each strip overlapping. Use a carpenter's level to gauge a line parallel to the ground. Mark this line on the plaster cast to indicate the correct front-to-rear balance of the horse's back. Figure C shows the finished cast removed from the horse.

must stand evenly, on all four feet, while the plaster is setting, and you will need to ask him to raise his back a little with a belly lift after you have placed all the strips—but before the plaster has set—to insure the mold is accurate.

While the plaster is setting, place a carpenter's level on the cast in the middle, about halfway down your horse's side. When the bubble shows "level," mark a line on the cast with a pencil. When you use the cast for trying saddles, always keep the line parallel to the ground, and the saddle will sit on the cast with the same front-to-rear balance as it will on your horse. Without this indicator, you may tip the cast too far down in the front or the rear.

Let the plaster finish setting. Is should feel warm, fairly dry to the touch, and should not bend as you begin to remove it. Remove it carefully. Once it's firm and completely dry (usually 24 hours later), it will be able to withstand having a saddle placed upon it, and even shipping. Note that this plaster mold will *not* support the weight of a rider.

The plastic cast eliminates the mess associated with plaster, but there can be drawbacks. Heat-sensitive plastic can lose its shape if it is heated again, and if the cast changes by only half an inch, that can mean the difference between an accurate and an inaccurate measurement. On a hot day, even the heat in your closed car or trunk can soften the plastic, and when shipping the cast, the temperature in trucks and airplanes becomes an unknown variable.

Measuring Saddle Fit

Devices are available that measure *the effects of the saddle on the back* rather than *back shape*. The problem with this type of measurement is that you have to interpret what the information provided means, and with these devices, many fitting problems look the same.

Some *measuring pads* purport to show where pressure points may be using a gel or other pressure-sensitive material. The problem is, if you use one of these pads, which are thick it can alter the fit of the saddle. The areas shown on the measuring pad as pressure points may be caused by a number of different reasons (see sidebar, p. 70). Interpreting each pressure point requires a great deal of saddle-fitting knowledge. For example, a saddle that fits well but needs reflocking in the cantle area will have the same pressure points as a saddle that is too narrow and is sitting low behind.

Thermography is sometimes used for evaluating saddle fit. Thermography reads the temperature of the skin and uses a type of camera that shows areas of heat. It can also be used—after riding in the saddle for a while—to read the temperature of the bottom of the panels. This device can be useful, but it is expensive, requires very careful attention to details, and can only tell *where* areas of pressure are, not *what caused* them. Also, if moisture from sweat is present or if a thick saddle pad is used, the information is inaccurate.

Computerized saddle-pressure measuring equipment is slowly bringing science and technology

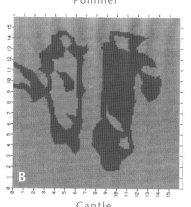
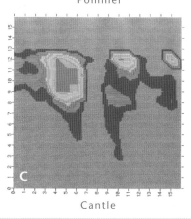
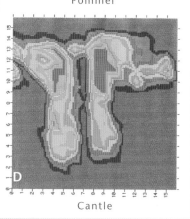

Pommel — Cantle

Computerized Saddle Pressure System

10.4 A – D Photo A shows the computer cable attached to a pressure-sensing pad under the saddle pad. Pressure is indicated by color according to pounds per square inch (psi). Blue is ideal; pink is acceptable; green more pressure than preferable; and red unacceptable. In B, you see a scan indicating ideal fit. Pressure is low, there is a wide space where the gullet is located, and the panels are large and in fairly even contact with the back. Figure C shows pressure concentrated over the stirrup bar area and particularly on one side. The saddle is probably too wide in front or in need of reflocking. In D, you see a very bad fitting saddle. It has a very narrow gullet, is touching the withers in the pommel area, shows intense pressure in the stirrup bar area, and the panel material appears to be very hard and unforgiving.

to the realm of saddle-fitting (figs. 10.4 A – D). It can measure pressures on the horse's back, resulting from the saddle and the rider. It is the *only* measuring device that can give information as the horse is being ridden. The computer allows you to actually see what is happening under the saddle while the horse is moving. You can see the effects of different panel materials and saddle styles. It is possible to compare different pads under the same saddle, or the same pad under different saddles. Much of the information in chapter 9 came from data gathered with computerized, saddle testing equipment.

The computer cannot tell you if the saddle is level, or the cause of pressure points—only that they are present. It also cannot tell you what type of saddle to purchase if the current one does not fit. For the vast majority of saddle-fittings, a well-educated hand and eye will do as good a job as any computer, so it is best to use it as one more piece of information, and learn to put all the parts of the puzzle together yourself.

Measured Caution

Evaluate other measuring devices on the market carefully. Many units claim that anyone can use them, but in reality, it takes instruction and practice to become skilled in the field of back measurement. A few measurements collected along a horse's back can give the *average* person a *general* idea of the appropriate saddle shape and fit. But remember, back shape changes under a rider, which eludes calculation, and there is no foolproof method for measuring backs in motion. At present, only the shape of the "still" horse can be measured, so be cautious when considering devices that claim to reflect the horse's back in motion.

11 Saddles for Various Sports

Once you are familiar with general saddle balance and its effect on the horse and rider, you can examine saddle problems unique to individual sports. English sports are usually performed in saddles that sit the rider close to the horse in order to feel every move he makes. The keys to selecting a saddle for your English sport are, firstly, that it fits your horse, and secondly, that it allows you to sit correctly for the activity you intend to perform.

To demonstrate that looks are not as important as whether the saddle allows you to ride correctly, examine figures 11.1 A and B. Here is a Western rider performing a sliding stop—a move performed predominantly in Western sports. In figure 11.1 A, the rider is in an English saddle that fits the horse well and allows the rider to maintain his position effortlessly. In figure 11.1

B, the rider is in a Western saddle that fits neither him nor his horse well and does not allow him to ride in a balanced way. If you observe the way the horse is moving under the English saddle, you can see that his hindquarters are significantly more engaged than under the Western saddle, and his back is so rounded he is almost lifting the rider and saddle into the air. Under the Western saddle, the horse's back is stiff and the rider is poorly balanced.

The lesson learned here is that *fit is more important than appearance in regards to performance.* Before we begin to assess specific saddle requirements (and design pitfalls) of various English sports, let me repeat something else I've said before. *The rider who uses minimal padding under the saddle to achieve correct fit will feel best connected to the horse.*

Saddle Type and Fit

11.1 A & B These photographs show how the type of saddle is really irrelevant to a sport, as long as it provides the horse comfort and the rider balance. In A, horse and rider are in complete harmony, performing a picture-perfect sliding stop in a well-fitting English saddle. Neither horse nor rider is comfortable in the Western saddle in B, as is proved by the rider's poor position and the horse's stiffness and lack of engagement.

The Horse's Pain-Free Back and Saddle-Fit Book

English Sports and Saddle Fit
Hunters and Jumpers

In the United States, the saddle style most commonly used on hunters and jumpers is the *close contact jumping saddle*. Riders seek the "feel" of the horse under their legs and seat, which the thin panels, minimal knee-rolls, and thin leather flaps typical of a close contact saddle allow (fig. 11.2). Hunter seat and jumper riders want to feel as close to the horse as possible and be able to attain a jumping position easily and securely.

There are several problems with this style of saddle. The thin panels do not adequately protect the horse's back from the tree, nor do they provide clearance on horses with moderate to high withers. These panels also tend to be small and unable to distribute the rider's weight effectively. The gullet is often narrow in an effort to allow the rider a close "feel," and the tree is generally short and narrow, which does not leave much room to adjust the panels so they distribute the rider's weight more effectively. Often, the seat is too narrow to support the rider's seat bones comfortably. Many of the popular—and expensive—new European-designed jumping saddles have panels with angles that are so steep, only their outer edges contact the back. The gullet is often wide at the back, but narrow near the stirrup bar area, which pinches the withers.

To compound these problems, riders often position the saddle *too far forward* and on the shoulder blades, restricting shoulder motion and creating more discomfort. This is usually done to improve balance over jumps because the stirrup

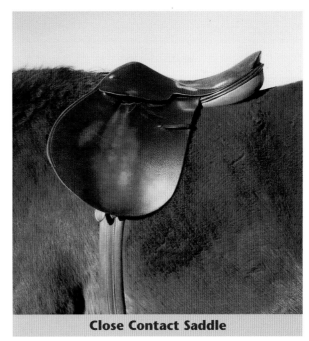

Close Contact Saddle

11.2 The type of saddle favored by hunter seat and jumper riders.

bar in a jumping saddle is typically placed *too far back* for safety, or the rider is in a saddle that is too small. Most riders, however, are not aware of *why* they place the saddle so far forward; they just do it because everyone else does. It is common to see a saddle slide back toward the correct place as a rider warms up, then, the trainers and fellow riders "kindly" inform her that her saddle has slipped back, so, just before going in the ring, she moves the saddle forward again. The rider may then wonder why the first three jumps are poor! When the saddle sits on the shoulder blades, the horse tends to travel with a high head and hollow back—the opposite of the relaxed frame desired in a hunter. This also decreases the horse's ability to focus on the upcoming jumps. Riders often use breastplates to secure saddles too far forward, which further inhibit free shoulder movement because they are adjusted so tightly (see *Breastplates*, p. 132).

There is a recent trend toward better close contact saddle design, and they can work very well if larger, thicker panels and wider gullets are used, and the stirrup bars are placed further forward to accommodate the rider's leg. These three changes eliminate the need for extra pads, allowing the rider to feel secure and close to the horse. A larger tree with flatter panels that conform to the angle of the horse's back disburses the rider's weight more broadly and provides a more comfortable seat, and longer tree points eliminate tipping down in front.

Dressage Saddle

11.3 A correctly fitted dressage saddle.

Dressage

A dressage rider, whose goal is to allow—and encourage—efficient use of the horse's back, also needs to feel her horse working under her. Dressage saddles need broad, flat panels that conform to the angle of the horse's back and a wide gullet to allow the horse maximum freedom to use his back. The horse has the best chance of being able to respond to the rider's aids and fluidly perform the requested movements when the rider is correctly balanced in the saddle (fig. 11.3).

Dressage saddles often fail to provide the rider with this ideal balance. One of the worst design flaws in dressage saddles are stirrup bars that are *too far forward*. Another typical flaw is *a long twist that slopes up to the pommel*, forcing the rider's weight to the back of the seat. Both of these tend to trap the rider in the chair seat position, perpetually behind the movement of the horse. Many riders experience back pain, often because they are trying to compensate for the forward stirrup bars or are struggling against the long twist, which jams them to the back of the saddle.

Dressage saddles usually have a deep seat, which requires a larger seat size to accommodate the rider comfortably (fig. 11.4 A). When the seat

Dressage Saddles and Rider Fit

11.4 A & B Because of the deep seat typically found in dressage saddles, riders often have difficulty selecting a size to correctly accommodate their legs, thighs, and buttocks. The saddle in A fits the rider well, but the too small saddle in B is forcing the rider's knee over the knee roll and her buttocks into the cantle.

is too small, the knee and thigh rolls push the rider's upper leg back and force her buttocks to the rear of the saddle, or push her knee out over the knee roll (fig. 11.4 B). If the saddle also has the stirrup bars in the wrong place, it will not allow the rider to compensate by adjusting her position.

The girth needs to be placed fairly far forward because dressage horses typically have a wide rib cage and a forward girth line (see p. 115). However, when the girth is forward, the cantle can move about, which creates friction. If you notice rubbed hair (especially during the winter), or superficial skin soreness after hard work, these are clues that the cantle is unstable. A dressage saddle with a V-system of billets is very helpful in this situation.

Eventing

Event riders may require as many as three different saddles for the three phases—dressage, cross-country, and stadium jumping—when they ride at upper levels of the sport. At the lower levels, riders can perform using two different saddles—one for dressage and one for cross-country and stadium (fig. 11.5). Since each phase is actually a different sport, saddles designed specifically for each phase will allow a competitor to ride her best. When competing at the lower levels, some are tempted to ride in one all-purpose saddle, but an all-purpose saddle is going to be less effective in multiple disciplines.

For security when jumping, a rider needs the saddle to feel narrow between her thighs. Most

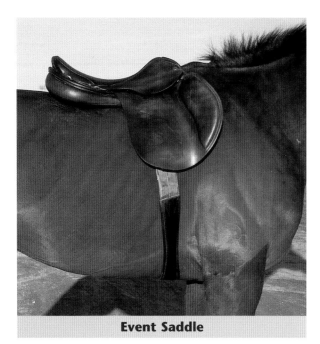

Event Saddle

11.5 The ideal event saddle has very forward saddle flaps and stirrup bars to help the rider feel secure in the forward position when riding cross-country for extended periods of time. The twist is built high above the base of the saddle to help provide a secure position with very short stirrups.

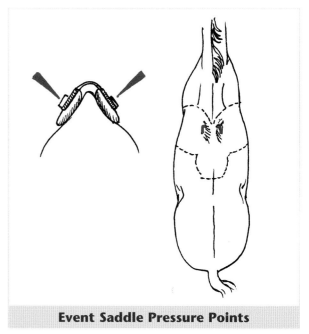

Event Saddle Pressure Points

11.6 A & B It is standard to make cross-country saddles with narrow gullets near the stirrup bar area, shown in A, not only for the rider's comfort but also to help hold the saddle in place. But, this pinches the sides and back of the withers, causing muscle atrophy so commonly seen in event horses.

cross-country saddle designers have succeeded in doing this but have sacrificed the horse's comfort by making the gullet and tree too narrow. The withers fit into the narrow gullet and hold the saddle in place nicely, but the surrounding muscles will atrophy because there is no room for their development (fig. 11.6 A & B). The solution is a wide gullet that clears the withers.

The rider must be able to stand in the stirrups of their cross-country saddle for long periods of time, positioning her weight over the stirrup bars and the front of the saddle. This tends to concentrate pressure on the horse's withers. Fortunately, the girth line on many event horses is located farther back than average, which helps counterbalance the forward weight of the rider (fig. 11.7).

Counteracting the Event Stance

11.7 Event riders stand in their stirrups during most of the cross-country phase. In order to keep the cantle down and the saddle secure with the rider's weight forward, it is necessary to attach the girth farther back on the saddle than is normal.

Ideally, the stirrup bars need to be very far forward, and, to give the rider the narrow, secure feeling she needs under her thighs, the twist needs to be built high above the tree.

Endurance and Trail Riding

The long-distance trail horse is perhaps the best specimen for studying saddle fit. An endurance rider spends more time in her saddle than any other rider. The longer you are in the saddle each day, the more critical optimum fit becomes. Also, because a horse's body weight and shape can change during a long ride, saddle fit can alter significantly during a relatively short period of time. A saddle that appears to fit for 50 miles may suddenly become a disaster at 75 to 100 miles, where even minor pressure points are accentuated by the increased length of time. Most importantly, the trail saddle needs broad, flat panels that conform to the angles of the horse's back and a wide enough gullet to allow the spine freedom to move.

One of the most common fitting problems seen with trail horses ridden in English saddles is that the popular breeds (Arabs, Morgans, Connemaras, and small, gaited breeds like Paso Finos, and Icelandics) have short backs that do not fit the Western-style endurance saddle. Dressage and all-purpose saddles are often made with panels and trees capable of fitting short backs, as well as with generously thick panels and a seat comfortable enough for long hours of riding. You can adapt either model into an effective endurance or trail saddle with the simple addi-

Pads that Go the Distance

In long-distance riding, pads can be especially beneficial as a soft interface between the saddle and the back. They are also useful in moving the sweat away from the skin. Sometimes, an endurance horse's back will blister under a particular pad, especially when rubber-like materials such as neoprene, synthetic fleece, or synthetic felt are used. This may be due to temperature increases (though research has not supported this theory), lack of air circulation, or the individual horse's skin reaction to the synthetic material. In general, the natural materials, especially wool, breathe better and have less chance of causing a reaction.

It is very difficult to prevent back pain in trail horses ridden over long distances mostly at a walk. Because the rider is basically stationary, the pressure is heavy and constant, as compared to the trot or canter where your position changes with each stride. If you usually go for long rides at the walk, it would be best to fit your saddle with a thick, wool fleece or an open-cell foam pad in mind.

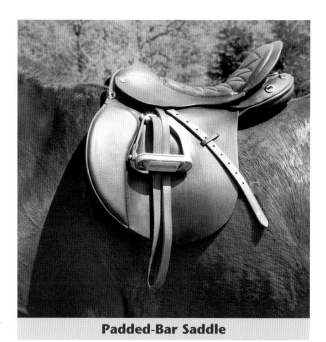

Padded-Bar Saddle

11.8 The padded-bar saddle, often used in endurance riding, has a Western tree covered with English panel padding. The panels extend beyond the cantle and can carry gear easily. The large, deep seats are designed for rider comfort.

panels may need to be reflocked several times during a busy riding season—it is better to reflock correctly and frequently than to overflock once a year or less.) A foam panel may be easier to manage, but foam does break down from heavy use (see *Panel Construction,* p. 29).

Several manufacturers have designed saddles for endurance riding that offer English-style seats on a Western-style tree. The bottom of the tree (called the *bar* in a Western saddle) is covered

tion of some D-rings or, in some cases, an attachment for a crupper.

Look for a saddle with thicker panels, made of either wool or foam. (Remember, wool flocked

with padding, similar to the panels in an English saddle (fig. 11.8). These saddles tend to have the desirable wide gullet and thick padding that offers protection from the tree. They also tend to have larger, deeper seats than regular English saddles, which riders tend to find very comfortable.

The main fitting problem with the *padded-bar saddles* is that the Western-style tree can be too long and flat, and may not conform to the natural shape of the horse's back. Note that sometimes, the padded bars are set at too steep an angle for a horse's back, and carefully check that there is no pressure on the loins. If the bar goes over the loins, but *does not* put pressure on the muscles, the saddle-fit is acceptable. These saddles also often place the stirrup bars too far forward.

Australian stock saddles are used for all types of trail riding, and in many ways, can be considered a hybrid of a Western and an English saddle (fig. 11.9). The panels and tree tend to be too long for smaller horses, but it is possible to shift the flocking away from the back of the saddle and prevent contact with the loins of short-coupled horses. The panels tend to be large and flat, and some of the newer designs offer fleece-covered panels. The trees run a bit narrow, depending on the brand.

There are two main types of trees available in Australian stock saddles: one closely resembles an English tree, while the other is basically a cross between a Western and English tree. The former is made of laminated wood as discussed on page 28. The latter is made with two bars

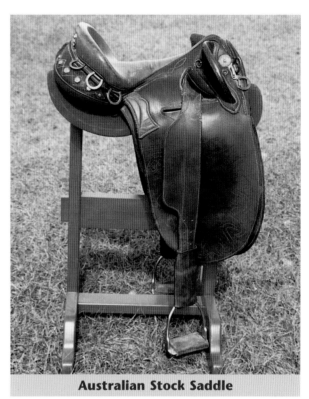

Australian Stock Saddle

11.9 Australian stock saddles are popular with endurance riders. The panels are usually covered with wool serge, allowing riders to make their own adjustments to the flocking.

along the bottom like a Western tree. The bars are finished with flocked panels, similar to the padded-bar saddle. The flocking can be wool, acrylic, or doe hair, which is unique to the stock saddle. Most stock saddle panels have a wool-serge covering (a heavy, loosely woven, wool cloth, described on page 30), and feature *over-girths*, which do not have elastic in them and should not be overtightened (see fig. 5.27).

When the saddle fits well, the overgirth is not required to keep it in place.

Like other saddles we've discussed, on most models the stirrup bars are set too far forward and the seat slopes toward the cantle, trapping the rider in a chair seat position. Traditionally, Australians rode this way to help them keep their seats in adverse working conditions, but it is hard on the horse's back. There are many good qualities to this type of saddle, but search for one that allows your leg to hang down in the correct position.

Treeless saddles can be useful for all types of trail riding because most pressure points are eliminated. Many horses move much better without a tree, and short-backed horses are easier to fit. While it is commonly believed that a tree distributes the rider's weight more economically, trail horses can go many miles in treeless saddles with minimal back soreness (see fig. 3.12 and *Treeless Saddles* p. 37).

Foxhunting

Foxhunters need a saddle that supports both horse and rider under the stress of galloping and jumping for long periods of time. The saddle needs to be especially comfortable to the horse in order to preserve his soundness and enjoyment of his job. Look for a saddle that has wide, thick panels so his back will be protected from the tree during long hours under saddle. The stirrup bars should be situated suitably for the jumping position (see figs. 6.1 A – C, p. 85), and the style of seat should be comfortable to the rider:

Soundness Problems on the Trail

Several soundness problems commonly seen in trail horses can be attributed, in part, to poor saddle fit. Endurance horses are especially susceptible to *suspensory strains* in the front legs. These can be caused by a saddle that slides forward or concentrates too much pressure on the shoulder blades when going downhill, a girth that is attached too far forward, or a saddle that is too narrow. Related causes of suspensory problems include: going down hills too quickly, letting your horse travel on his forehand, and a horse that travels with a high head and a hollow back. *Pain in the front feet and heels,* and even *navicular disease,* can result as well.

---

some prefer a flatter seat and others a deeper, more padded seat.

I often see riders with their legs in the chair seat position and their weight concentrated toward the cantle due to poor or uneducated riding habits. As some riders become tired, they tend to push their feet forward, forcing more of their weight against the cantle. Many horses that misbehave while hunting, especially those that constantly jig and fuss, are responding to back pain.

Pony Club Games and Gymkhanas

Ponies and horses used for a variety of games on

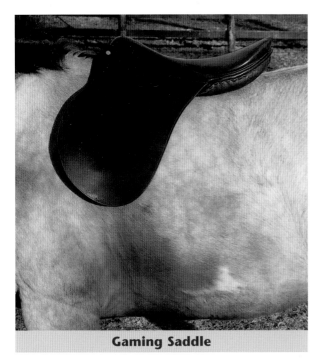

Gaming Saddle

11.10 Gaming saddles need to be flat so the rider can quickly dismount and lightweight so the horse can maneuver obstacles.

horseback need saddles with fairly flat seats (fig. 11.10). In the course of these games, the rider has to make quick moves, dismount and remount, or lean over to pick up various items. Look for a saddle with a flat seat—such as a close contact saddle—with a wide tree that will fit ponies. Thin panels work well, since ponies tend to have low withers, and help improve stability of the saddle.

A *racing exercise saddle* is often used because it is lightweight and flat. However, it only has a half tree that ends just behind the stirrup bars and tends to be very narrow. Gymkhana ponies tend to have broad backs, so be aware that these half-tree saddles rarely come close to fitting them.

Polo

Polo players need particularly stable saddles because they gallop and make sudden stops and turns. They ride with long stirrups, similar to dressage, so it is especially important that the stirrup bars allow the rider to keep his legs under his hips to maintain his balance. The player appreciates a somewhat deep seat for security, but one that allows him to move as he swings the mallet. The saddle needs to be especially durable since the twisting forces applied during the game are much higher than in other sports, with the rider often leaning far off to one side or the other.

A dressage saddle can work well because the required stirrup length is similar. Look for a dressage saddle with relatively flat knee and thigh rolls and a deep seat. Some riders may find they prefer a saddle with thicker knee rolls for added stability, but be sure the seat size is large enough, and the flaps are long enough, to accommodate the length of the legs. Dressage saddles with very straight saddle flaps will not be appropriate for polo, as the coinciding stirrup length will have to be too long.

Most polo saddles in use today are very cheaply made with non-spring trees, which tend to break easily. The extreme forces on the saddle break the reinforced metal head and gullet plate

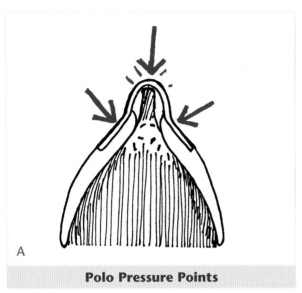

Polo Pressure Points

11.11 A & B Polo saddles are usually made with high, narrow gullets that are clamped down on the withers for stability. The points of painful pressure can be clearly seen in A and B.

as well as the extra reinforcing plate used for the sport. The saddle generally has a narrow gullet and a high pommel, and riders try to stabilize it by clamping it onto the withers (fig. 11.11 A & B). Most polo ponies have narrow backs and high withers, so the narrow gullet squeezes tightly against the bone, causing sores and calluses. The horse also receives a painful poke in the withers when making a fast turn or stop because the tips of the points of the tree are typically left uncovered in polo saddles. Horses that are sore in the withers tend to be more reluctant to stop and turn quickly because that is when they experience pain, and a polo pony that will not turn is of no use to a polo player.

12 Fitting Multiple Horses: Professionals, Riding Schools, and Camps

The key to locating a saddle that works on many horses is to simply find one that is well designed and crafted according to the principles in this book, and then fit it to the type of horse you ride most often. Keep in mind when fitting multiple horses that there are consistent back characteristics within breeds (see chapter 8). While of course every horse in a breed will not have the *same* conformation, many horses in one breed will have *similar* back shapes. So, if you ride a certain type of horse, there is a good chance that the same characteristics will be shown by all the horses you ride.

The professional trainer who rides many different horses may not realize it, but her livelihood actually depends on saddle fit. A client hires a professional with the expectation that her show horse will win or her problem horse will improve. Frequently, "training" problems are due to poor saddle fit and back pain. A trainer who pays attention to saddle fit, even with a limited budget for saddles, can easily acquire a good reputation for fixing problem horses.

I repeat: It is impossible to fit all horses with one saddle, and no matter what anyone says, all the pads in the world will not make one saddle fit all. However, if you are riding many horses and you want to do the best job possible, two or three well-designed saddles will allow you to fit the majority of horses. The better the design of the saddle, the more horses it will fit. Investing in a second or third saddle may seem expensive, but it doesn't take many lost clients or commissions to equal the purchase price of a good saddle. You will more than recover your investment if you sell one additional horse, or sell a horse for more money than he was previously worth, because you fit his saddle correctly.

The key is to have two, or ideally three, tree widths in the style and brand you prefer. You may want your best saddle to be the size you most commonly require for the type of horse you ride, so purchase a cheap leather or synthetic saddle in the size you least commonly ride. For instance, if you ride Andalusian dressage horses, you will rarely, if ever, need a narrow saddle. If you ride Thoroughbreds, you may require a full range of widths, and a variety of pads and shims to adapt each saddle to the different horses (see A *Level Seat*, p. 66).

Once you have selected your saddles, collect a set of shims, an open-cell foam pad, and a closed-cell foam pad. These items should enable you to fit most of the horses you ride. Add other pads to your collection as the need arises. With each horse, go through the basic steps of fitting your saddle, then improve the fit with pads if needed.

Fitting many horses on a minimal budget is the primary concern of schools and camps as well. To complicate matters, the horse populations in these places usually change on a regular basis. Here are some strategies for making saddle-fitting manageable.

The first step I recommend is to *permanently mark each saddle and pad* with a number, using any marking system you wish. (Don't use names. It's easier to keep the list current using numbers, which can stay the same even if horses change.) Ideas for marking saddles include using a perma- nent black marker directly on the leather, hanging tags on the saddles, or attaching the tradi- tional metal plates to the back of the cantles. Lightweight pads (cotton quilt or single fleece) do not need to be marked, but all thick or spe- cialty pads and shims should have numbers writ- ten or sewn onto them.

The next step is to *match each horse, as well as possible, with a saddle that fits, and record the numbers*. Do the same for saddle pads and shims. One saddle may fit several horses adequately, but will probably require a different configuration of pads to enhance the fit for each individual. In the school or camp situation, the creative use of pads and shims can even help make it possible to fit a horse to several appropriate saddles. For example, if a horse is commonly used for both small children and adults, or for some jumping, it may be best to find at least two saddles that fit him (one child and one adult-size, or one for flat- work and one for jumping).

When each horse has a saddle-and-pad com- bination that works reasonably well, *make a list detailing the horse and the numbers of his saddle and pad, or pads*. If shims are being used, draw a little diagram of exactly where the shims should be placed under the saddle. This list needs to be posted in the tack room or grooming area where everyone can easily see it. Keep extra copies of the list so that if it is lost, you can immediately supply a new copy. If you post it outside, put it in a sturdy, resealable plastic bag to protect it from the elements. The list will probably need to be updated frequently.

Once you have fit the various horses, then consider the riders. Schools often accommodate different-sized riders using the same saddle-and-horse combinations. Refer to page 92 for ideas on fitting different-sized riders to the same saddle.

School saddles require regular reflocking, depending on how often they are used and what type of riding they are used for. A saddle being used for three hard lessons a day, including jumping, will need to be reflocked much more frequently than a therapeutic riding saddle used at the walk for a half-hour, three days a week. Reflocking is an expense that many riding establishments think they cannot afford, but it is actually cost effective. The expense of feed and shoeing is a regular, unrelenting cost of owning horses. If they have back and lameness problems due to bad saddles, your costs escalate and your incoming cash flow is lessened. So, select one saddle to be reflocked annually, bi-annually, each quarter, or month, depending on how many saddles you have and how often they are used. If you have access to a competent saddle-repair person who understands reflocking, schedule him or her to come regularly to monitor all the saddles. Organizations that rely on donations might arrange with this saddler to reflock the saddles during times of the year when other work is slow.

Saddle Economics

Saddles that fit well do not necessarily have to be expensive. Riding schools and camps usually cannot afford a tack room full of expensive saddles, yet they can still ensure good fit with a little bit of effort. If you have a particularly valuable—in other words, a very safe, sane, and healthy—schoolhorse, it may be worth investing in a well-fit saddle for him. The cost of a good saddle is small compared to the cost of replacing a money-making, top-notch schoolhorse. Learn to hunt for saddle bargains at the local tack shops, auctions, bulletin boards (many a nice saddle has been found quietly posted at the local grocery store), and the Internet. Beware of donations, though occasionally a good saddle will appear. More often than not, a major structural flaw is the reason the saddle is being donated.

A *treeless saddle* can be beneficial in many school and camp settings, and for many riders in therapeutic programs, as they are versatile and fit many horses (see pp. 37 and 174). *Hard shell pads* are another economical way to ease saddle fit on multiple horses (see p. 148).

13 A Practical Approach to Finding Your Saddle

The economics of good saddle fit is a valid concern. If you have a problem with the saddle you already own, or you have just begun your search for a saddle that fits you and your horse, or you have a young horse that isn't ready for his permanent saddle, you could feel overwhelmed. Do not feel alone if you do not have thousands of dollars in your saddle budget. The average horse owner is not rich, and most of us need to be very careful how we spend our money. I can offer some practical ideas to help you find a permanent saddle or devise an appropriate temporary fix until your horse is ready— or you have some money saved.

Beginning the Search

Borrowing Saddles

You might be surprised at the number of people who have extra saddles or who no longer ride but cannot bear to part with their saddle. Often you can work out a mutually beneficial arrangement that allows you to use the saddle in exchange for cleaning and conditioning the leather. Perhaps you can have some necessary repairs or reflocking done. The cost to you is significantly less than that of purchasing a new saddle, and everyone wins in such an exchange.

If you board in a stable with other riders who use the same type of saddle as you, some people are willing to share their saddles on a temporary basis. This way, you can gain a few months while you wait for your horse to change shape.

Obviously, you must take good care of a borrowed saddle. Do not put it on an unpredictable horse, and don't ride in it for six hours in the rain. Strive to return the saddle in better condition than when you first borrowed it.

Trading Saddles

If several people in your barn, riding club, or neighborhood are interested in refitting an old saddle or finding a new saddle, organize a *group saddle-fitting party*. You may find that some people can trade saddles, and some may offer ideas for pads or shims, and everyone might end up with an appropriate saddle. Money can also be exchanged as part of a trade, as one person's saddle may be more expensive than another's. This is a particularly good solution in clubs with many children. Not only do horses change, but children outgrow saddles quite rapidly, and a child in a saddle that doesn't fit has a difficult time learning to ride properly (see sidebar, p. 110). Group saddle-fitting and trading sessions could become an annual tradition.

Used Saddles

Very few items retain their value today, but used saddles in good condition are some of them. You can ride in a saddle for ten years and sometimes sell it for more than you originally paid for it! So, if you own a used saddle that does not really work for either you or your horse, consider selling it and buying another used saddle for about the same price. Though it is often tempting to keep your old saddle for sentimental reasons, the sale of it can help the funding of a far more appropriate, much more comfortable, and—a few years down the road—much more profitable saddle.

If you are considering a used saddle, check it over very carefully. Be sure the saddle is sound before you consider riding in it. If you are selling your saddle, advertise in tack shops, horse newsletters, the local paper, national magazines, or on the Internet (all good sources for finding a saddle, too). You can *consign* the saddle with a tack shop. While selling the saddle yourself entails responding to calls and showing it to interested parties, selling it on consignment usually means sacrificing some money for commission. However, it will have a better chance of selling in a location with a lot of people traffic.

If you are connected to the Internet, you have access to many possible buyers and sellers, even if you live in a remote area. Selling over the Internet means you should be prepared to accept a returned saddle, and when you're the buyer, make an arrangement so you can return the saddle if it does not work for any reason. Be aware that you will have to pay shipping back and forth with any mail order, which can become expensive. There are some national used saddle stores where you can send your saddle for consignment or list it in their database and pay a commission if it sells.

Buying and selling used saddles can be an excellent, if sometimes time-consuming, method of assuring that your horse has a saddle that fits as he goes through transitions in shape.

New Saddles: Working with Tack Shops

Typically, when saddle shopping, prospective buyers enter a tack shop and a salesperson assists them in locating a saddle. Unfortunately, sales staff is often unfamiliar with many of the concepts integral to proper saddle fit, so it is important that as the buyer, you become an educated consumer. Gain experience by borrowing friends' saddles and trying as many different saddles as you can on lots of different horses.

While there is an ever-growing number of saddle types and brands available, depending upon your discipline, your choices may be limited by what is available in your local tack shop. Be patient and check around. You might find a tack shop a little further away that has the brand you want. The Internet can make it much easier to shop for specific styles of saddles, if you are willing to deal with the time and money involved to ship saddles back and forth. Attend horse shows and symposiums where you can see and compare multiple styles, especially if you have somewhat unusual needs.

Many tack shops do try to assist with saddle-fitting, but staff usually receive very little valid training. It often simply involves fitting the rider—without stirrups—on a stationary plastic horse. The stands used in tack shops will not balance a saddle the same way as your horse will, so even if it feels great in the shop, you will still need to put the saddle on your horse.

One way to get a better idea of how the saddle will fit on your horse is to take a small line level, about 2 to 3 inches long (see figs. 5.13 A – C, p. 67), place a folded-up bath towel across the plastic horse under the back of the saddle, and adjust the towel until the level tells you the center of the seat is approximately in the center of the saddle (fig. 13.1). Once the saddle is balanced in the shop, you can better sense how it may feel

Trying Saddles in Tack Shops

13.1 You can get a better idea of how a saddle will feel on your horse if you try balancing it in the tack shop first. Bring a towel and a line level with you when you saddle shop, and adjust the towel under the cantle until the level tells you the center of the seat is in the center of the saddle. Then you can try it out.

on your horse, and you will be able to immediately eliminate some candidates.

Many tack shops will let you take one or more saddles home to try, provided you leave them some form of security or payment. Some shops even have a place where you can bring your horse and ride on the premises. You can learn a lot by seeing a variety of saddles on your horse, so if you find more than one candidate, take as many as you can home to try. Remember, you can learn from an incorrect fit because you get better at recognizing what is correct.

Demonstration Saddles

A common practice among saddle fitters, company representatives, and some tack shops is to offer *demo saddles* for you to try out. While an excellent idea in theory, in practice, it can be very misleading.

Trying a demo saddle allows you to ride in a saddle representative of the style and brand that interests you. You can borrow the saddle for a short period of time, check the fit carefully, have a lesson in it, and get some input from your instructor or knowledgeable friend on how well you ride in it. Then you can decide if you want a model like it. Realize, however, that the demo saddle is not the same saddle you are going to buy! The version you actually purchase may not fit anything like the demo model you tried because of variations in saddle manufacturing. In many cases, you have already committed to purchasing the new saddle before you have had the chance to examine or test it. And, to make matters worse, if you tried the demo saddle, the saddle you buy is often non-returnable. Circumvent such problems by getting a written guarantee that the saddle you buy will be totally satisfactory to you and will fit your horse correctly.

Be sure to take excellent care of the saddles or you will end up owning them, whether they fit or not. Tack shops generally do not allow you to make any marks on a new saddle. There *are* ways to ride in a saddle without leaving evidence, as long as the shop will allow girth marks on the billets. It is impossible to girth up any saddle without leaving marks, though thick, round rollers on the girth's buckles will leave fainter lines.

Protect the saddle during your test ride by wrapping the stirrup leathers in socks, plastic wrap, or another smooth material. Duct tape, or any type of tape, can help hold these protective coverings around the leather, but be careful the "sticky" part does not touch and mark the leather. Rubber bands work well. Some synthetic saddles mark more easily, so be especially careful with them. Use a thin, clean saddle pad, so you can read the pressure patterns and keep the saddle clean.

During your trial period, you might want to plan to take the saddle to a top-quality saddler for a prepurchase evaluation (see p. 185), especially if you have questions the sales person cannot answer. If the shop objects to having someone else review the saddle, be suspicious!

Finally, don't give in to sales pressure, and *never* buy a saddle you have doubts about. You will probably have to live with it for a long time, and if it is not correct, it may take several months for back pain or behavior problems to show up in your horse. That late in the game, there is probably little or no chance of returning the saddle.

Custom Saddles

Custom saddles are often a good solution for accommodating a difficult-to-fit horse or rider. However, they are expensive, and you must be as careful about selecting a custom saddle maker as you are about fitting the saddle. If you have a complex fitting situation with *both* yourself and your horse, you will usually spend less on one custom saddle than you will buying several ready-made saddles that do not work for either of you.

Keep in mind that if you have a custom saddle made for one horse, it may not fit another. Sometimes, the panels on a custom saddle can be changed to match the shape of a new horse using the same tree size.

If you decide to purchase a custom saddle, you should require a *written guarantee* that the saddle will fit both you and your horse. If the saddler is from another state, or country even, stipulate that you can return the saddle for adjustments, or get a refund, or possibly another saddle if there is a major problem that cannot be resolved. Be certain that, should you need, there is a way for you to collect on the warranty without spending more in legal fees and travel than you did on the saddle.

Working with Saddlers and Saddle Fitters

Perhaps you are not ready to commit to a custom saddle, but sometimes a standard stock saddle will fit you or your horse better after some minor alterations. Avoid creating additional problems by using a reliable and well-educated saddler.

Buyer, Beware

When investigating custom saddle options, keep your eyes open and do not fall for hard pressure sales pitches or hype that does not make sense to you. Gimmicks are used in custom saddle-fitting as frequently as in other types of sales. One particular sales pitch to avoid is making your saddle uneven to fit an unevenly built horse. Once you have an uneven saddle made, the saddle will constrict your horse, and he will never be able to become balanced. Also be wary of the "easily adjustable" or "changeable" tree (see p. 29). In general, if the sales pitch makes claims that do not adhere to the solid basics of saddle-fitting, be extremely cautious.

Some custom saddle makers take measurements of you and your horse, then return to their shop and modify a stock saddle. Estimate how many custom saddles are being produced by your saddler. Custom saddles take time to make, so the saddler who is turning out a huge number of saddles in a relatively short period of time either has a huge staff, or is actually modifying stock saddles. If the saddle maker really understands saddle fit, you may still get a saddle that works well; but you shouldn't be paying for a totally custom saddle when you're actually getting a semi-custom saddle.

There are many people in the saddle-fitting business who, though they may be very good at leather repair, actually have had little training. You are within your rights as a consumer to ask saddlers about their qualifications and education before you entrust any saddle to them. High-quality saddlers are usually willing to discuss any aspect of their education and work with you, and should be willing to work with your trainer or veterinarian, as well. Be cautious: just because someone talks a great deal does not mean they are educated or skilled, and just because they are well-educated, doesn't mean they are skilled. Check with references regarding their degree of satisfaction and the quality of the saddler's work. Converse with the saddler before leaving your saddle with him, and ask him to explain everything he plans to do, and then form an agreement regarding mistakes or defects in his work. A good saddler is willing to stand behind his work and correct alterations if there is a problem.

Finding a saddler to make simple repairs or adjustments to your saddle can be as difficult as finding a saddle fitter. A good repair job should be virtually invisible—a patch of leather sewn on the outside of a saddle to cover a worn place is not an example of a quality repair. A reflocked saddle should not look as if it was opened up and put back together. Stop by a potential repair person's shop. Saddles that have been repaired and are awaiting pick-up are usually available so you can see his work.

Interest in correct saddle-fitting is growing, and the demand for quality work is not yet being met in the United States. There is hope, however. The Master Saddler's Association, originally started in England, now offers an extensive course in the United States (see *Resources,* p. 211).

Caring for Your Saddle

Once you find—or decide you already own—your dream saddle, you need to properly care for it to extend its working life span. It is not easy to replace a saddle, especially one that really works. And, it only makes sense to protect a major investment.

Use plain, glycerin saddle soap for basic cleaning. After cleaning, restore the leather's natural moisture in order to keep it supple and strong. Top quality leather dressings replace the natural animal fats removed by the tanning process and needed by the leather, usually with a natural oil—normally cod liver oil with natural animal tallow fats. Oils, such as neatsfoot, actually weaken the leather by penetrating in between the fibers, causing them to rub against each other. They can also cause the leather to become damp and heavy. Some of the popular compounded products contain oils and other ingredients that can rot the stitching, while also degrading the leather (fig. 13.2).

Healthy leather should be flexible and moisture resistant, but not waterproof. If the products you use seem to be to be making the leather stiff or the stitches rot, change products, then consider where you live. Leather needs can vary from region to region, depending on the climate and use of the saddle. If you live in an

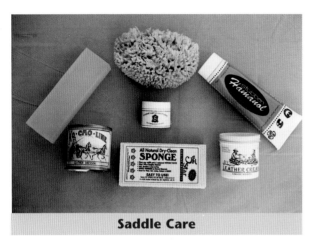

Saddle Care

13.2 Keep an assortment of saddle cleaning and conditioning materials on hand.

extreme climate, pay particular attention to your leather. For example, in the very damp, eastern part of Texas, mold grows extremely quickly, while in Hawaii, the salt air and sun dries the leather out rapidly. Andy Foster offers this trick: think about your own skin, and treat your leather accordingly.

Realize that your safety depends on maintaining leather and replacing worn parts. Go over your saddle thoroughly several times a year, checking for any worn or cracked spots. Well-cared-for leather will last for many years.

14 Caring for Your Horse's Back

Good saddle fit is one of the most important contributions you make to your horse's well-being. However, your horse's comfort—and consequently, his performance—also depends on the condition of his feet, mouth, head, and body. Many apparently unrelated equine-management and care topics relate directly to back pain. It is possible to blame your saddle when another issue is actually the culprit.

Do not be discouraged if you carefully correct saddle fit, and your horse still has problems. Keep in mind that if a poorly fitting saddle has been used on your horse for any length of time, his consequent back pain can remain for years. And, of course, there are many reasons for back pain other than saddle fit. Bones are held together by soft tissue—muscles, tendons, ligaments, and joint capsules—and these tissues are

very susceptible to injury and strain. Though some back pain is from actual injury or degenerative changes to ribs or vertebra, most is caused by damage to soft-tissue.

In my experience, significant back pain from a bad saddle or an injury can require several months or more of treatment and rehabilitation. In some lucky cases, when the saddle was the reason for the pain, correcting the fit eliminates the problem without additional treatment. Other times, rehabilitative bodywork must be considered. Traditional Western medicine often fails to recognize or resolve back pain, so most of the treatments discussed in this chapter are considered *alternative*, or *complementary medicine*. They have an excellent track record for treating, and in many cases, curing back pain, no matter what the cause. Of course, always consult your

Potential Causes of Back Pain Other than Saddle Fit

- Trauma in the pasture—as simple as slipping in mud or on wet grass.
- The everyday stress of normal work.
- Accidents in the stall—getting cast, for example.
- Playing hard, especially with a larger, stronger companion.
- Pulling back when tied, thereby straining neck and back.
- Confinement, cannot stretch or roll, leading to stiffness.
- Poor rider techniques.
- Training devices that restrict free motion.
- Being an ex-racehorse—whole body has been stressed.
- Too little warm-up time.
- Fast starts, especially if the horse is off-balance.
- Being ponied with head held tightly in the rider's lap.
- Mechanical hot walker—keeps the head and neck up and the back hollow.
- Traumatic, difficult birth, and especially assisted births.
- Poor conformation, or conformation not suited to sport.

regular veterinarian in all health and pain-related matters as well.

Some of these methods you can do yourself, while some therapies are best undertaken by a trained professional. As with all forms of medicine, there are competent and inept practitioners, so check references carefully. Keep the lines of communication open, and remember, a good practitioner should be willing to tell you when he has done all he can and advise you to seek other help. If you feel the practitioner is competent but your horse is not responding, or if he is achieving poor results because of inability, be proactive on your horse's behalf and consult someone else. (See *Resources*, p. 211, for addresses of organizations that certify and teach alternative medicine to qualified individuals.)

In many cases, getting a horse back on the path of health and comfort is a long-term project that involves multiple steps and a team of people working together. It is best to work with a veterinarian as the leader of the group to develop an appropriate therapy or rehabilitation program, but in reality, some veterinarians are not interested or may not approve of the therapies you wish to pursue. If this is the case, take the time to learn as much as you can, proceed carefully, and involve competent, educated professionals to help you along.

Stretching

Stretching your horse's muscles is an excellent way to begin to heal his back—and increase your horse's flexibility in general. Just about everyone can do stretching exercises, though if you have your own back problems, find someone else to do them for you. All you need is information, a bit of time, and some patience.

The primary rule is *never force a stretch*. If your horse resists or pulls against the stretch, the muscle you are trying to relax tightens and shortens instead of lengthening. In this instance, move with your horse, or put his leg down for a moment, then start over. Patience is required, so if you or your horse has a different agenda (turnout time for him, dinner time for you), it is best to leave the stretches for another day.

Hold each stretch for 30 seconds or so, longer if your horse is comfortable, less if not. Wait for your horse to relax into your hands, then stretch him a little further. Follow the *"never force"* rule, and you can stretch horses in any direction without harm. A complete exploration of the subject is beyond the scope of this book, but I'll give you a list of useful stretches to try with your horse. For more in-depth study of stretches from the ground, consult *Stretch Exercises for Your Horse: The Path to Perfect Suppleness* by Karin Blignault, and learn valuable ridden exercises in *Simplify Your Riding: Step-By-Step Techniques to Improve Your Riding Skills* by Wendy Murdoch. I also recommend Linda Tellington-Jones' TTEAM videos (see *Resources,* p. 211).

Basic Leg Stretches

1. Begin with the front legs. Place your hands behind one knee and lift the leg forward, bending the knee. Bring the leg out in front of the horse as if you are stretching the girth area. Hold for 30 seconds or so.
2. Next, pick up the foot in the normal hoof-cleaning position. Pretend a pencil points off the end of the toe and draw circles in the ground with the imaginary pencil. Release the leg slowly. (The TTEAM method calls these *Leg Circles*; they are quick and easy to do as you tack up each day.)
3. Pick up the hind foot as if you are going to clean it, and again draw circles with the imaginary pencil pointing from the toe.
4. Finally, do a "non-stretch, stretch." Pick a leg up, the same way as with the *Leg Circles*, and just hold the leg in a position the horse is comfortable with, allowing him to relax the limb into your hand. Be patient; it may take a minute or more before you feel the weight of the relaxed leg. Only do this stretch when you and the horse are relaxed and not in a hurry. This avoids a "pulling" battle.

Proceed slowly and keep movements small while your horse gets the idea.

Belly Lifts

Belly Lifts are excellent for both increasing abdominal muscle tone and stretching back muscles (see figs. 1.4 A & B, p. 8). If your horse is uncomfortable doing this stretch, be very cautious and keep an eye on his feet to avoid getting kicked. If your horse accepts this exercise, make it a regular part of your routine by adding a belly lift after you finish grooming individual sections of his body: neck, belly lift; shoulder, belly lift; and so on.

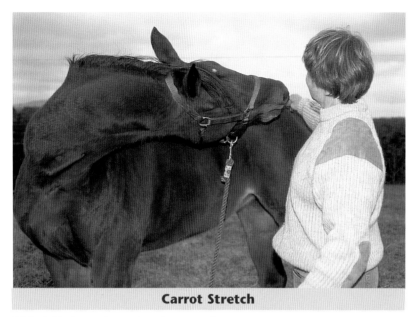

Carrot Stretch

14.1 This horse is performing a perfect "carrot stretch," reaching all the way around to the hip bone.

ing him squarely on an even surface and measuring from the ground to the *lowest* point in the center of your horse's back with a measuring stick. Remeasure that spot in several months and compare the difference.

Carrot Stretches

Easy and extremely beneficial, *carrot stretches* are, for obvious reasons, often a horse's favorite exercise. Ask your horse to bend and reach for bites of a carrot held at the level of both hips and both stifles (fig. 14.1). Due to stiffness in his neck and back, your horse may not be able to stretch all the way around to his hip on one or both sides. If this is the case, reward him when he has stretched as far as possible. Next, encourage him to stretch his head and neck forward and down between his front legs to receive another carrot. This safely stretches all parts of his back and neck. You can also be creative with your stretches, holding the carrot any place your horse can comfortably reach, such as next to his shoulder, rib cage, or in front of him so he stretches forward.

When you first teach your horse carrot stretches, position him so there is a wall on one side so he cannot turn in circles. Once he knows the routine, he will usually perform the carrot stretch anywhere, even out in the field. If you

You can increase the flexibility of the rib cage by performing a *sideways belly lift*. Standing near your horse's elbow, reach your fingers past the center of the horse's girth area and as far beyond the sternum to the other side of the ribcage as you can. Then pull *up and toward* the side you are standing on. The area just behind the shoulder blade on your side should fill with muscle, and the ribs should bend toward you, similar to the way they would when you ride in a circle or perform a lateral movement. This exercise can help if you are having trouble bending your horse evenly in both directions.

Keep track of how much flexibility your horse's back gains from these exercises by stand-

perform the carrot stretch exercise regularly, you will notice an improvement in his range of motion. These are not good exercises if your horse tends to be "mouthy" or bites, and for some clever horses, it is best to save the carrot stretch until after you ride, otherwise, the whole time you are tacking up, he will be bending and stretching, looking for a carrot.

Massage Therapy

Massage therapy can be beneficial to horses with back pain because it relieves muscle tension and spasms. For some, massage is all that is needed to correct back pain; others will need deeper treatment, like acupuncture or chiropractic therapy. Regular massage therapy sessions will ensure supple back muscles. And, it is realistic for you to learn to do basic massage that will complement a professional massage therapist's work. The more you can learn about massage, the better and more consistent your horse's performance will be.

Therapeutic massage has been performed for thousands of years in many different cultures and is gaining in popularity in the equine world. Keeping the muscles limber and flexible is very important to an athlete's soundness, longevity, and performance. Football players, for instance, may come off the field and go directly to a massage therapist so their muscles do not tighten up after playing, and many marathon runners will stop during a race for 2-minute massages to prevent tightness or to loosen a cramping muscle.

Sport horses are benefiting from the same kind of approach. Suppling your horse's muscles

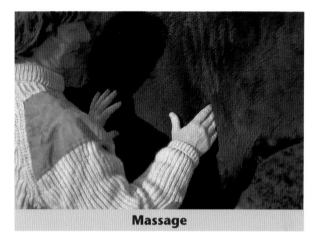

Massage

14.2 A small specific area can be massaged to help loosen an entire muscle.

before he enters the show ring will enhance his performance. Massage can prevent muscles from tightening and speed recovery after a hard workout by increasing blood flow and interrupting muscle spasms. It can also loosen up scar tissue and adhesions that form after a muscle, tendon, or ligament injury.

There are many different forms of massage, and all forms, if done correctly, can be beneficial to the horse. Massage therapy typically consists of various stroking techniques. A therapist will seek tight or sore places in the muscles, and work them loose with her hands or elbows. Specific small areas, known as *trigger points*, can be massaged to help loosen an entire muscle (fig. 14.2). A therapist will also include stretching of muscles, tendons, and ligaments as part of the massage, to ensure free range of motion.

At present, equine massage therapy courses in the United States generally only offer one week of training—nowhere near the amount of time necessary to learn about the variety of problems seen in horses. There are several, newer training courses that are addressing this need, however. The best way to select a competent massage therapist is to find one that has been certified for human massage, completed at least one of the two-week or longer equine courses, and as an added plus, is a horse person herself.

You can evaluate the effectiveness of massage treatment by watching and reading your horse's reaction. He should seem to enjoy the process and be relaxed and should feel suppler when you ride him the next day. It is expected that sometimes a horse will be sore for a few days afterward, depending on the extent of his muscle injury, tension, or spasm. But if most horses massaged by a particular person are sore the next day, or if they appear tense during the session, avoid that practitioner. An effective therapist should produce significant improvement in your horse in one to four treatments. If you are not getting results, more diagnostics may be needed to find the problem, and always consult your veterinarian.

Physical Therapy

Physical therapy is non-invasive treatment for injuries using *various combinations* of lasers, ultrasound, electrical stimulation, magnetic therapy, hydro (water) therapy, heat, cold, stretching, and massage. Many of the modalities used in equine physical therapy were originally developed for humans, which ensures that extensive scientific review and testing was done before any of the devices were approved. Because muscles, tendons, ligaments, and bones react in similar ways across species, these applications can certainly be effective for horses, though the protocols may differ. Currently in equine medicine, physical therapy techniques are less accepted and less widely available than in human medicine, but a well-trained human physical therapist can actually be an excellent resource for treating back pain in horses.

Part of the reason physical therapy has not been well received is that there has been no formal equine teaching program, but this is changing (see *Resources*, p. 211). Many untrained people, including veterinarians, may claim to be physical therapists, but to date, most of them learned to use their equipment by reading the owner's manual or being briefed by a manufacturer. Few untrained, lay practitioners have the knowledge to properly care for injuries, and it is possible to do more harm than good.

Select a physical therapist carefully, asking where she got her training and how long she trained (a few weekend courses is insufficient). A physical therapy degree is ideal, and a veterinarian who has studied physical therapy extensively is great. Many human physical therapists are becoming interested in equine physical therapy and are doing an excellent job. In the interim, owners can safely use *heat* and *cold therapy*, which are simple and very beneficial.

Cold Therapy

14.3 You can treat an area of the back with a large ice boot typically used for a leg. It can be secured with a surcingle.

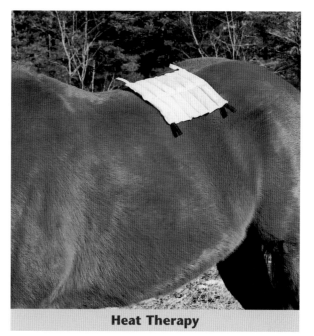

Heat Therapy

14.4 Add heat to a horse's back by placing a hydrocollator (heated in hot water) on the treatment area. If the hydrocollator is extremely hot, wrap it in a towel to protect the back.

Cold Therapy

Cold therapy is used to decrease pain and blood circulation, consequently it prevents swelling in an *acute*—or recent—injury such as a pulled muscle or a bruise. Cold, in the form of ice or water, is best used several times a day during the first 48 hours. Do not exceed 20 minutes for each session. After 30 minutes, increased circulation can occur, causing increased swelling. Cold hydrotherapy entails running a hose over the injured area. Ice is best applied using a wet towel or a commercial cold pack that has a wet surface against the skin (fig. 14.3). Dry cold wraps are much less efficient at cooling. In cold weather, running cold water over the back will chill a horse, so it is best to use an ice pack. Cold can also be applied to muscle spasms: massage ice cubes over a spasm for 15 to 20 minutes.

Heat Therapy

Heat therapy increases circulation in an injured area, reduces pain, relaxes muscles, and increases the amount of stretch in scar tissue. Heat is used in *chronic* injuries—those conditions that have been present for more than a week. Back pain is usually chronic—often has been present for years—and responds well to heat therapy.

Heat is best applied with a hot, moist compress for 20 to 30 minutes, one to three times a day. For moist heat, fill a bucket with hot water (not too hot to put your hand in), and soak a large towel. Wring the towel lightly, and apply directly to the area of soreness, then, as it cools, reheat it. You can also use a microwave to heat a wet towel. An inexpensive hydrocollator can be purchased from a pharmacy and placed in hot or boiling water (fig. 14.4). This is a very efficient source of moist heat and will stay hot for over 20 minutes. It can even be pinned to your horse's blanket, but carefully wrap it in a towel, and check it frequently to protect the skin from burning.

If you have a steady supply of warm water in your barn, you can perform hydrotherapy by hosing the back and neck under pressure for about 20 minutes. Horses love this type of treatment.

Dry heat does not penetrate as well as moist, so is much less efficient and probably not worth the effort.

Magnetic Therapy

Magnetic therapy can increase circulation and relieve chronic back pain. It is useful when owners have exhausted all other options for pain relief. Magnetic therapy *does not* correct the underlying reasons for back pain, so a horse will probably return to his previous level of stiffness if you discontinue use.

Electro-magnetic body blankets are currently popular, but quite expensive. Generally, the benefits of these blankets include: increased circulation, warm muscles, and relaxation related to the release of *endorphins*—the natural opiate-like compounds that are a normal by-product of exercise. Endorphins are released by the biochemical reactions that occur when the electromagnetic energy is applied to the skin and muscles.

The more affordable approach involves placing magnets directly over your horse's painful area. They are best applied for a short duration—less than 2 hours, once per day. The goal is to provide a stimulus, then allow the body time to heal on its own. Some manufacturer's representatives are advocating very long treatment times, even overnight, but application of magnets to the horse for more than 8 hours a day has not been studied and may be detrimental.

The research on magnets for medical use shows that you need to place the *negative* side against the skin to treat *chronic* conditions and the *positive* side against the skin for *acute* problems. When treating chronic back pain, you can safely use the negative side of any inexpensive magnet for many months, but an acute problem can be treated with the positive side for no more than a few hours at a time, once or twice a day, for no longer than five days.

A standard (*unipolar*) magnet—like a refrigerator magnet—has two poles, a *North* and *South*—or a *negative* and *positive*, to be more accurate. When you purchase this kind of magnet, its sides may or may not be labeled. To accurately determine which side to place against your horse's skin, use an inexpensive compass. The negative side is the one that attracts the North pole of the compass, or is "North-seeking," so mark it with an "N." And vice versa. Magnetic strength is called *gauss*. In general, magnets that are 2000 to 3000 gauss will be the most useful.

Some of the unipolar magnets are becoming available in easy-to-use wraps. You can make your own by sewing magnets into an old blanket or leg wrap. Magnets sold as *bipolar*—meaning there are alternating negative and positive poles facing the skin—are available in many different shapes and are placed inside convenient wraps. Remember, however, the positive side should *never* be placed on a chronic injury, so avoid using bipolar magnets on your horse's back.

Professional Physical Therapies

Some forms of physical therapy should really only be done by professionals. In some cases, you can work with a professional who will help you perform regular treatments at home on your own. The physical therapist should give you very clear instructions as to how use the piece of equipment she has prescribed. Be sure you understand and follow instructions exactly. More is *not* better, and careful research has been done to determine the correct settings and times for each piece of equipment.

Lasers

Lasers are perhaps the safest, most useful, and most versatile of all the physical therapy equipment used for the treatment of back pain. A *cold laser* sends a beam of light into tissue, stimulating the metabolism of the cell. (*Hot lasers* are used in surgery to cut tissue.) This can be used in a general way to relieve pain and increase circulation or by a trained acupuncturist on acupuncture points. With proper instruction, this device is safe to use at home and has value in treating wounds as well as muscle and tendon injuries.

Ultrasound

Therapeutic *ultrasound* units send high-frequency sound waves into deep tissue and provide the deepest source of heat available. This therapy can be very useful for back pain, especially for large muscle spasms and scar tissue. The operator must be knowledgeable about this modality as great harm can be done if it is used incorrectly. The high-frequency sound waves can damage deep muscles and bones.

Electrical Stimulation

Electrical stimulators conduct a gentle electrical current into muscle, serving as an effective pain reliever and also improving blood flow to damaged muscles. Because they exercise a specific muscle or group of muscles without exerting the horse, these stimulators are very useful in the rehabilitation stage of an injury or in treating localized nerve damage.

Acupuncture

Acupuncture is one of the most effective treatments for equine back pain. For optimum benefit, it should be combined with other therapies, such as stretching and chiropractic work. Acupuncture is considered the practice of medicine, and most states specify that it can only be done by licensed veterinarians.

Acupuncture is based on the principle that another, invisible, circulatory system exists in the body. Like blood in the cardiovascular system and electricity in the nervous system, there is also energy, or *Chi*, that flows through the body along pathways called *meridians*. *Acupuncture points* occur in specific locations on the body along these meridians and can be measured in concrete terms: A device—essentially a modified ohmmeter—can detect a measurable decrease in electrical resistance at each acupuncture point, locations the Chinese have specifically identified for centuries. An important acupuncture meridian is actually directly affected by poor saddle fit. The *Bladder Meridian* is located about 4 inches from the spine along both sides of the horse's back—right where the saddle sits, and it contains acupuncture points that connect to all the other pathways in the body (fig. 14.5).

Many scientific studies have examined how acupuncture works. In a very simplified way, the meridian system can be compared to a bio-electrical system. Acupuncture points act like "dimmer switches," and when a point is blocked, the amount of energy that flows through that point is decreased—in other words, the "lights are turned down." An acupuncture needle is inserted at the appropriate point to "turn them up again." You can, however, have *too much* Chi flowing through a point. Now think of an acupuncture point as a gate. If the gate is opened too widely, excess energy can pass through; if opened narrowly, too little flows through. The ideal is an even, steady flow.

Acupuncture is most commonly performed by stimulating points with needles, but a cold laser can be used if your horse does not like needles. *Acupressure* is a massage technique using acupuncture principles, stimulating the points with finger pressure. It may take many more treatments to relieve back pain, however.

If acupuncture is working for your horse, and you have corrected saddle fit, you should see improvement in the symptoms within four treatments. If not, more diagnostic tests should be done, though some problems do require more extensive therapy—maybe over a six-month period. To determine if the cause for a poor response is your horse or your practitioner, carefully observe your horse's responses during treatment. He should be fairly content and certainly not in pain. You should feel free to ask your practitioner questions and discuss the case, including further problems, a lack of response, and other possible courses of action.

Chiropractic Therapy

Chiropractic therapy is the science of restoring motion to a joint—the point where two bones meet and the soft tissue (nerves, muscles, tendons, and ligaments) around it. The neck, back, pelvis, and in many cases, the lower legs are the most commonly treated areas. The spine consists of a long column of bones—neck, thorax, lum-

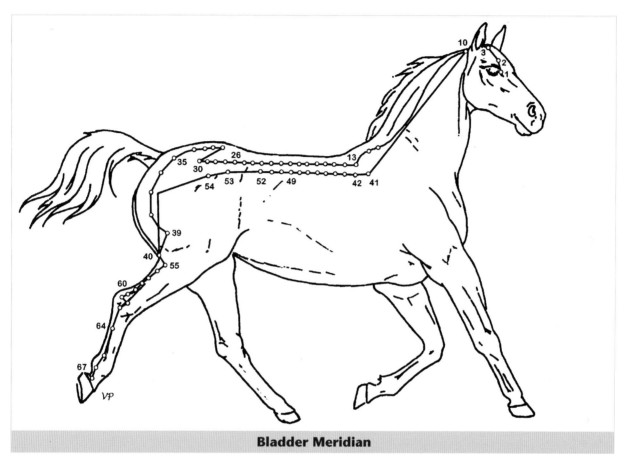

Bladder Meridian

14.5 The Bladder Meridian runs from the eye to the top of the hind foot. The part of this meridian that is located directly under the saddle contains important acupuncture points connecting to other meridians, so an ill-fitting saddle can potentially block the flow of energy throughout the horse's body.

bar, and sacrum—several joints, and *discs*, which act as cushions between the bones. When a horse becomes sore because of an ill-fitting saddle, he compensates for the pain by dropping his back and stiffening his spine. Muscles, tendons, and ligaments gradually tighten and scar over time until performance is seriously affected.

Chiropractic treatment is an excellent therapy for stiffness and back pain (figs. 14.6 A & B). Horses are natural athletes and can remain very supple throughout their lives if properly cared for. If the spine stays flexible, the rest of the body benefits, especially the lower legs. Veterinarians and riders alike often attribute stiffness to age,

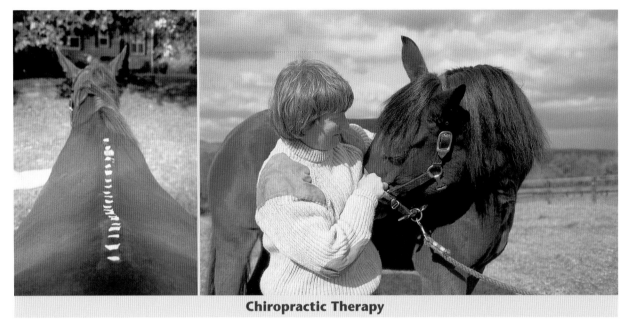

Chiropractic Therapy

14.6 A & B The horse in A has a spine that has been pulled out of alignment by tight muscles, so much so that the bones of the spine do not line up correctly or function smoothly. While this horse was rideable, he had problems bringing his hind legs underneath him in collected work or when jumping. This horse's work improved considerably after some chiropractic care, including gentle adjustments to the neck, as I am doing in photo B. I am placing my hand over a specific vertebra and giving it a short, quick thrust.

but in truth, most horses, regardless of age, can regain their flexibility and normal fluid spinal motion through chiropractic care.

Each time your horse moves his back, the cartilage and discs soak up joint fluid (*synovial fluid*)—like sponges soaking up water—pumping in nutrients and carrying away waste. Rigidity, or loss of motion between the bones—called *subluxation*—decreases the normal pumping action between the vertebrae. This slows, or even prevents, the flow of nutrients to the discs and car-

tilage, causing them to degenerate—commonly known as *arthritis*. The nerves, tendons, ligaments, and muscles surrounding the vertebrae are also affected, becoming irritated, inflamed, or scarred, or have spasms.

To restore motion to the joints, a chiropractor performs an *adjustment*—a short-lever, specific, high velocity, controlled thrust into a joint with his hand or an instrument called an *activator*. The activator looks like a small metal syringe and delivers a rapid force to a very specific area.

If the thrust is correctly aimed, it does not take a great deal of force. There is a form of chiropractic practiced by those who are not educated in correct techniques that uses a crude kind of adjustment called *manipulation*. This involves violent, forceful movements of a joint, often with the assistance of rubber mallets, boards, and tractors. Avoid anyone who uses violent techniques. If possible, observe a practitioner at work before allowing him to treat your horse. As with other practioners, ask about his training, certification, licensure, technique, and references.

Usually you will see improvement in your horse within four chiropractic treatments. If not, reevaluate the diagnosis. Though a few adjustments may be slightly uncomfortable for your horse, the overall experience should be a pleasant one. Based on your chiropractor's recommendations, maintenance therapy is advised. Monthly to quarterly treatments may be necessary to prevent a recurring loss of motion.

Nutritional Therapy

Many people are unaware that *nutrition* affects their horses' back health. Although *nutritional therapy* is a subject that requires a book of its own to discuss adequately, I have provided a basic introduction of nutritional issues you might want to learn more about.

In my experience as a veterinarian, a horse who is fed good quality hay and grain made *without* byproducts, preservatives, molasses, or sugar has muscles with better tone and less soreness.

Educated vitamin and mineral supplementation is necessary for muscle health. All soils, except those of good organic farmers, are depleted of many nutrients. Unfortunately, there is little research available regarding how nutrients specifically affect muscles, though it is known that *calcium*, *phosphorus*, *potassium*, and *magnesium* are important. *Selenium* and *vitamin E* play an important role in muscle health and are deficient in the soils throughout much of the United States. (A few places do have *excess* selenium, so research your locale before adding supplements containing selenium.) If your horse has tight, hard, and painful muscles and is susceptible to *tying-up* or *myositis*, he may be deficient in one of these nutrients.

An important part of any nutrition program is to separate where your horse obtains *minerals*, and where he gets *salt*. Commonly-used, red, mineralized salt blocks are about 94% salt. Horses actually require far more in the way of minerals and will obtain insufficient amounts from the block alone. A few companies make low salt mineral mixes, but it is best if you can find a mineral supplement *without* salt, and then feed salt separately (fig. 14.7).

A healthy intestinal tract improves the digestion and absorption of all nutrients. A horse that has been treated with antibiotics may absorb nutrients poorly due to the antibiotics killing the good bacteria needed for digestion. The use of high quality *probiotics* (beneficial intestinal bacteria) is one way to improve intestinal health.

Many of the popular *joint supplements* are also beneficial for muscles. Though their primary

Salt and Minerals

14.7 Here are examples of salt (white) and salt-and-mineral (red) blocks, and, in the middle, powdered minerals. I recommend that horses obtain their salt and minerals from separate sources.

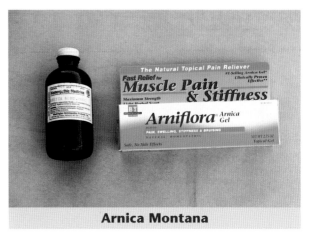

Arnica Montana

14.8 Arnica montana is a homeopathic medicine used to treat stiff muscles and joints. It is available in pill or gel form.

action is on the joints, healthy joints improve the ability of muscles to perform optimally.

Herbal Medicine and Homeopathy

Many other alternative therapies can be beneficial in improving the health of the musculoskeletal system. *Herbal medicine* and *homeopathy* can be effective, though perhaps to a lesser degree than other therapies we've discussed. Some high-quality, anti-inflammatory herbal formulas can be quite helpful. Always carefully evaluate an herbal company before using their products, and find out what kind of training their herbalists have received.

Homeopathy is a complex complementary modality that uses diluted materials placed on small pellets, which are ingested (see *Resources*, p. 211). Homeopathic medicines are best prescribed by a veterinarian trained in homeopathy except for simple injuries. However, I will mention *Arnica montana*, a useful, usually side-effect-free remedy that can be purchased from any health food store (fig. 14.8). Arnica helps stiff, sore muscles and injuries, usually reducing swelling and shortening the healing time. It is supplied in small tablets (or gel for topical use), and you can feed your horse six to eight of them up to three times a day for five days. If the problem has not lessened, it is best to consult a homeopathic veterinarian.

Shoeing for a Healthy Back

Correct shoeing is one of the most important aspects of keeping a horse sound and his back healthy. Each horse—and each foot on each horse—is unique. The local environment and how the horse is used add further complexity to the subject.

When the feet are comfortable, the horse's upper body is also comfortable. When the toes are long and the heels low and sloping forward, the back of the coffin bone drops down slightly at the rear of the foot, tugging the flexor muscles and tendons at the back of the leg down. The flexors connect to an area near the stifle, then the *psoas muscles* travel across the hip to the underside of the rib cage just behind the saddle. When the psoas muscles are tight, the rib cage area becomes tight, making it difficult for the horse to raise his back (fig. 14.9). The same concept holds true for the front legs. The downward pull on the flexor tendons puts tension on the muscles of the rib cage (*serratus ventralis*).

In many instances, the back can be helped by shortening the toe and bringing the *break-over point* (the rounded part where the horse's foot leaves the ground) back in a *Natural Balance* style (see *Resources*, p. 211). Simplified, the concept of Natural Balance shoeing is to support the coffin bone, and thus the entire column of leg bones, with the shoe. To achieve the desired foot shape, the farrier sets the break-over point of the shoe back to a place just in front of the coffin bone. The sole is left intact (see sidebar, p. 206). The shoe may appear to be set quite far back,

compared to what you may be accustomed to seeing. Over the next three or four shoeings, the wall of the foot will reform to the shape of the coffin bone, eliminating the long toes, low heels, or flares commonly seen.

Orthotics, wedge pads, bar shoes, and other additions to the bottom of the feet can be beneficial in specific instances (figs. 14.10 A & B). Very basically, your horse's toes should be short, and their angle should approximately follow that of the pastern. The foot should not grow over the edges of the shoe before the next reshoeing. The heels should grow well, follow the same angles as the toe, and not be crushed or *under run.* (An under run heel is one where the tubules of hoof horn grow forward instead of down.)

In some cases, good shoeing can be the key that unlocks a major problem, while in others, it is just a small help. It is always important to keep the feet in mind, however, as they are a major factor in back health.

Conventional Medicine

The common *conventional treatments* prescribed for back pain are *rest, anti-inflammatories,* and *muscle relaxants.* Rest will usually make a back feel better, but shortly after the horse returns to work, the problems will resurface—especially if saddle fit has not been corrected. Anti-inflammatories tend to reduce pain for a few days while the horse is being dosed, but performance never really improves the way it can if acupuncture and chiropractic are the primary treatments. Anti-inflammatories, particularly *phenylbutazone,* have some

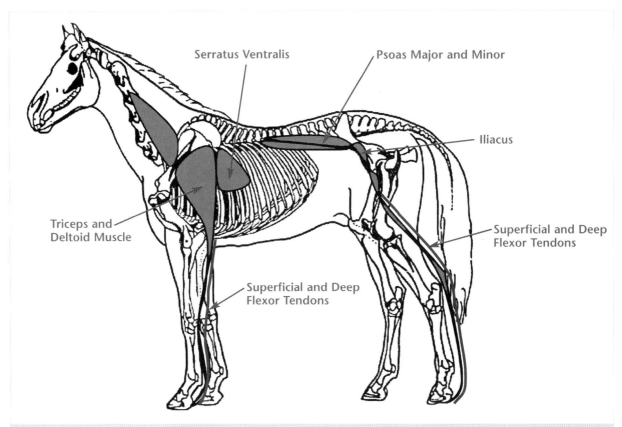

Serratus Ventralis

Psoas Major and Minor

Iliacus

Triceps and Deltoid Muscle

Superficial and Deep Flexor Tendons

Superficial and Deep Flexor Tendons

Muscles Connecting the Foot to the Back

14.9 Important muscles and tendons connect the horse's feet to his back. In the front leg, the superficial and deep flexor tendons (red line) run from the foot to the triceps and deltoid muscle at the back of the shoulder. The shoulder blade is then connected to the rib cage by the serratus ventralis. If, due to a foot imbalance, these tendons and muscles are strained or tense, the horse's rib cage will be pulled to one side or the other. In the hind leg, the superficial and deep flexor tendons (red line) run from the foot up near the stifle to the iliacus—a small muscle at the bottom of the hip bone. The iliacus connects to the the psoas muscles, which directly connect to the bottom of the spine and end in the saddle area. Tension or strain in these muscles or tendons makes it difficult for the horse to use his back properly.

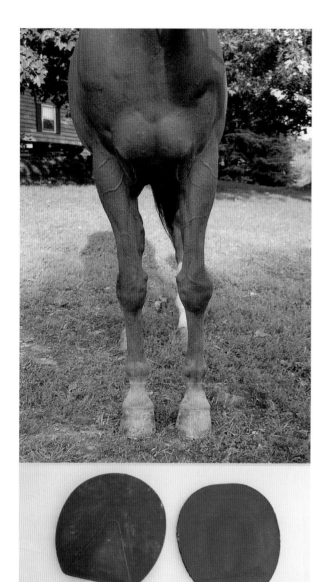

Orthotics

14.10 **A & B** Orthotics look similar to ordinary protective pads but are usually only applied to one foot. This horse has knees that are unlevel and is a good candidate for orthotics.

significant side effects on the gastro-intestinal tract and can be detrimental to many horses, especially when used frequently. Muscle relaxants can make the horse feel better for a short time, but may have some long-term negative effects if muscles become abnormally relaxed.

Conventional medicine can be useful in the diagnosis of back pain, though even if your horse displays very clear symptoms, the tests can be "inconclusive." In some cases, diagnostic tests can help *rule out* certain problems—especially lower leg lamenesses—as being a source of the back pain.

Radiographs (X rays) can be taken to check for bone spurs, arthritic changes, or fractures, but in many cases, it is not possible to view the important parts of the spine, and to radiograph the back, your horse must be taken to a clinic with a large enough x-ray machine.

Thermography has shown some promise in diagnosing back pain. This technology measures skin temperature, and most practitioners use it to search for areas of heat. However, many horses with back pain show areas of *decreased* temperature where their primary pain is located, indicating a lack of circulation, which can actually be more painful.

Scintigraphy shows areas of *increased* circulation and cellular activity, which occur during inflammation. Since many cases of back pain display *decreased* circulation, scintigraphy does not always provide an answer but can rule out fractures.

Diagnostic ultrasound, the most promising of diagnostic tools for examining the back, was pio-

Comparative Foot Structure

Farriers and veterinarians studying the feet of both wild and domesticated horses have discovered a number of indications that the back of the foot is supposed to do most of the work.

- The back of the frog has two sensory nerves where the foot first contacts the ground—if it lands heel-first. These nerves are not located anywhere else on the foot.
- The bars of a wild horse's foot are strong and visible. Well-shod feet have the same structures present.
- The heels on wild horses grow down to meet the ground, rather than forward, as is seen on many domesticated feet. Again, well-shod feet have similar heels.
- In the wild, dirt usually packs firmly in and around the clefts of the frog in the back part of the foot. It forms a flat surface to contact the ground and support the coffin bone. This evidence shows that the hoof would be better supported if humans left feet packed with clean dirt (of course not with manure and shavings, which can lead to thrush).
- Barefoot horses, both wild and domesticated, have a thickened callous over the front of the coffin bone at the toe. Shod horses can also have this callus if it is not trimmed away. A farrier can maintain the integrity of the sole by only trimming away the dead, crumbly sole and leaving the live sole—like trimming your fingernails short, but not too short. If you trim in this manner, the toe actually builds a thicker, protective callous. If the sole callous is removed, however, the horse, whether shod or not, can have sore feet because the coffin bone actually drops down slightly inside the hoof. The bone can then become bruised because the sole is too thin to protect it.

neered in France and is being used in the United States by veterinarians taught by Dr. Jean-Marie Denoix. This technology can reveal ligament problems, bone spurs, other arthritic changes around the joints, and the presence of *disc disease*—a condition that was previously not thought to occur in horses.

Someday, there may be better methods and more effective technology to help us definitively diagnose back pain. In the meantime, we must learn to use a combination of techniques to help our horses achieve and maintain good health and balance.

Problematic Management Practices

Horse management is a complex process. Many management and training practices affect your horse's comfort level, and consequently, performance. Even after you correct saddle fit, your horse's performance may not improve unless other issues are also changed. Examine your management practices to identify other potential contributors to equine back pain and behavior problems.

Ponying with a horse's head twisted around to the lead pony's rider physically strains the muscles in the neck, back, and hindquarters. Long-lasting pain and stiffness occurs. Unnatural stress is also placed on the joints and tendons in the lower legs, contributing to many of the injuries so common on the racetrack. Tracks in many parts of the world, notably England, Ireland, and Hong Kong, do not depend on ponying except for the most unruly individuals. In the United States, however, almost every horse is ponied to the starting gate of a race and is often ponied during training. When ex-racehorses later become riding horses, many of the common behavior problems directly relate back to this practice.

Excessive longeing and round pen work can stress the entire musculo-skeletal system, including the lower legs. A horse should not be worked in one position, with his head and neck flexed in one direction, without frequent changes in direction and position.

The multitude of *training devices* on the market is endless, ranging from benign to abusive. Equipment such as *tie downs, draw reins, side reins,* and *chambons* are examples of training devices that are commonly used incorrectly. Training devices generally cause at least one joint to brace against them. If a single joint tightens in resist-

Potentially Problematic Management and Training Practices
■ Ponying
■ Excessive longe work
■ Round pen work—especially with one- to three-year-olds
■ Training devices
■ Inappropriate muscle care
■ Failure to warm up and cool down
■ Mechanical hot-walkers
■ Excessive swimming
■ Tight blankets
■ Deep ring footing
■ Confinement

ance to a training aid, the entire spine loses its normal motion. Training devices also generally keep a horse in the same unnatural position for long periods of time, and muscles fatigue quickly when held in the same position, even for a few minutes. The safest way to use any training device is for only a few minutes, then allow the horse to rest or move freely for a few minutes, and repeat. This is known as *interval training* and has been shown to be a very effective method of training in many sports, both human and equine.

Appropriate muscle care is vital to healthy muscles and performance. Many horse owners focus on the horse's legs and spend very little time caring for the muscles of the upper body.

Every owner can learn a few basic stretches to do with their horse (see p. 190).

Warming up and cooling down play important roles in keeping the muscles loose and pain-free. Human athletes have long incorporated pre- and post-performance programs in their training regimens, and this policy is easily applied to horses in all sports. One research study conducted in England showed that horses that were trotted for 20 minutes after hard exercise cleared *lactic acid* (a byproduct from exercise that can cause muscle pain) from their blood significantly faster than horses that were walked or stood still. To reduce injury and maximize performance, include adequate warm-up and cool-down periods in every ride.

Mechanical hot-walkers hold the head and neck up in the air, which forces the back to hollow. These are often used immediately after exercise, when the horse needs to stretch his muscles, not tighten and shorten them. If you can't hand-walk your horse, make time for stretching immediately after he comes off the hot-walker. Innovative new hot-walkers are becoming available, and though expensive, they often provide excellent alternatives to traditional hot-walkers (see *Resources*, p. 211).

While *swimming* is valuable for rehabilitating injured horses, it is less beneficial for routine conditioning. It does provide exercise without stressing the legs and offers a break from the normal routine, but horses swim in a hollowed-out position, which inappropriately develops upside-down neck and back muscles. *Pulling* through the water emphasizes the shoulder muscles, and the hindquarters aren't correctly conditioned because there is little to *push* against. Tendons, ligaments, and bones are strengthened by concussion, and therefore will not be conditioned from swimming.

Inappropriate blanketing can create back pain. *Cut-back blankets* that rest behind the withers (fig. 14.11 A), and blankets that are either *too small* or *too large*, produce vice-like tension between the back of the withers and the points of the shoulders. Your horse's stride will shorten significantly as the shoulder muscles are compressed, even after the blanketing season has ended. The shoulder joint becomes painfully tight and loses free motion, which the horse compensates for by tightening up his entire back. *Tight surcingles* and *overgirths* used to prevent blankets from slipping also restrict the withers, which will often become stiff and sore.

Blankets should fit as loosely over the shoulders as possible. You can tell whether your blanket fits correctly by checking the front buckles after a day outside—they should still be easy to open. The most effective blanket shape covers the withers and rides slightly up onto the neck (fig. 14.11 B). This style tends to hang well, leaving the shoulders free to move. Fit can sometimes be improved in an older blanket by sewing darts in the center of the neck area, allowing the blanket to hang away from the shoulders. You can also add a gusset to the shoulder, although this will require adding extra material, and a heavy-duty sewing machine (fig. 14.11 C). Be

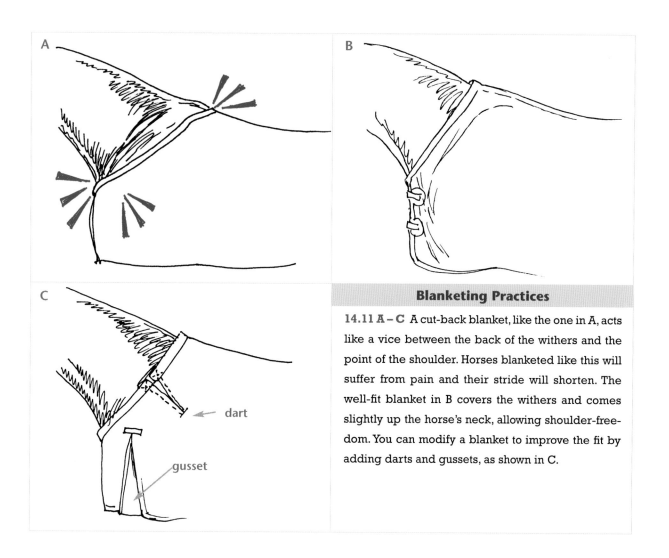

A

B

C

dart

gusset

Blanketing Practices

14.11 A – C A cut-back blanket, like the one in A, acts like a vice between the back of the withers and the point of the shoulder. Horses blanketed like this will suffer from pain and their stride will shorten. The well-fit blanket in B covers the withers and comes slightly up the horse's neck, allowing shoulder-freedom. You can modify a blanket to improve the fit by adding darts and gussets, as shown in C.

sure that the top of the gusset begins *above* the shoulder joint. There are also many new lightweight, durable blankets available that eliminate the twenty-to-thirty pounds of material that older blankets would put on the horse's back.

Ring footing is often a cause of back pain, especially when it is too deep. Your horse moves through deep footing just like you would walk on the soft part of the beach, and there is danger that tendons, ligaments, and muscles can become strained.

One of the most *appropriate* management practices is to *turn horses out* to buck, roll, and play—movement is necessary for back and joint health. Horses that stand in stalls, especially those with overhead fly sprayers, become stiff from immobility—the equine equivalent of a "couch potato." Overhead sprayers not only spray toxic chemicals onto your horse's food and water supply, but the reduction in the fly population means he does not need to swish his tail and stomp his feet, movements that help keep him limber. Regular turnout often reduces, or eliminates, the need for excessive longeing before competition, as well as the expense and frustration of trying one herbal relaxation formula after another. *Allow your horse time to be a horse,* and reap the benefits of better performance and health.

In Conclusion

Regardless of daydreams and clearance sales, the best saddle to buy is the one that *fits*. This means it has to fit both *you* and *your horse*. Finding the right saddle is a process. The only way to improve your horse's well-being and your relationship with him is to take your time, and find the best-fitting saddle your money can buy. *Educate yourself* rather than expect a salesperson to make your decision for you.

Saddle-fit responsibility doesn't end there. Check your fit regularly to avoid future problems. Pay attention to your horse and listen when he tries to tell you that something is wrong. Maintain your horse's health to the best of your ability, either by finding qualified practitioners or learning how to do bodywork yourself. I hope this book provides you with some of the tools you need to find your dream saddle, keep your horse's back pain free, develop a lasting partnership with him, and achieve your goals, whatever they may be.

Resources

For the Horse

Anatomy and Physiology

Zoologik System®
Equikin
2198 W 15th Street
Loveland, CO 80538-3597
(800) 950-5025
(970) 667-9047
www.anatomyinclay.com

Natural Balance Shoeing
Equine Digit Support System, Inc.
506 Hwy 115
Penrose, CO 81240
(719) 372-7463
www.hopeforsoundness.com

Computerized Saddle Pressure Measuring Equipment

Novel Electronics, Inc.
Pliance Horse System
964 Grand Avenue
St. Paul, MN 55105
(651) 221-0505
www.novel.de/pdf/flyer/eng/horse_eng.pdf

SaddleTech
2995 Woodside Road
Suite 400
(650) 631-8400
Woodside, CA 94062
www.saddletech.com

Tack and Equipment

Centaur Equinecisers & Hot Walkers
5761 Ridgeview Avenue
Mira Loma, CA 91752
(800) 962-8050
www.hotwalkers.com

Lauriche Saddlery
22 Station Street
Walsall, West Midlands
England WS2 952
+01922-626430

Master Saddler Association
2698 Jennings Chapel Road
Woodbine, MD 21797
(301) 570-3100
www.mastersaddlers.com

Mylers, Inc.
2043 Good Hope Road
Marshfield, MO 65706
(800) 354-3613
(417) 859-0177
www.mylerbitsusa.com

Seams Right Saddle Pads
Seams Right, Inc.
P.O. Box 550
Jefferson, Maryland 21755
(800) 690-7237
(301) 473-4477
www.seamsright.com

Bodywork and Therapy

Information and links to other alternative medical sites:
www.altvetmed.com

Academy Of Veterinary Homeopathy
PO Box 9280
Wilmington, DE 19809
(866) 652-1590
www.theavh.org

The American Academy of Veterinary Acupuncture
66 Morris Avenue
Suite 2A
Springfield, NJ 07081
(973) 379-1100
www.aava.org

American Holistic Veterinary Medical Association
2218 Old Emmorton Road
Bel Air, MD 21015
(410) 569-0795
www.ahvma.org

American Veterinary Chiropractic Association
442154 E 140 Road
Bluejacket, OK 74333
(918) 784-2231
www.animalchiropractic.org

Chi Institute of Chinese Medicine
9700 W. Hwy 318
Reddick, FL 32686
(800) 891-1986
www.tcvm.com

International Veterinary Acupuncture Society
P.O. Box 271395
Ft. Collins, CO 80527-1395
(970) 266-0666
www.ivas.org

Veterinary Botanical Medicine Association
6471 Tamiami Canal Road
Miami, FL 33126
www.vbma.org

For the Rider

Education, Training, Practitioner Listing

D'Al School of Equine Massage
627 Maitland Street
London, Ontario
Canada N5Y 2V7
(519) 673-4420
(877) 327-2952
www.darcylane.com

Equine Sports Therapy Programs
9791 NW 160th Street
Reddick, FL 32686
(352) 591-4735
www.equinesportsmassage.com

Equinology, Inc.
P.O. Box 1248
Grover Beach, CA 93483
(805) 474-9044
www.equinology.com

Midway College
Equine Physical Therapy Program
512 E. Stephens Street
Midway, KY 40347
(859) 846-4421
www.midway.edu/degreeprograms/equine.html

TTEAM Training USA
PO Box 3793
Santa Fe, NM 87501
(800) 854-8326
www.tellingtonttouch.com

Rider Bodywork

American Society for the Alexander Technique
P.O. Box 60008
Florence, MA 01062
800-473-0620
(413) 584-2359
www.alexandertech.com

Feldenkrais Educational Foundation of North America
3611 SW Hood Avenue
Suite 100
Portland, OR 97239
(866) 333-6248
(503) 221-6612
www.feldenkrais.com

The Rolf Institute of Structural Integration
5055 Chaparral Court
Suite 103
Boulder, CO 80301
(800) 530-8875
(303) 449-5903
www.rolf.org

American Massage Therapy Association
820 Davis Street
Suite 100
Evanston, IL 60201-4444
(847) 864-0123
www.amtamassage.org

Association for Network Care
444 Main Street
Longmont, CO 80501
(303) 678-8101
www.associationfornetworkcare.com

Centered Riding, Inc®.
P.O. Box 12377
Philadelphia, PA 19119
(215) 438-1286
www.centeredriding.org

The Murdoch Method, LLC
Equiband™
(866) 200-9312
www.wendymurdoch.com

Recommended Reading and Viewing

(Note: *Anvil Magazine* back issue articles can be read online at www.anvilmag.com.)

Alon, Ruthy. *Mindful Spontaneity: Lessons in the Feldenkrais Method.* Berkeley: North Atlantic Books, 1995.

Becker, Robert, and Selden, Gary. *The Body Electric: Electromagnetism and the Foundation of Life.* New York: Quill, 1998.

Blignault, Karin. *Stretch Exercises for Your Horse: The Path to Perfect Suppleness.* North Pomfret, VT: Trafalgar Square Publishing, 2003.

Bromiley, Mary. *Equine Injury, Therapy, and Rehabilitation.* 2nd ed. Boston: Blackwell Scientific Publications, 1993.

Clayton, Hilary M. *Conditioning Sport Horses.* Veterinary Practice Publishing Company, 1991.

de Némethy, Bertalan, and Coleman, Alix. *Classic Show Jumping: The de Némethy Method.* New York: Doubleday Publishing, 1988.

Denoix, Jean-Marie, and Pailloux, Jean-Pierre. *Physical Therapy and Massage for the Horse.* 2nd ed. North Pomfret, VT: Trafalgar Square Publishing, 2001.

Dwyer, Major Francis. *Seats and Saddles, Bits and Bitting, Draught and Harness, and the Prevention and Cure of Restiveness in Horses.* New York: The Rider and Driver Publishing Company, 1886.

Edwards, Elwyn Hartley. *The Saddle in Theory and Practice.* London: JA Allen & Company, Ltd., 1990.

Edwards, Rob. "Interview with Gene Ovnicek." *Anvil Magazine.* September 1996.

Hannay, Pamela. *Shiatsu Therapy for Horses.* North Pomfret, VT: Trafalgar Square Publishing, 2002.

Harman, Joyce C. "Bitting for Comfort and Performance." *TTEAM Up with Your Horse.* 2(2): 1998.

Harman, Joyce C. "Does your blanket fit?" *Practical Horseman.* December 1996.

Harris, Susan. *Horses, Gaits, Balance and Movement.* New York: Howell Book House, 1993.

Harris, Susan, and Brown, Peggy. *Anatomy in Motion I: The Visible Horse.* North Pomfret, VT: Trafalgar Square Publishing, 2000, videocassette.

Harris, Susan, and Brown, Peggy. *Anatomy in Motion II: The Visible Rider.* North Pomfret, VT: Trafalgar Square Publishing, 2000, videocassette.

Hourdebaigt, Jean-Pierre. *Equine Massage: A Practical Guide.* New York: Howell Book House, 1997.

Jeffrey, Dale. *Horse Dentistry: The Theory and Practice of Equine Dental Maintenance.* Glenns Ferry, ID: World Wide Equine, Inc., 1996.

Kainer, Robert A., and McCracken, Thomas O. *Horse Anatomy, A Coloring Atlas.* Loveland, CO: Alpine Publications, Inc., 1998.

Meagher, Jack. *Beating Muscle Injuries for Horses: 25 Common Muscular Problems, Their Cause, Correction, and Prevention.* Hamilton, MA: Hamilton Horse Associates, 1985.

Murdoch, Wendy. *Simplify Your Riding: Step-By-Step Techniques to Improve Your Riding Skills.* Cedar Ridge, CA: Carriage House Publishing, 2004.

Norris, Noel C. *The Book of Magnetic Healing and Treatments.* Brookline, MA: Redwing Book Company, 1995.

Ovnicek, Gene. "Applying the Equine Digit Support System." *Anvil Magazine.* October 1996.

Ovnicek, Gene. "The Life Cycle of Laminitis: Part 1." *Anvil Magazine.* February 1999.

Ovnicek, Gene. "The Life Cycle of Laminitis: Part 2." *Anvil Magazine.* March 1999.

Pasquini, C., Reddy, V.K., and Rutzlaff, M. *Atlas of Equine Anatomy.* Pilot Point, TX: SUDZ Publishing, 1991.

Porter, Mimi. *The New Equine Sports Therapy.* Lexington: Eclipse Press, 1998.

Pullen, Gabrielle. "Reading the Bottom of the Hoof." *Anvil Magazine.* June 2000.

Schusdziarra, Heinrich, and Schusdziarra, Volker. *An Anatomy of Riding.* Briarcliff, NY: Breakthrough Publications, 1985.

Scott, Mike, Converse, Anne, and Tocci, Peter. *The Basic Principles of Equine Massage/Muscle Therapy.* Bolton, MA: Massage/Muscle Therapy Publications, 2003.

Self, Hilary P. *A Modern Horse Herbal.* Boonsboro, MD: Half Halt Press, 1996.

Shafarman, Steven. *Awareness Heals: The Feldenkrais Method for Dynamic Health.* San Francisco: Addison Wesley & Benjamin Cummings Publishing Company, 1997.

Spencer, Nancy. *Basic Equine Stretching.* Equitronics Production, 1993, videocassette.

Stashak, Ted S., and Hill, Cherry. *Practical Guide to Lameness in Horses.* Philadelphia: Lippincott, Williams & Wilkins, 1995.

Steinkraus, William C. *Reflections on Riding and Jumping: Winning Techniques for Serious Riders.* North Pomfret, VT: Trafalgar Square, 1997.

Swift, Sally. *Centered Riding.* North Pomfret, VT: Trafalgar Square Publishing, 1985.

Swift, Sally. *Centered Riding 2: Further Exploration.* North Pomfret, VT: Trafalgar Square Publishing, 2002.

Tellington-Jones, Linda. *Improve Your Horse's Well-Being: A Step-By-Step Guide to TTouch and TTeam Training.* North Pomfret, VT: Trafalgar Square Publishing, 1999.

Tellington-Jones, Linda. *Solving Riding Problems with TTEAM Tape 1: From the Ground.* North Pomfret, VT: Trafalgar Square Publishing, 2000, videocassette.

Tellington-Jones, Linda. *Solving Riding Problems with TTEAM Tape 2: In the Saddle.* North Pomfret, VT: Trafalgar Square Publishing, 2000, videocassette.

Wanless, Mary. *For the Good of the Horse.* North Pomfret, VT: Trafalgar Square Publishing, 1997.

Zidonis, Nancy A., Soderberg, Marie, and Snow, Amy. *Equine Acupressure: A Working Manual.* 3rd ed. Larkspur, CO: Tallgrass Publishers, LLC, 1999.

Index